T0352414

# ASIAN AMERICAN IS NOT A COLOR

# ASIAN AMERICAN IS NOT A COLOR

## CONVERSATIONS ON RACE, AFFIRMATIVE ACTION, AND FAMILY

OIYAN A. POON

BEACON PRESS
BOSTON

BEACON PRESS
Boston, Massachusetts
www.beacon.org

Beacon Press books
are published under the auspices of
the Unitarian Universalist Association of Congregations.

27 26 25 24     8 7 6 5 4 3 2 1

This book is printed on acid-free paper that meets the uncoated paper
ANSI/NISO specifications for permanence as revised in 1992.

Many names and identifying characteristics of people and schools
mentioned in this work have been changed to protect their identities.

Lyrics by Chris Iijima from "Asian Song" are printed here
with permission.

Text design and composition by Kim Arney

*Library of Congress Cataloguing-in-Publication Data
is available for this title.*

Hardcover ISBN: 978-0-8070-1362-5
E-book ISBN: 978-0-8070-1364-9
Audiobook: 978-0-8070-3525-2

# CONTENTS

CONCLUSION

Asian American Identity
Is a Solidarity Ethic and Practice   171

ASIAN
AMERICAN
IS NOT A
COLOR

# "BUT ASIAN AMERICAN ISN'T A COLOR"

To my daughter, Té Té:

When you were just three years old, the world around us felt like it was burning down, and simultaneously felt full of possibility. In 2018 we were in the midst of the Trump presidency. Our government was cruelly separating children and babies from their families at the US-Mexico border, incarcerating them for fleeing intolerable conditions in their homelands that could be traced to a history of US military interventions in Central America.[1] We attended a rally in Colorado to protest the family separations and inhumane treatment of asylum seekers and immigrants. You wore your favorite rainbow glitter butterfly shirt in solidarity. We talked about how butterflies migrate to survive and in search of possibilities for thriving. This was not your first protest. Your father and I had brought you to several protests before, in solidarity with the Black Lives Matter movement. Between the time you were born in 2015 and when you turned three, law enforcement officers had killed thousands of people, with Black people the most likely targets.

Movements were building both in opposition to racism and to forge a more humane and just world. Your father and I often discussed the news of the day, our worries and dreams for the future. With NPR on the radio in the background one night, you asked me, "Mama, are we Black?"

"No, we're not Black," I answered.

"Are we White?" you asked.

"No, we're not White," I said, suspecting what you would ask next.

"Then what are we?" you wondered out loud.

"We're Asian American," I responded. "Can you say 'Asian American'?"

"Asian kAH-merican," you slowly pronounced in your sweet three-year-old toddler voice. You precociously pushed back, "But Asian kAH-merican isn't a color!"

I was stunned into silence by your innocent wisdom. Your very succinct and true observation highlighted the absurdities of race and racism in ways that my decades of scholarly training and professional career as a race scholar had not. I knew we would have these conversations about race and racism as you grew up. I just did not anticipate them to come so soon, so early in your life—less than forty months into our journey as mother and daughter. Simultaneously pleased and startled by how astute your observation was, I remember fumbling through some sociological explanation about how race is a social construction, while my thoughts ran all over the place. *What a brilliant observation! How did she know enough to ask about race in this way? Has she been hearing messages about race and racism in preschool? From TV? Listening to me and her father talk about the news? All of the above?*

I explained that Black and White[2] are colors like in your crayons, but when we're talking about people, we know that Black people's skin tones can be different shades of brown, and White people's skin tones aren't often white like fresh snow. I told you that Asian Americans have all different kinds of skin tones too. I reminded you that your Auntie Taz is also Asian American. She's Bengali American and her skin is like warm sand—a deeper shade than our golden light-brown skin tone. Before I could continue, you had already moved on to talking about an episode of *Daniel Tiger's Neighborhood* or some other toddler pop culture.

I hadn't finished telling you about how humans have all kinds of beautiful skin colors, but our society has been shaped by a history of people with light skin tones, particularly from western Europe, colonizing and exploiting lands and people with more melanin than them around the world. And this history of human relations and oppression, power, and racial meanings had created these socially constructed notions of race and color and racist hierarchies that granted people with lighter skin color and European phenotypes more affirmations of their humanity and opportunities for material wealth in an unjust system of racial capitalism.

This history also meant that colors like black and white became references to groups of people whose relationships are mediated by racial power and contemporary legacies of historical exploitations and oppression. In talking about Black, White, and Asian American people, we hadn't even yet discussed Indigenous, Latinx, Arab, and Middle Eastern peoples; these names aren't colors either, but they too are imperfect and contested terms used in reference to evolving identities and groupings of people.

I also wanted to emphasize to you that in the face of colonial conquest, conflicts, war, violence, famines, injustices, and oppression, people have always come together to survive, resist, fight back, thrive, and create new possibilities, and we come from these legacies of political struggle and freedom dreaming.[3] I had no idea how to communicate this to you when you were three, or to anyone else not steeped in the history and sociology of race and ethnicity. I made a mental note to myself that the next time you had a question about race, I would be ready to explain the loaded social meanings of skin colors.

In summer 2020, during the COVID-19 pandemic, we moved back to Chicago—your birthplace—after three years of living in Colorado.[4] You came into childhood consciousness in northern Colorado. You loved your friends and teachers there, but I missed my friends, teachers, and community in Chicago—a city of big problems and Big beautiful Shoulders.[5] You were five years old when we moved to a rare racially integrated neighborhood on the city's Northwest Side, where our neighbors next door were Black, Filipino, South Asian, Latinx, and White. The predominantly Asian American places like your grandfather's neighborhood in Quincy, Massachusetts, Boston Chinatown, the San Gabriel Valley, or Argyle in Chicago were all faded moments in your pre-pandemic memory.

On our first visit to Chicago Chinatown in that first year of the COVID-19 pandemic, your father hopped out of the car and jogged into Chiu Quon Bakery on Wentworth to pick up some pastries. In the car, we waited for him and watched masked people, bundled up for the brisk fall weather, hustling in and out of restaurants, boba cafes, hair salons, Chinese herbal medicine shops, and green grocers. The busy street was full of double-parked cars and their blinking hazard lights, canopied by red and gold tasseled lanterns set up for tourists, who had avoided, and maybe even scapegoated, the neighborhood and Chinese American community for the pandemic. You asked me, "Mama, why does everyone look like us here?" I sucked in my breath and as fast as I could (knowing your attention span was short) fumbled my way through a mini lecture about the history and contemporary legacies of anti-Asian immigration laws, racial covenants and racial segregation, ethnic enclave economies, gentrification, and community cultural wealth.[6] In the back of my mind, I wished your father—a Chicago urban planner—was in the car to help answer your questions. Again, I was not ready to give you a developmentally appropriate explanation. I sank in the driver's seat, looked out the window at masked people who generally shared our shades of light brown and "eyes that kissed in the corners"[7] in a deeply segregated city, and silently lamented about how complex race and racism are to explain and understand.

How do you teach a kindergartener about the histories and contemporary legacies of race and racism in a way that affirms her humanity and agency? Suddenly, I wished I had studied early childhood development and education in addition to my scholarly expertise areas—higher education, critical race theory, and Asian American studies. Critical questions from my dissertation committee at UCLA, journal article reviewers, and discussants and attendees at academic conferences and symposia had nothing on your young mind. Of course, afterward when I told all these stories to my friend Sarah Park Dahlen (a professor and expert on children's literature), she suggested I probably could have just said that race and racial categories, like Black, White, and Asian American, were all made-up ideas. I could have just explained that these ideas were used to make up rules that positioned White people to seem superior, so they could have things that others could not, and that these ideas were used to hurt and keep other people and whole communities and neighborhoods down. I could have told you that a long time ago people with power made up meanings and rules out of colors to justify these inequalities and unfairness.

Your auntie, Dr. Sarah,[8] made it seem so simple, but we knew it wasn't all that simple, especially as a so-called anti-CRT movement was beginning to grow. In 2021, just one short year after racial justice activists responded to the police murders of Breonna Taylor and George Floyd and mobilized against anti-Black racism, some parents began protesting the false notion that schools were teaching "CRT" (critical race theory). This was a reactionary blowback against growing advocacy and changes for more racial equity—fairness—in our society, and it confused me for two reasons. One, I had never heard about CRT until I started pursuing my PhD in my early thirties. Two, and more importantly, I could not understand how these fellow parents were so opposed to having their children make sense of the racialized world around them. You were just a toddler when you started asking me questions about race and racism, and research has shown us that you were not alone. As social psychologists have asked, "If babies and toddlers can detect race, why do so many parents avoid talking about it?"[9] What were these "anti-CRT" parents saying when their children asked them about race and racism?

There is another reason I'm so confused by my fellow parents who are "anti-CRT." In 2021 Asian Americans across the country started mobilizing and successfully advocated to bring Asian American history to K–12 schools. I was involved in supporting efforts in both Texas (yes, the same Texas that "banned CRT") and Illinois.[10] I am excited to observe similar efforts in Connecticut, Ohio, New Jersey, New York, and other states.[11] I have been deeply disappointed to observe some fellow Asian American parents protest "CRT in schools" yet simultaneously advocate for Asian American studies in schools. Asian American studies *is* the field of inquiry seeking to understand the racialization and experiences of Asian Americans at the intersection of transnational migration, empire and colonization, and patriarchy. Asian American studies also importantly examines and spotlights what can be learned from Asian American agency and cultural productions of resistance and transformation within these contexts.

All of this has highlighted for me that we need *more* learning, understanding, and dialogue about race and racism, not less. Even as a toddler you had questions. My responsibility is to help you learn, explore, and create meaning that will shape how you act in this world in relation to those around us.

You were so young when you started asking different forms of a question I have pondered over a lifetime—a question many like us have confronted and answered in different ways for centuries. *What does it mean to be Asian American?* Although it's probably not developmentally appropriate for a three- or five-year-old, this book is my way of exploring this question, and continuing our conversation you started.

Your questions often remind me of my own journey of racial consciousness. Growing up in a working-class White immigrant town in western Massachusetts, I understood at a young age what Toni Morrison meant when she said, "In this country, American means White. Everybody else has to hyphenate."[12] In elementary school, recent Portuguese and Polish immigrant classmates would often verbally taunt me, mocking my eyes or cornering me on the playground with singsong racist and sexist rhymes like "Chinese, Japanese, dirty knees, look at these!" while pointing at their chests. As I got older and sometime after the start of Hollywood's 1980s trend in films about the American War in Vietnam and Southeast Asia, including *Platoon* and Sylvester Stallone's Rambo movies, the jeers became more sinister. White classmates would shout "Chink! Go back to China!" or "Go back where you came from, gook!" as I walked the intimidating gauntlet of school hallways.

Confusing questions of race didn't always arise in explicit ways. I remember a sunny Massachusetts spring day in 1988, when my sixth-grade classmates and I were stuck inside getting ready to take a state standardized test. Before the test had even started, my twelve-year-old fingers froze with the yellow no. 2 Ticonderoga brand pencil hovering over the demographic question: Black, White, or other? I raised my hand to get the teacher's attention, and asked Mrs. S, "Which one am I?" Mrs. S hesitated briefly before telling me to mark "other." Claiming "other" didn't sit well with me, as I wrote in my preteen diary that night: "What does 'other' mean? Other what?"

In school in the multicultural 1990s, my teachers taught me not to talk about race or racism. Their lessons countered the questions I had and national recognitions of Black History Month and the growth of public discourse on racism. Black History Month programming on TV, even in brief public service announcements, offered tiny moments of the anti-oppressive messages I craved. When a high school teacher assigned a book report on an autobiography or biography of our choosing, I selected *The Autobiography of Malcolm X*. Although the teacher rejected my choice, I read the book without someone to guide me.

Around the same time, I happened onto Ronald Takaki's *Strangers from a Different Shore* at the public library. As I read both books in secret, I felt nauseous and ill equipped to make sense of the historical accounts of systemic oppression and collective Asian American struggles for justice I was reading. In college I finally took my first Asian American studies class, and I reread Takaki's book with the expert mentorship of a professor[13] and in community with a diverse group of fellow Asian American students. I began to understand how my individual experiences were rooted in the toxic soil of systemic racism that intersected with other systems of oppression like misogyny, xenophobia, capitalism, anti-Black racism, and settler colonialism. Racism is not simply an interpersonal phenomenon that requires a "racist bone" in one's body. It is structurally built into laws and everyday practices and norms over time. Solving the problem of racism requires cross-ethnic and cross-racial relationships, learning, and movements to bend the long arc of the moral universe.[14]

This course set me on a path to pursue a career of inquiry through graduate school and into a career as a race scholar. I had, and still have, many questions and wonderings about how racism works, why it persists, and how to contribute toward social justice movements for change. I became an educator, motivated by a desire to offer the next generations the affirmations and guidance I hungered for throughout my journey to make meaning of the world around me.

What does it mean to be Asian American? This is not just a question you posed when you were three years old. It is a question with which many have struggled. It has been central to my life and career. So I decided to sit down and write a book addressed to you, my daughter.

In this book I offer my concerns and hopes about how Asian Americans are shaping the future of race relations and possibilities for a more just world. I do so by telling some of my own story and journey as a professional race scholar and politically engaged community member. I write about racial politics. I center the knowledge based on research I am most known for: the racial politics of college admissions and affirmative action, and how Asian Americans have been deeply and emotionally engaged in these debates since the 1970s. In this arena of ongoing and current debates, I have been a key player since 2005, conducting research on the relationship between affirmative action and Asian Americans, and advocating for race-conscious policies that affirm diversity.[15]

I am far from the first to write a book to explore this existential question, but I'm not giving you hot takes that only center my personal observations and opinions. For what it's worth, I think there are too many hot takes in this world that don't account for or engage with research and evidence in thoughtful ways. I will not give you easy answers in this book. In fact, I don't have any settled answers. I want this to be a continuation of ongoing conversations. I hope this book will raise more questions for you, and that we can talk through them, learn together, and grow in our intergenerational understandings that might support the creation of new insights and possibilities. I write this book, drawing from what I've learned over the last few decades through research, which I started over a decade before you were even an idea in my heart. I want to share what I have learned from the past—Asian American histories—and how it has helped me make sense of the present—our confusing contemporary world. By making sense of both history and present, we might create new insights— bold dreams—to lead our actions for creating new possibilities. To do so, I trace the affirmative action debate among Asian Americans in this book.

## ASIAN AMERICAN "IDENTITY WRESTLING" AND THE AFFIRMATIVE ACTION DIVIDE

At the 2022 American Education Research Association conference in San Diego, I attended a standing-room-only lecture by Professor Emeritus Carol Lee, who explained that civic engagement is identity wrestling. In the poorly lit, beige-walled convention center ballroom, Dr. Lee played a video of opera singer Marian Anderson's masterful 1939 performance of "My Country, 'Tis of Thee" at her outdoor concert on the steps of the Lincoln Memorial. I reflected on Anderson's beautiful act of defiance—to offer the world a concert when the Daughters of the American Revolution refused to allow her to perform in Constitution Hall, in an effort to maintain anti-Black racism and White supremacy. I felt chills, as the recording of Anderson's voice rang out in the convention hall, when I noticed that the contralto had changed the third line of the song from "of thee I sing" to "of thee we sing." My heart swelled with inspiration as Dr. Lee explained that Marian Anderson was engaged in a civic act of identity wrestling through her art.

Listening to Dr. Lee, I realized that Asian Americans are engaged in heated identity wrestling matches. We wrestle to make our identities and perspectives exist in this world and be recognized. We assert our existence and rights, through a long history of litigation and courtroom battles. We also live in an exciting era of Asian American pop culture and creative pursuits garnering mainstream recognition. There are now more comedy specials by Asian American comedians like Hasan Minhaj, Ali Wong, and Jo Koy, children's books by Asian American authors and illustrators like Bao Phi and Thi Bui, major movies like *Crazy Rich Asians*, *The Farewell*, *Everything Everywhere All At Once*, *Shang-Chi and the Legend of the Ten Rings*, *Turning Red*, and *Raya and the Last Dragon*, and TV and reality shows like *Never Have I Ever*, *Ms. Marvel*, *Fresh Off the Boat*, *House of Ho*, and *Family Karma* than I can count. When I would go to Asian American film festivals in the late 1990s and early 2000s, it was just a dream that we would see our cultural productions appreciated outside of Asian American communities. The exciting upsurge of cultural productions offers an increasing plenitude of Asian American narratives[16]—a diversity of viewpoints that may not always agree with each other. In the affirmative action debate, Asian Americans are wrestling with many different and conflicting views, perhaps reflecting the varied social, cultural, and economic conditions experienced across Asian diasporic communities.[17] At the heart of the differences is a disagreement over where anti-Asian racism comes from and the best solutions for dismantling it. There is no unified viewpoint among this conglomeration of ethnic groups with linked yet disparate histories and cultures called Asian Americans.

The question "What is (anti-Asian) racism?" is another way to ask the question: What does it mean to be Asian American? The existence of race, racial categories, and identities is in deep relationship to the presence of racism. Racism shapes what race means; race makes racism possible. Answering these questions is complicated, when we live in a society that uses simplified and narrow metrics of socioeconomic status to determine the existence of racism.

Overall, Asian Americans are the racial group with the highest levels of educational attainment and household income in the US. Simultaneously, some Asian American ethnic groups—Cambodian, Hmong, and Laotian— have some of the lowest levels of educational attainment and income in the country. Paradoxically, Asian Americans suffer the highest rates of suicide, and among college students Asian Americans express the lowest sense of belonging and satisfaction in survey studies.[18] These statistics illustrate a more complex picture. They do not lead to easy answers about how race and racism affect Asian Americans. They certainly do not suggest that Asian Americans have been liberated from racism in both their educational experiences and in other social realms.

Racism cannot be narrowly determined and defined by access to college degrees or household income. In the years after the start of the COVID-19 pandemic in March 2020, alarming reports raised public concern over a rise of anti-Asian violence. This new self-reported data on racial harassment and violence adds to the continuing Islamophobic violence targeting Muslim and South Asian Americans following September 11, 2001. Still, there are differences and conflicts between Asian Americans and how we understand racism and what to do about it.

For example, the anti–affirmative action Chinese Americans I interviewed agreed that racism, and anti-Asian racism, are real problems. However, we find ourselves on opposite sides of a debate over affirmative action—one of the few policy tools that remains[19] for addressing systemic racial inequalities in employment, public contracting, and education. One of my mentors, public policy professor Paul Ong, called this conflict the Asian American affirmative action divide. This divide, especially related to education access, is emblematic of a larger debate over what constitutes anti-Asian racism and how to end it.

There are many other policy issues that Asian Americans care about, and I could have focused on any number of them. However, as an Asian American community insider or close observer can tell you, raising the question of affirmative action—and especially race-conscious college admissions—in Asian American spaces might elicit a range of highly intense emotions. This relatively niche policy issue is like a third rail for some Asian Americans. If you want a pleasant and conflict-free Asian American holiday dinner, I suggest not talking about affirmative action. Since the early 2010s, I've noticed a deep emotionality in this debate that gets at the Asian American condition and our existence as a racial group.

What does it mean to be Asian American? To answer this question, I offer a narrative deep dive into the affirmative action debate, specifically in Asian America. In 2016, right before Donald Trump was elected president, I led an interview study of Asian Americans across the country who were leaders and central members of Asian American organizations active in legal and policy debates over race-conscious admissions. They told me their personal life histories and experiences with race and racism, their values, and what they believed about education and college access policies.

These thirty-six individuals represented a diversity of identities. They were immigrants, the children, grandchildren, and great-grandchildren of immigrants and refugees. They identified across a spectrum of ethnic identities—Burmese, Cambodian, Chinese, Filipino, Indian, Korean, Taiwanese, and Vietnamese. They represented a range of economic class backgrounds. The majority of the thirty-six supported affirmative action, but seventeen of them opposed the policy. All of them agreed that racism and racial inequalities were problems. They also believed they represented Asian American interests. However, they didn't share a common understanding of the nature of racism. Without a common notion of the problem, it felt like there were different understandings of what it meant to be Asian American.[20]

I dip into the stories of these thirty-six people alongside my own personal stories to answer our central question: What does it mean to be Asian American? Although Asian Americans represent a relatively small population, listening and learning about what Asian Americans believe about race, racism, and what to do about it can reveal so much about how racism works in the US. Affirmative action is among the best policy debates to reveal how Asian Americans are engaged in identity wrestling. Their engagement in ongoing political contests over the legalities of one of the few remaining policy tools to address racial inequalities reveals peculiar contours of racism in America.

In affirmative action debates, Asian Americans are not just fighting over what should become of race-conscious policies in college admissions; we are wrestling over what it means to be Asian American.[21] On one hand, advocates for affirmative action represent an ethnically diverse and intergenerational panethnic coalition of Asian Americans. They work across racial lines with other people of color to articulate and advance an expansive racial justice agenda that seeks both incremental and transformative systemic changes. On the other hand, opponents, who represent few outside the Chinese American community in their campaigns, are weaponizing the Asian American identity. They generally see no problem with how systems, such as highly rejective[22] college admissions, work to reinforce racial inequalities that benefit them. Instead, they assert that the responsibility for increasing college access for Black, Latinx, Indigenous, and Southeast Asian American students lies with these marginalized communities and individuals. They just need to work harder. Or they will say that the PK–12 education system is to blame for college access inequalities and that college admissions practices should not change. Interestingly and increasingly, many of these same people are opposing policy changes in PK–12 to increase access to quality education across racial groups of students.[23]

The affirmative action debate highlights tensions between the diverse political ideologies and understandings of race and racism among Asian Americans. The complex fractures among Asian Americans in this policy debate reflect differences within the population along the question of whether the state should respond to racism, and how it should address the problem in relation to Asian Americans. How the affirmative action conflict is settled within Asian America bears deep racial consequences that reach beyond this relatively small population and well into the future of race and public policies in America.

## OVERVIEW

Individuals who recognize racism as a problem make varied choices in responding to it, based on how they understand racism, how it works, and how they perceive their relationships with people who are racially different from them. The ongoing debates over affirmative action between Asian Americans illustrate this point well. Policy opponents believe that the system of college access works well, and that Asian Americans are well represented in highly desirable undergraduate institutions based on individual will, determination, and grit. Therefore, they believe that if a racial group is underrepresented it is strictly due to a lack of personal, individual ethic. Moreover, they may view any policy that seemingly undermines the value of individual grit to be unfair. There is often a refusal to acknowledge that systemic inequalities and injustices can render even the most herculean individual effort insufficient. Through this logic, policy opponents assert that there is no public duty or moral obligation to change systems that reproduce racially unequal outcomes.

Supporters of affirmative action recognize that the educational system is rife with racial inequalities and needs to be changed to be fairer and more equitable, particularly in a racially diverse society. Therefore, actions need to be taken to change unfair systems to affirm diversity and equity in our society. Relying on a diverse democracy framework, policy supporters contend there is a public and shared responsibility in a democratic society to critically interrogate and change systems that perpetually reproduce inequalities.[24] They believe that our fates are linked together, across demographic lines.

In sum, for affirmative action opponents, the solution to racial inequalities is found in changing individual values and attitudes to help individuals work harder in systems that are presumed to be fair. For affirmative action supporters, racism is a systemic problem that calls for changes to unjust systems. These fundamentally different paradigms of racism and racial inequalities lead to very different social visions and goals. They are also not new differences between Asian American agendas seeking to assert our rights and place in the US. Disagreements over how to confront racism among Asian Americans are not new, especially in the US court system.[25] How Asian Americans articulate their rights in US society and social institutions has broad implications, as I discuss in chapter 1.

Throughout this book I seek to honor the humanity and dignity of fellow Asian Americans who hold ideological and policy disagreements with me. At the same time, I offer a personal yet evidence-based case for why I am persuaded to invest in an expansive agenda centering cross-racial solidarity as the only way to fully affirm the dignity of Asian Americans. I started the research project on which this book is based in 2016. As a new mom at the time, I found myself shifting my gaze and desires toward shaping a better future, for my child and generations after mine. To figure out how to contribute toward movements to build a new world, I wanted to understand the stories, experiences, and resulting views of fellow Asian Americans across the affirmative action divide. How did our histories produce our present-day differences in how we imagine what a fair, just, and humanizing society could be like?

I learned that we have chosen different pathways to fight for our communities, with different implications and visions for the future. Despite our disagreements, we are motivated by a sense of love for communities and families in what we are fighting over and for. I now wonder how the affirmative action divide might forge entirely new possibilities for the future for both Asian Americans and society more broadly.

Although every chapter opens and closes directed to my daughter, Té Té, I invite anyone else to read and join our conversation. I have organized this book as an exploration of the past, present, and future of Asian Americans and race in America. Asian Americans across the affirmative action divide offer various models and possibilities. There are many Asian American stories—historical and current ones—about how we choose to confront anti-Asian and other forms of racism and oppression. What we learn about racism and how we understand it as a problem and our visions for the future shape the choices and investments we make toward that future.

## MOTHERING AND THE FUTURE

Dear Té Té,

I have been reflecting on the past and present and what it means to be an Asian American scholar and activist, who is now first and foremost a mother to a third-generation, mixed-ethnic Asian American daughter. Motherhood has moved me into a space of thinking deeply about the future. You are my embodiment of my hopes and dreams for the future. You are a diasporic third-generation Asian American, whose working-class maternal grandparents immigrated from Hong Kong and whose professional-class paternal grandparents immigrated from Thailand—after the 1965 Immigration Act. Your childhood conditions are so different from mine, and yet they are so similar. I grew up in a financially unstable home in a working-class, predominantly White immigrant, suburban community. You are comfortably middle-class, growing up in a predominantly Latinx urban community in a state that requires one unit of Asian American history be taught across K–12 classes. You talk with me about race, racism, and other systems of oppression. I did not grow up discussing racism with my immigrant parents, but that did not mean we did not experience intersectional racist and misogynist violences. We just rarely talked about it together. Instead, I often felt a mix of shame, rage, hurt, and confusion. I turned to the public library for quiet answers in books on racism and anti-racist leadership and movements, which felt like illicit readings, because I had never encountered such words to make sense of the social world in school or at home. You have Disney heroes like Raya who identify as Southeast Asian like you. However, media representations will not save us, no matter how exhilarating they are.

We still confront anti-Asian violence, which has been increasingly documented during the COVID-19 pandemic, and is so familiar to me, your father, and our extended diasporic families. And we discuss how intersectional anti-Asian racism, while vile and requiring that we take up burdensome battles, is not the same as anti-Black racism, nor as settler colonialism, especially as we are settlers on Native American lands.[26] Still, our conditions and experiences are interconnected and complexly entangled.

When you were two months old, on June 17, 2015, a White man murdered nine Black parishioners during Bible study at the Mother Emanuel African Methodist Episcopal Church in Charleston, South Carolina. I remember driving home to you, through Uptown Chicago, with the elevated tracks above me on a cool and overcast day, when I heard the radio announcer listing the names of the slain, including Clementa Pinckney. Your first name is pronounced the same way as that of the late pastor and state senator Pinckney, and hearing your name brought me to a deeper level of sorrow, lament, and rage. With postpartum hormones coursing through me, I did not know parenthood could intensify emotions that way. It wasn't the first time I had mourned and raged in solidarity against White supremacy, anti-Black violence, and murders, but it was the first time I'd experienced it after becoming a mother who had just brought new life into the world. Hearing your homophonic name spoken among the murdered people took me to a dark emotional place.

Asian American is not a color. You were very right at such a young age. We are not Black. We are not White. Still, our fates are linked with others through a multilayered and adaptive web of systemic oppression. They have brought me to invest in desires for solidarity to end systems and cycles of violence and injustices, even if we might not directly, immediately, or obviously benefit. Asian American is a political identity historically created on a foundational commitment to solidarity for racial justice.

There are some out there who would say that Asian American is not a real identity. Such assertions are gaslighting rhetoric, because sociopolitical systems that include policies, laws, and state acts have contributed toward a creation of an Asian racial group across ethnic lines. For example, immigration laws after the Civil War targeted Chinese migrants and evolved over time to create an Asiatic Barred Zone in 1917, codifying anti-Asian xenophobia that continues to live on in our contemporary world.

Although government actions and systemic oppression created some contextual grounds for the creation of Asian America, know that young Asian Americans across ethnic identities created the Asian American identity—a cultural production and project of collective, community resistance to oppression, spanning diverse and at times divergent narratives. Before the civil rights era of the 1960s and 1970s, there were no "Asian Americans." During the civil rights movement in the US, college campuses were dramatically increasing their enrollments of students of color.[27] Some students, who identified distinctly along ethnic lines (i.e., Chinese, Filipino, Japanese, and Korean), rejected the term the US government and other dominant organizations had given them: Oriental. College students like Yuji Ichioka and Emma Gee who are often credited with creating the phrase "Asian American" came together in community to create new possibilities and a new identity.

There is no denying that Asian Americans have been racially targeted and oppressed across ethnic identities, and that we have collectively fought together for our rights historically. The question is: What do we do about intersectional anti-Asian racism today? When we have a sense of what one form of racism is, what do we do about it when it is visited on others in different forms? What are our responsibilities in relationship with fellow humans in this world?

My hope is that this book, alongside many others, will support you as you continue growing, learning, and making meaning of this world—as you navigate it as a Chinese (Hong Konger) and Thai American girl. We live in a society that will demean your humanity, misunderstand, misrepresent, and gaslight you on your experiences of confronting and navigating the intersections of racism and patriarchy, which will target you in particular ways that are different from how they target other systemically marginalized people. In my lifetime, I have been persuaded to recognize cross-racial solidarity as the most viable and promising practice of resistance to racism. I don't just want you to navigate or confront systems of oppression; I hope you will build relationships to participate and contribute toward collective movements against intersecting systems of oppression that target Asian Americans and many others, to forge new possibilities and futures.

After all, the practice of solidarity across differences for justice has been a key feature of what it means to be Asian American. Asian American is not a singular color, as you observed when you were just three. It's made up. Just like all other racial categories, it has no biological basis, and its existence relies on how power shapes the relations and relationships between people in the world. At the same time, Asian Americans and Asian America are very real.

As a panethnicity—a challenging practice of cross-ethnic solidarity—Asian American identity is an idea and an aspiration, a means for political solidarity that relies on constant negotiations and renegotiations between ethnic communities (e.g., Bengali, Cambodian, Chinese, Hmong, Indian, Lao, Pakistani, Taiwanese, etc.) within a larger context of how race and power operate.[28] When I first started learning about the historical articulation and development of Asian American panethnicity in college, I felt a sense of excitement to know that people like me had a role in the civil rights movement. I have sometimes romanticized this story of political unity and power building to fight White supremacy and other systems of oppression. However, it would be incorrect to assume that Asian American is a settled term or a unified group. There are many different understandings of race, racism, and what it means to be Asian American.

This book is my offering to restart and continue our conversation about what it means to be Asian American. I invite you to engage with my storytelling about my experiences, observations, wonderings, and research. I hope you reach insights that might affirm and encourage you to continue asking questions about the world around you and engage in dialogue with people who will challenge your understandings.

# CHAPTER I

# THE ANCESTORS AND
# THEIR CONTRASTING DREAMS[1]

Dear Té Té,

Every time we visit my family in Boston, we try to schedule some time at Forest Hills, where my mom and paternal grandparents are buried, and where the immigrant first-generation of my family here have all purchased plots for their final resting place—in a place where they have created home and community. Forest Hills is a beautiful and serene cemetery easily mistaken for a well-curated park on the southwestern side of Boston. Opened in 1848, it features a sculpture garden on arboretum-like grounds, with the grave markers and tombs of some of Boston's most notable individuals and families, including poets, authors, playwrights, artists, civil rights activists, athletes, politicians, and business leaders. In summers starting in the late 1990s, the cemetery hosted an annual Japanese-style lantern festival on a pastoral pond.[2] It is an extraordinary hidden gem in the city, away from most of the touristy destinations noted in travel guides.

Our ancestors are not buried with the most notable occupants at Forest Hills, such as poet e. e. cummings and playwright Eugene O'Neill. Instead, they are in a wide-open hillside with no trees to block the view of the adjacent city neighborhoods and Franklin Park, set apart by the American Legion Highway and the Arborway (MA-203). To get to our ancestors' resting places, you first enter the cemetery through a long winding driveway lined with a majestic canopy of pine, maple, ash, and honey locust trees. The entryway to the cemetery, marking the border between the city and the bountifully landscaped cemetery, is a sandstone castle-like gate. To the right is a red-roofed, old-style masonry finished chapel. Once you pass the gate, you are presented with multiple meandering pathways in all directions.

Every spring since my grandfather died in 1986, our family has visited Forest Hills for the Ching Ming springtime tomb-sweeping memorial holiday to burn incense and paper money and to offer foods to our ancestors in the afterlife. Generally held in April when the trees are mostly still bare and the bitter winds would sweep across the hillside, Ching Ming was a sort of annual family reunion picnic with everyone bundled up and eating Chinese BBQ and pastries from Chinatown. As a kid I would often sit in the car to stay warm, bored without any electronic devices, waiting for the adults to finish their time together at the grave site.

To get to the Chinese section of the cemetery, you must first find your way through the mazelike botanical section of the cemetery and head toward the left. If you get distracted by the beautiful blossoms in spring or the elaborate tombs of the wealthy, you can easily become lost. There weren't many graves in the Chinese section in the 1980s.

We only knew about the cemetery because my grandfather used to take the T (Boston's public transit system) all over the metropolitan area to explore his new home after my grandparents immigrated. They, along with my aunt, moved from Hong Kong to Boston in 1980 through the family reunification immigration pathway created by the 1965 Immigration and Nationality Act, which was signed by President Lyndon Johnson just fifteen years before their arrival. One day my grandfather took the train to the end of the Orange Line—to Forest Hills. Walking around the neighborhood, he happened on the gates into the cemetery. Afterward, he told his wife and children—my father, uncles, and aunt—that he would like to be buried there. Since the 1980s the cemetery's numbers of graves marked with Chinese and many other Asian surnames have grown exponentially, paralleling the growth of the Asian American population in the Northeast and across the US since 1965.

My brothers and I have always been enthralled by this cemetery. My favorite time of year to visit has always been the autumn when the tree canopies in the wealthy and mostly White section of the cemetery are ablaze with colors, and the weather is still warm enough to enjoy being on the hillside by our ancestors' graves while reflecting on the past. Your uncle Felix has an award-winning podcast episode about the ginkgo trees and their fallen seeds that lined the entrance to the cemetery and some of our core childhood memories set at Forest Hills.[3] The ginkgo trees are no longer there and only exist for us in faded recollections. For me, I have always been fascinated by how even in death, Boston's people are racially and ethnically segregated in the cemetery.

Asian Americans have been changing the landscape in the US in small and big ways. At Forest Hills cemetery, as the Asian surnames increased on gravestones each year, my family and I noticed new amenities, like water faucets and large metal bins to accommodate cultural practices of burning papier-mâché houses, cars, smartphones, and other materials to support the ancestors in their journeys in the afterlife. We didn't need to bring our own bins and water jugs anymore. More than twenty years after my grandfather passed, the cemetery started putting up a large multilingual Chinese, Vietnamese, and English sign every spring next to the entryway to welcome people celebrating Ching Ming.

During our trip to Boston for the 2019 winter holiday and to start 2020 together with family, while the grown-ups discussed preparations for our visit to Forest Hills, between figuring out where we would buy flowers, have lunch, and buy pastries, you asked where we were going the next day. I explained to you that we would be visiting my mom at the cemetery. You asked if you would get to play with her. I clarified that she was no longer alive, and you would only see her tombstone marking where her remains were buried. It wasn't your first visit, but it was the first time you asked questions. You were four years old, and it seemed that you suddenly realized that I had a mom you had never met and that she was not physically present in our lives. She died in 2013, about two years before you were born.

Later that night as we settled into bed, you turned to me and whispered, "Mama, I don't want you to die." Then with a quivering voice, you said, "I don't want to die." You started sobbing, and I started crying too, overcome by emotions. In some ways, your innocence about life started eroding that day, with the realization of death—that none of us will be physically breathing and interacting with the physical world forever. I remembered that I was also four years old in Massachusetts when I had the same realization. I remember walking into our living room with green shag carpet to find my mother crying while seated next to a cream-colored corded rotary phone, on the black-and-white plaid stitched fabric sofa. She had just received a phone call from Hong Kong and learned that her father had died. I remember crying that night in the bathtub with my saline tears running down in droplets into the warm water that enveloped me. I realized that my mom would not be with me forever and wondered what it would be like in a coffin, not fully understanding death. As you cried, I comforted you, knowing the overwhelming feelings you must have been having. I cried too, as I mourned this erosion of your innocence and grieved over knowing that you had never felt my mother's physical presence in your life.

Holding you that wintry night in Boston, I told you that our ancestors never completely leave us, and that I would always have some presence in your life and beyond. I know this, I told you, because when you were two years old, we were in a hotel in Nebraska during our move from Chicago to Colorado. I woke up early in the morning to you sitting in bed, looking up into the corner of the room and talking. In my early morning haze, I couldn't make out what you were saying. When I asked you who you were talking to, you turned to me with your chubby toddler cheeks and matter-of-factly said, "Your mom." I was shocked into silence and threw a pillow to wake your father and tell him what had just happened. Whether you truly had an encounter with my mother's spirit or just had a moment of fanciful imagination and storytelling when you were two years old, we will never know. But after I explained that our ancestors continue to stay with us, you calmed down and fell into a deep sleep.

The past is always present. In reading historical accounts, I am convinced that what our ancestors and elders did in the past has created the conditions of our present. And what we do in the present—what will become history—will shape the future. This thinking raises the question: How do we become good ancestors?[4] I don't think there is a right answer to this question, but I have learned from Indigenous scholars that there is a community-accountable way that centers intergenerational collective dreams and desires in future making.[5] To show you what I mean, I offer a story of selected "litigious Asian Americans"—ancestors who acted in ways that have shaped our present conditions of race, immigration, and education rights. It has always struck me how central courtroom battles have been to Asian American struggles for civil rights in the US, including rights to immigration and citizenship, property, civic participation, and public school attendance. The courts became a strategic arena for Asian Americans to fight for their rights when other opportunities were foreclosed.[6]

## LITIGIOUS ASIAN AMERICANS

The night before her October 2018 testimony in federal district court (US District Court for the District of Massachusetts) in the *SFFA v. Harvard* case, Sally Chen—one of eight students who testified on record about the importance of race-conscious admissions to diversity's benefits in education—received an email of encouragement from Oscar-nominated filmmaker and Harvard alumna Renee Tajima-Peña that read, "Knock em dead tomorrow. Remember Yick Wo, Wong Kim Ark, Mamie Tape, Fred korematsu [*sic*] and all our ancestors who spoke truth to power in the courtroom."[7] According to Chen, "Tajima-Peña linked my efforts to a lineage of Asian American civil rights victories, illustrating a proud history of progressive activism, litigiousness, and resilience."

Tajima-Peña's list could have included many other Asian Americans who have entered the court of law to defend and define the rights of Asian Americans. These litigious Asian Americans have not always shared the same legal strategies. They have pursued different approaches to claim Asian American rights in relationship to others, namely, White and Black people, in the US racial hierarchy. Studying the histories of these different cases illuminates different contours of racial ideologies and desires motivating their litigation.

Some litigious Asian Americans have entered the courts to litigate for the rights of Asian Americans that center their own self-interests within a presumed static unjust racial hierarchy. Others have, unintentionally or intentionally, argued for their rights in ways that would simultaneously advance the rights of people in general by questioning hierarchical norms. Sometimes I think about these two groups as the former arguing for "just us" and the latter advocating for justice. "Just us" is an agenda that starts from an acceptance of a status quo system and racial hierarchy of inequalities that restrict access to the top of the racial order to those who possess Whiteness. Those who advocate for their rights from a "just us" framing care little about how their visions of the future and actions might reproduce inequalities for people other than themselves. To me, justice requires a fundamental rejection of systemic norms and can be accompanied by an analysis that recognizes that we are not alone in a shared society, and our actions bear implications for ourselves *and* others. To claim an agenda of justice requires serious contemplations of social interconnectedness, a recognition of linked fates, and an investment in solidarity to transform norms and systems to be more equitable for all.

To be sure, people's legal histories and motivations are never as simple as a dichotomy between "just us" and justice. I cannot say with certainty what motivated historical litigious Asian Americans in their legal efforts. Still, as a non-historian, I find it illuminating to contrast some Asian American legal cases using this framework to think about how different Asian American arguments for their rights bear implications for our society beyond this relatively small population—for better or worse.

## A BRIEF HISTORY OF LITIGIOUS ASIAN AMERICANS, RACE, CITIZENSHIP, AND PUBLIC EDUCATION

Long before there was a United States of America, as early as the 1500s, voluntary and involuntary Asian immigrant settlers, starting with Filipinos, created communities and shaped the contours of social and political life. They interacted with the people in the places where they settled—Native Americans, African Americans, Latinx, and Whites—navigating the always precarious racial dynamics of different local places. From the time early Asian settlers arrived in the US, they cultivated new cultures and projects of resistance. Some entered the arena of the US court system as a site of resistance, to counter racial requirements for US citizenship.

Whiteness has been a long-standing requirement for US citizenship, starting with the founding of the nation. The 1790 Naturalization Law declared that "any alien being a free white person, who shall have resided within the limits and under the jurisdiction of the United States for the term of two years . . . and making proof to the satisfaction of [any common-law court] that he is a person of good character" may become a US citizen. It was the first time the new settler-colonial state had defined eligibility for citizenship as restricted to White people (i.e., White male property owners from northern and western Europe). White women's citizenship in the US was contingent on marriage to White male citizens, until the Cable Act of 1922. Racial prerequisites for citizenship remained until 1952.[8]

With the 1857 *Dred Scott v. Sandford* decision, the US Supreme Court declared that the descendants of enslaved Africans could not become US citizens. A few years later, in 1866, shortly after the end of the Civil War, Congress passed the Civil Rights Act granting African Americans legal citizenship. In 1868 the ratification of the Fourteenth Amendment affirmed that "all persons born or naturalized in the United States, and subject to the jurisdiction thereof, are citizens of the United States and of the State wherein they reside." Furthermore, Congress stated in Section 7 of the 1870 Naturalization Act "that the naturalization laws are hereby extended to aliens of African nativity and to persons of African descent." Congress chose to exclude Asians and Native Americans from the right to become naturalized US citizens after some deliberation leading up to the 1870 law, leaving the status of these groups ambiguous and uncertain.[9] This uncertainty of belonging in the US continues to follow contemporary Asian Americans who are often viewed as perpetual foreigners.[10]

Rising anti-Asian sentiments in the late 1800s and early 1900s led to several immigration laws that severely limited and effectively shut down Asian immigration to the US until 1965. In the 1875 Page Act, Congress barred the immigration of Chinese women, reasoning that they were likely to engage in prostitution and present threats to public health. In 1882 President Chester Arthur signed the Chinese Exclusion Act into law, barring Chinese people from entering the US. The 1917 Immigration Act created the Asiatic Barred Zone, prohibiting immigration from almost all of Asia and the Pacific Islands to the US. Japan and countries "owned by the United States adjacent to the continent of Asia," which included the Philippines, were exceptions to the barred zone. This law expanded the principles central to the Chinese Exclusion Act across most of the continent of Asia. These government acts begin forming historical foundations for the basis of shared cross-ethnic concerns and interests among Asians in the US.

By the 1920s, anti-immigrant sentiment had grown to a fever pitch. At the 1924 Ku Klux Klan convention, Georgia governor Clifford Walker called on the nation to "build a wall of steel, a wall as high as Heaven," to stop immigration from Asia. That same year, the Johnson-Reed Immigration Act effectively ended immigration from Asia until 1965. With this law, the barred zone expanded to include Japan, and quotas capping the number of immigrant visas to people who were eligible to naturalize as US citizens from the Eastern Hemisphere were significantly tightened. No quotas were placed on the number of immigrants from the Western Hemisphere. In 1946 the Luce-Celler Act placed restrictive quotas of a hundred visas each year on immigration from the newly independent Philippines and India, which would gain its independence from the British Empire in 1947.

In 1952 Congress passed the Immigration and Nationality Act, also known as the McCarran-Walter Act, which effectively abolished the Asiatic Barred Zone and ended the "alien ineligible to citizenship" category in US immigration law. However, it continued to maintain a strict quota system that sustained severe immigration restrictions on Asia. Finally, in 1965, Congress ended national origin, race, and ancestry as bases for immigration and naturalization with the passage of the Immigration and Nationality Act. Many historians have drawn links between the Black-led civil rights movement—its influences on transforming notions of race and rights—and the liberalization of immigration and citizenship laws in 1965. Some have also suggested that Cold War tensions between the US and the Soviet Union motivated the changes to immigration pathways for foreign scientists to contribute toward US global interests.[11]

Throughout this history, Asian Americans have pushed back against racist laws related to race, rights, citizenship, and education through the legal system. In studying these cases, I started noticing seemingly different goals. The plaintiffs in *Ozawa v. United States* (1922), *United States v. Thind* (1923), and *Lum v. Rice* (1927) were pursuing the inclusion of

Asian Americans—Japanese, Indian, and Chinese Americans—at the top of a presumed stable racial hierarchy in the United States. On the other hand, Asian litigants in *United States v. Wong Kim Ark* (1898) and *Lau v. Nichols* (1974) were pursuing the transformation of norms in legal interpretations to who could participate in US citizenry and public schooling. Wong and Lau both identified as Chinese, but their legal victories transformed national policies in citizenship and education to expand the rights of all people in the US, not just Chinese Americans or Asian Americans.

## LITIGATING TO CLIMB THE RACIAL HIERARCHY

The historic US Supreme Court cases of *Ozawa v. United States* (1922), *United States v. Thind* (1923), and *Lum v. Rice* (1927) particularly demonstrate efforts to assert Asian American rights to move up in the US racial hierarchy. In immigration, citizenship, and schooling, the law maintained racial exclusion and segregation until the mid-twentieth century. Like other racially marginalized people, Asian Americans fought for their rights using the legal system. In doing so, Takao Ozawa, Bhagat Singh Thind, and the Lum family argued that the state should treat them like White Americans and thus afford them the privileges and status of Whiteness required for both naturalizing as US citizens and attending segregated White schools. Although this book focuses primarily on race and education access, these historical cases demonstrate the links between immigration, citizenship, and education. For instance, Gong Lum was an undocumented immigrant; his wife Katherine had immigrated to the US as a servant, and their children were US citizens by birthright.

Within a social context of increasing xenophobia targeting Asian immigration in the early 1900s, Takao Ozawa and Bhagat Singh Thind fought the exclusion of Asians from citizenship in the federal courts. Separately, they both argued that they had met the racial condition of Whiteness required for obtaining US citizenship. The Supreme Court rejected both men's claims to Whiteness in decisions that were only months apart from each other, revealing how race is socially and flexibly constructed.

Takao Ozawa immigrated in 1894 and completed a college degree at the University of California Berkeley. Presenting his personal plea to become a US citizen, Ozawa submitted a brief to the court that read, "In name, General Benedict Arnold was an American, but at heart he was a traitor. In name, I am not an American, but at heart I am a true American."[12] In the brief he explained how assimilated he was to White American culture; how he married an educated, American wife; attended a White church and had his children attend a White school; and only allowed his children to speak "the American (English) language at home." Basically, he presented an argument full of respectability politics to demonstrate how his character was compatible with a culture and society of White dominance.[13] Moreover, his attorneys argued that Ozawa and other Japanese were "white in color."[14] Nonetheless, the Supreme Court ruled against Ozawa. Justice George Sutherland, himself an immigrant but from England, explained, "The words 'white person' were meant to indicate only a person of what is popularly known as the Caucasian race," and skin color is not the same as race.[15]

Three months after the Ozawa ruling, Bhagat Singh Thind arrived at the Supreme Court, likely with some added confidence in his case as a result of Justice Sutherland's opinion equating Whiteness with "the Caucasian race." Relying on popular racist theories like Blumenthal's theory of man and A. H. Keane's racial typology, which classified Asian Indians as "Caucasian," Thind argued that he met the racial prerequisite of Whiteness to naturalize as a US citizen. Unfortunately for Thind, the court decided that Whiteness should not be decided based on "science" but rather on common social understandings of Whiteness. Three months after the Ozawa case, Justice Sutherland further defined Whiteness in the Thind ruling. He wrote, "What we now hold is that the words 'free white persons' are words of common speech, to be interpreted in accordance with the understanding of the common man, synonymous with the word 'Caucasian' only as that word is popularly understood."[16] In other words, the court decided that Asian Indians may be "Caucasian" according to A. H. Keane (and his racist science), but they were certainly not "White," thereby rejecting Thind's petition to become a US citizen. I always think of this case whenever I hear someone today use the term "Caucasian" to describe someone who is White. According to the Supreme Court, they are not the same.

A few short years after these racial prerequisite cases for naturaliza-tion, the Supreme Court would revisit the question of where Asian Amer-icans belonged in the US racial hierarchy, as related to the administering of racially segregated public schools. By the 1920s, over 1,200 Chinese Americans resided in the Mississippi Delta region, where Jim Crow had replaced chattel slavery as the system of racial oppression and White dominant social order after the Civil War. Legally affirmed by the Supreme Court decision in *Plessy v. Ferguson* (1896), public facilities such as train cars, buses, and public schools were racially segregated between Whites and African Americans.

It was in this context that Katherine and Jeu Gong Lum decided to test the school segregation laws of Mississippi in 1923, by sending their US-born daughters, Berda and Martha, to the local White school in Rosedale, Mississippi. After one year of attendance at the new Rosedale Consolidated High School, the two girls were sent home by the principal, who notified their family that their attendance at the White school was no longer permissible. By the time school started again in September 1924, President Calvin Coolidge had signed the 1924 Immigration Act, and Rosedale Consolidated High School had received its state accreditation, requiring compliance with state rules and regulations, which included reserving the high school for White students. As Chinese Americans, the Lums did not easily fit into the Jim Crow racial classification of "colored," a racially demeaning term that commonly referred to African Americans.

In response, the Lums chose to engage in a legal fight, with an under-standing that they were risking the family's safety and grocery business. Because Jeu Gong was an undocumented Chinese American immigrant, they knew the government could find out and separate him from his wife and children. They also knew that their business creditors could retaliate against their business and livelihood. However, they chose to take the risk, because they did not want to accept inferiority to Whites or be grouped with Black people in the racial hierarchy. In Katherine Lum's words, "I did not want my children to attend the 'colored' schools. If they had, the [Rosedale] community would have classified us as Negroes."[17] According to journalist Adrienne Berard, Katherine believed that fighting for the rights of Chinese Americans to attend White schools was a fight for "the privileges afforded to whites." However, the Mississippi Supreme Court ruled that segregated schooling served "the broad dominant purpose of preserving the purity and integrity of the white race," not of other races. Upholding the lower court ruling in 1927, the US Supreme Court in *Gong Lum v. Rice* reaffirmed the constitutionality of separate facilities by race, between White and non-White, citing its ruling in *Plessy v. Ferguson* (1896) to justify the maintenance of excluding Chinese Americans from White schools. In the court's opinion, Berda and Martha's rights as Chinese Americans were not violated, since they were allowed to attend public schools intended for students who were not White, "separate from those provided for the whites."[18] The *Plessy* ruling was therefore not just applicable to segregating facilities for White and Black people; it was also relevant to keeping White people separate from all other people who were not deemed White. The Lums and other Chinese American children could attend a Black school, create a Chinese school, or go to school anywhere but with White children, because they were not White.

I have sometimes wondered whether Ozawa, Thind, and others could have argued that they were people of "African descent" to meet the racial prerequisite established in the 1870 Naturalization Act. Could that have been a strategic option for gaining US citizenship? In more than fifty federal cases over the racial prerequisite for citizenship filed by Asian Americans, Latinx, and people of Middle Eastern descent, only one chose to claim they were a person of African descent in court.[19]

However, like Ozawa and Thind before, the Lums understood the realities of racism and the racial order. They fought to climb a racial hierarchy toward Whiteness. As African American studies professor Imani Perry has observed in Mississippi, where Chinese Americans, African Americans, and White people have lived side by side since the 1800s, racism is a system of stratification designed to motivate "those who are neither at the top nor the bottom [to] work mightily to preserve their position in the middle."[20] For some Chinese Mississippians, "Black people are so stigmatized, it feels imperative to maintain a distance from them."[21]

Ozawa, Thind, and Lum pursued a kind of racial equality where they could possess White privileges and be treated like Whites. Their fight was for Asian Americans to cross what W. E. B. Du Bois had named the color line and gain rights reserved for Whites, leaving the unjust and dehumanizing racial order intact to continue the systemic oppression of other people of color. Their political choices and actions inherently aligned with the deep-seated social reality that "the American Dream is at the expense of the American Negro," as articulated by James Baldwin in 1965. None argued against broad de jure (i.e., legally sanctioned) racial barriers to US citizenship or the existence of racially segregated and therefore unequal schools. They worked to be included in the system of White supremacy and granted the rights and privileges that Whites have in it.

Maybe Ozawa, Thind, and Lum didn't realize they could choose to lead a systemically transformative path for racial justice, instead of implicitly accepting the status quo racial hierarchy. Given the possibilities and limitations they faced, and without studying the archives of their cases, I cannot definitively say that they were hoping to reposition themselves alongside White people in the social order. However, they only had to look back to the 1898 Supreme Court case of Wong Kim Ark for a legal case that led to radically transformative change to previously accepted norms. After all, this ruling was why there was no question of whether Martha and Berda Lum were US citizens in *Lum v. Rice* (1927). In contrast to Ozawa, Thind, and Lum, other Asian Americans have led systemically transformative projects.

## LITIGATING TO TRANSFORM AND EXPAND RIGHTS

In both *United States v. Wong Kim Ark* (1898) and *Lau v. Nichols* (1974), Chinese Americans fought and won their game-changing cases and helped reshape policy conditions and rights for all in the US. Wong Kim Ark was born in San Francisco to Chinese immigrants in 1873. Five years before his birth in 1868, Congress ratified the Fourteenth Amendment, which states, "All persons born or naturalized in the United States, and subject to the jurisdiction thereof, are citizens of the United States and of the State wherein they reside." He was nine years old when the Chinese Exclusion Act became law in 1882. In response to the rise of anti-Chinese hostilities, Wong's parents moved their family to China in 1890, but he returned to San Francisco a few months later with little trouble and made a living as a cook. In 1894 he traveled to visit his family in China, but on his way back, John Wise, the customs chief in San Francisco, denied his reentry, detaining him on different boats in the San Francisco harbor for five months until he was released on bond.

With the aid of a Chinese benevolent association, Wong Kim Ark retained an attorney and filed a federal lawsuit claiming a constitutional right to citizenship in the US, based on his place of birth—under the legal theory of *jus soli* (i.e., citizenship based on birthplace). Wise and the US government argued that Wong was not a US citizen, because his parents were not US citizens—relying on a theory of *jus sanguinis* (i.e., citizenship based on biological parents' nationality).[22] Moreover, they argued that the 1882 Chinese Exclusion Act barred him from entering the US.

When the case reached the US Supreme Court, it seemed the justices were searching for a reason to deny birthright citizenship to Asians born in the US. The rambling majority opinion presented an extensive review on how European nations defined "natural-born citizen." In the end, the court ruled in an overly wordy way that Wong Kim Ark was constitutionally indeed a US citizen by place of birth. Because of Wong's legal battle, the principle of birthright citizenship regardless of race became legal precedent.

Wong Kim Ark's legal victory transformed what it means to be a US citizen, dismantling racial barriers to birthright citizenship.[23] However, legal racial barriers to immigration for Asians and other people of color not from the Western Hemisphere would remain until the middle of the twentieth century. After centuries of racial restrictions in immigration and naturalization, the 1965 Immigration and Nationality Act brought forth an unprecedented increase of immigration from Asia and other non-European parts of the world. By the 1970s, many Chinese and Latinx immigrants settled in San Francisco, and immigrant and emergent multilingual children enrolled in San Francisco Unified School District (SFUSD) in large numbers. According to case facts in *Lau v. Nichols* (1974), "2,856 students of Chinese ancestry who were not proficient in English" had enrolled in the school district.[24]

Rather than address these children's varying educational needs, SFUSD chose a one-size-fits-all, English-only approach in their curriculum. The school district confronted their ethnically and linguistically diversifying student population with a sink-or-swim challenge: figure out how to succeed in schools that were essentially English-only, with minimal to no help developing English language skills, or discontinue formal schooling. Many emergent multilingual Asian American and Latinx students struggled through school without appropriate and adequate educational programs.[25]

After years of advocacy and demanding that SFUSD provide bilingual education for immigrant children, their families and advocates of immigrant student rights in SFUSD filed a federal lawsuit on behalf of about eighteen hundred Chinese American children. In *Lau v. Nichols* (1974), a kindergarten student named Kinney Kinmon Lau served as the name and face of the case. In its unanimous decision, the US Supreme Court ruled that the San Francisco school district had violated the Civil Rights Act of 1964 and discriminated against them "on the ground of race, color, or national origin."[26] Additionally, the court stated, "there is no equality of treatment merely by providing students with the same facilities, textbooks, teachers, and curriculum; for students who do not understand English are effectively foreclosed from any meaningful education." Equal treatment can essentially maintain systemic exclusion and inequality.

Notably, the choice to center Chinese American students was a racially strategic one. According to Edward Steinman, the lead attorney for Lau, the case was "*Lau v. Nichols* and not '*Gonzalez*' *v. Nichols*" because he and San Francisco civil rights activist and Berkeley Asian American studies professor emeritus Ling-Chi Wang "thought that the courts might have an easier time dealing with [Chinese American children] than children from Spanish-speaking backgrounds."[27] In other words, they were strategically capitalizing on an image of Asian Americans being more sympathetic than Latinx children were, in the eyes of the mostly White judges and justices.[28] The strategic gamble paid off, and the implications of the *Lau* ruling in the Supreme Court have affected larger numbers of Latinx students than Asian Americans. This lawsuit systemically transformed public schooling to benefit all emergent multilingual students, including the Portuguese and Polish immigrant students I grew up with in Massachusetts in the 1980s. In California this victory was especially remarkable, given the long history of exclusion of Chinese Americans from public schools until 1885 and segregation in education.[29]

The same wager in strategically deploying Asian Americans as a more sympathetic plaintiff likely would have failed just a few decades earlier. There had been a dramatic shift in racial views and stereotypes of Asian Americans from the first half of the 1900s—when the US had effectively banned immigration from Asia—to the second half of the same century— when Asian Americans came to be viewed as a "model minority."[30] By the 1960s media and political powers began shifting their racial narratives away from Asians as undesirable immigrants who brought immorality, crime, and disease. They reframed Asians as a quiet, accommodating, and hard-working population, just as the Black-led civil rights movement was at a high point. In the middle of the civil rights movement in the 1960s, mainstream news outlets like the *New York Times* published stories and essays about long-suffering Asian Americans who were able to achieve middle-class status through the dint of their grit and hard work, not complaining about racism.[31] This new, seemingly sympathetic, racial typecasting of Asian Americans offered a new way to undermine racial justice efforts, offering a foil and contrast to racial stereotypes of African Americans as undeserving and unreasonably entitled in their demands for changes to public and economic institutions, state and federal government agencies, and public life more generally. In lauding a "model" minority in relationship with the White majority, these racialized narratives and claims paternalistically frame and define another minority as implicitly or explicitly delinquent and deficient. The model minority stereotype leads to further marginalization of already racially subjugated populations.[32] There is a flattening, oversimplification, and rejection of the complexities and full stories of people and complex systems of racial power.

## LEGACIES OF LITIGIOUS ASIAN AMERICANS

Our litigious Asian American ancestors fought many struggles in the courts. I often wonder whether they had a clear vision of the future in mind or if they were simply focused on their specific cases. In all likelihood, there were a lot of ideas mixed into their experiences. I wonder what Wong Kim Ark was thinking and feeling when he decided to move to China in the 1960s, long after he had struggled through his legal battles that changed the parameters of citizenship and race in the US. What led him to decide to leave? What would he have to say about politicians in 2018 trying to end birthright citizenship?[33] Why did the Lum family not fight for the full integration of public schools rather than just to have Chinese Americans accepted into White schools? What would they think about the rapid re-segregation of schools and complicated patterns of Asian American public school enrollments today? Asian Americans are most often enrolled in schools that are majority White, majority Black, or majority Latinx. At the same time, schools with relatively large and growing numbers of Asian American students sometimes motivate White families to leave for Whiter schools, where they perceive more "commonalities" with other students and families.[34] What were the Lum family's desires for the future, and how does our contemporary world compare to their visions? Regardless of their intent, they had different views of and realities in their world and what needed to change.

The court system served as a central arbiter of how Asian Americans have been positioned in US social hierarchies and systems of power. In the historic cases of litigious Asians in US history—Wong Kim Ark, Takao Ozawa, Bhagat Singh Thind, Katherine, Jeu Gong, Berda, and Martha Lum, and Kinney Lau—there were key differences between how they engaged in theories and projects of change that bear relevance to the racial order in the US. Underlying these different ancestors' actions were desires for change and their intended and unintended consequences. We have a long legacy of political struggle as Asian diasporic immigrant settlers and descendants in the US, who have actively mobilized to claim dignity, belonging, and rights through different pathways.

Our ancestors had limited choices and strategic opportunities available to them. Much has been accomplished through many movements—the civil rights movement and ethnic studies movements, to name just two examples—and strategic efforts in community organizing and advocacy for civil rights and justice across ethnic and racial groups. Their work in challenging and transforming racial power have made more options and opportunities available to Asian Americans for pursuing change. Litigation is no longer one of the few avenues through which Asian Americans can advocate for their rights.

However, in education some Asian Americans are now participating significantly in lawsuits claiming anti-Asian discrimination in public magnet school enrollment policies that do not lead to large numbers of Asian American representation. For example, some Asian Americans are key players in *Association for Education Fairness (AEF) vs. Montgomery County Board of Education* and *Coalition for TJ v. Fairfax County School Board*.[35] In the AEF complaint, a judge in the US District Court for the District of Maryland dismissed the case in July 2022, finding no evidence that race-neutral changes to the Montgomery County Public Schools (MCPS) magnet school program admissions policy "disparately [impact] Asian American students or had been implemented with discriminatory intent."[36] Similarly, in May 2023 the US Court of Appeals for the Fourth Circuit ruled in favor of the Fairfax County School Board, finding no evidence of negative impacts on Asian American students in the enrollment policy changes at Thomas Jefferson High School that allowed the school to draw students from all middle schools in the district.

Interestingly, these contemporary Asian American litigants do not use their individual names, like Gong Lum or Kinney Lau did. Instead, they have been involved in forming organizations (e.g., AEF and Coalition for TJ) or supported organizations founded and led by White conservatives (e.g., Pacific Legal Foundation and Students for Fair Admissions) in lawsuits aimed at sustaining systems and processes that reproduce relatively high representations of White and Asian American students in selective public schools and colleges.

In each of these contemporary organizations' federal complaints, the litigants have deployed narratives of Asian Americans as victims— hard-working and high-achieving students who deserve the spoils of academic competition, presumably unlike stereotypes of Black and Latinx students. As District Court Judge Xinis observed in the dismissal of the AEF case, in 2013–14 "Black and Hispanic students represented nearly half of the MCPS student body, yet they accounted for less than 15% of the magnet school seats. Conversely, Asian American students represented just 14.8% of the MCPS student body yet occupied nearly half of the seats." This demographic pattern remains similar across the educational institutions and their related present-day lawsuits. There is a concerning weaponization of "Asian American" against other students of color in the distribution of educational opportunities. Using the courts as a tool to defend one's rights looks different from a clearly subjugated position, as Asian Americans were in the last century, than now, when on the whole Asian Americans occupy a very different position.[37]

I have often wondered if what these Asian Americans are doing could be considered opportunity hoarding—when parents use their available capital and assets to ensure opportunities for their children at the expense of others.[38] Perhaps it would be too easy and ungenerous to judge and dismiss these fellow Asian American parents as being so foul in their behaviors. After all, Charles Tilly's concept of opportunity hoarding and subsequent education studies applying the theory have generally centered White parents, with few studies examining Asian Americans.[39] In his study to understand how Indian American parents strategically navigated education systems for high achievement, sociologist Pawan Dhingra applied the concept of concerted cultivation.[40] He distanced Asian immigrant parental behaviors from opportunity hoarding and explained that "White middle-class parents try to 'hoard opportunities' by keeping academic inequalities in place (e.g., tracking, school choice) when their children are on top."[41] He went on to contrast dynamics between White and Asian American educational striving by stating that "when whites lead academically, other students must be taught to catch up. When Asian Americans achieve more than whites academically, they must be taught to calm down." Although I am persuaded that Asian American parents practice their own style of concerted cultivation, I remain uncertain that some Asian Americans are not engaged in opportunity hoarding through their policy and legal advocacy.

That said, I do want to be clear that many contemporary instances of Asian American activism in education have also pursued expansive notions of racial equity and justice, through cross-racial coalitions, as I share later in this book. There has never been just one strategy Asian Americans have pursued to advance our rights. We can see how differently Asian Americans fight for our place in this society by listening in on how Asian Americans vehemently disagree with each other over race-conscious policies in college admissions.

In these twenty-first-century legal debates over race, education, and belonging, there are generally two different groups of Asian Americans engaged in identity wrestling with different ideas of what it means to be Asian American in relation to other people and American social institutions. They are the latest generation of litigious Asian Americans. Time will tell what the choices and actions of these opposing forces of litigious Asian Americans will produce for the future. Before diving too deeply into the differences between Asian Americans across the affirmative action divide, in the next chapter I center our commonalities. Even when we are bitterly arguing with each other and talking over each other, it is important to remember each other's humanity and what we share, to begin unraveling what it is that we are each trying to set out for the future.

## ANCESTORS, ACTIONS, AND THE FUTURE

Dear Té Té,

One of my happiest days was Commencement Day in 2010. My mentors Don Nakanishi and Danny Solórzano—two of my academic ancestors—hooded me and ceremoniously granted me the rights and privileges earned with my PhD, in front of the faculty, my peers, and all our families and friends at UCLA on a typically gloomy June[42] day in Westwood. Afterward, looking at me with wonder, my mom remarked, "When I was a girl in Hong Kong working in factories, the best I could dream for myself was to work as an office girl. Today, my daughter has a PhD." We hugged as I teared up. She rarely showed emotion, so I'm quite certain I don't remember her shedding a sentimental tear.

What I also remember is the celebratory family dinner in Boston three months earlier when I had officially filed my dissertation and received email confirmation from the university that I had completed all requirements for my doctorate. As we sat down to a home-cooked meal on a cold Boston night, my father and brothers congratulated me on earning my PhD. There may have been a toast. Those memories are hazy now, but I distinctly remember my mom quietly eating. Noting her silence and alluding to the stereotypical dreams of so many Asian immigrant parents hoping to raise (medical) doctors,[43] your uncle Chester asked our mom, "Aren't you so proud? One of your kids is a doctor!" In between bites, your grandmother coolly stated, "Wrong kind of doctor." And we all busted out laughing. Like you, my mother always was able to keep me grounded. It was her way of reminding me not to think of myself as being better than anyone else. I had the privilege of a lot of formal schooling, but that didn't mean I was more intelligent than someone like her who didn't have opportunities to continue her education past grade school. Although she had pointed out how different my vocational possibilities had been from hers, my mom had never pushed me in my academic goals. In fact, she often raised questions about why I would forgo a professional salary and do several more years of schooling beyond a college degree. She would never understand the career path I would take. I was not living any dream she had for my life, but she was glad I was healthy and happy before she passed.

You didn't know my mom. She was a fighter and survivor. She was the youngest of six children, born in Zhongshan, China, right after World War II. Her older siblings told me stories of how she would take cleaned frog bones and make necklaces with them, and how she started cooking for herself when she was nine years old because her mother would leave early each day to watch her grandchildren, neglecting her youngest child. And her father, I have been told, was often absent from the home, drinking and gambling. My cousins have told me that he was mean, which I have taken to imply that he may have been abusive.

My mother survived a famine, eating bugs and bark to survive, before she and her family migrated with other refugees to the British colony of Hong Kong. Barely finishing elementary school, she worked in wig factories and garment factories as a teen. In her twenties she and a friend opened a small tailoring shop, attracting young men clients with their skills in fashion. The miniskirts I always saw my mom wear in pictures from that time probably didn't hurt business either.

When asked why their parents immigrated to the US, many Asian American children of immigrants say that their parents moved halfway across the world away from everything they knew for their children to have a "better life." I know that I have assumed and said the same thing about my parents. However, when I take time to think about what I know about my mom, I cannot say that she moved here for me or my brothers.

She unabashedly told anyone in her social circles through laughter that of the three of us, only one of us was planned. I was her first child, but not the planned one. She flew on a plane for the first time in her life for over twenty-four hours in December 1974, recently married to my father, whom she hadn't seen in over three years since he had left Hong Kong in 1971 for college in Boston. Barely knowing how to speak English, she got on a plane with her new husband—a practical stranger—and set out on an adventure. In my mom's story, I was not her dream come true.

Each time I remember my mother, on visits to her grave in the segregated Asian section at Forest Hills, I reflect on what I know and don't know of her life's journey and dreams. What made her decide to marry a man she hadn't seen in over three years? What ideas of her future life in America did she have? What I do know, as her daughter, is that she wanted her children to be healthy and happy. She wanted us to be polite and kind to people around us. She didn't want us to ever experience hunger and economic hardships like she had. She supported her children to do well in school, not necessarily to go to some fancy college with name-brand cachet, but so we could find a financial stability that she never had. She also loved having an active social life with fellow Chinese American immigrants in western Massachusetts. Weekly mah-jongg potluck parties that went well past midnight appear in many photos from my childhood. She loved to host and cook for friends. She was often the life of the party. I can still see her high cheekbones lit up with her brilliant smile whenever she was with her friends.

She is just one of our ancestors who made choices given their circumstances. My parents, like all parents (including me), are not perfect—far from it. I do know, however, that throughout our lives as parents, we do what we can with what we have, what we know, what we value, and all within our contexts and conditions. Each of our daily choices and actions are like forks in the infinite multiverse of possibilities.[44] Many small and large interconnected choices and actions have shaped each of our specific realities. How we choose to act will also create new possibilities for ourselves and for others whom we will never know. How will we act as ancestors who are birthing new future possibility arcs?

Back in December 2019, when we went to visit my mother's grave site, we solemnly set a bouquet of flowers and did our best to stick lit incense into the frozen winter ground in front of the tombstone. You learned to put your hands together in prayer and bow three times to the grave. We listened as your grandfather talked to his late wife in Cantonese as if he were waking her from a slumber, telling her that he was there with her children and granddaughter. We ate roast pork, bao, pineapple buns, and egg tarts we bought in Chinatown while you and your uncle Chester's dog Pepper wandered around and between tombstones, many marked with Chinese characters. I hope you will continue to pay your respects to the ancestors, and that you will also consider how our present was shaped by ancestors with whom we have no blood ties, recognizing the wholeness of all of our imperfect stories and choices.

# CHAPTER 2

# COMMONALITIES ACROSS THE AFFIRMATIVE ACTION DIVIDE

*Do We Even Know What
We Are Arguing About?*

Dear Té Té,

When I was pregnant with you, your father and I decided not to find out your sex. We didn't want to get swept into the pink or blue socialization. People would look at us funny when we told them we didn't want to know our baby's sex. One time a stranger in a laundromat, after some casual talk, scolded me for not finding out your sex: "If you don't know if you're having a girl or a boy, how will people know what kinds of gifts to buy the baby? That just seems rude to your family and friends who want to support you."

When you were born, we dressed you mostly in primary colors and made sure you had a full range of toys and books, not just clothing, toys, and books "meant" for girls or boys. We hid Disney princess toys and books, or regifted or donated them (sorry, friends and family!), because I really didn't want "Cinderella [to eat] my daughter."[1] But as author Peggy Orenstein explained in her book, we were helpless in the wave of pink glitter crashing in on our home through gender socialization.

As soon as you could express yourself, around when you were eighteen months old, we gave you options in clothing. Without fail, you gravitated toward pink, lavender, sparkles, and lace. We didn't often watch TV or movies with you at home, but when you were three years old you came home from preschool singing and imitating the dance moves from that earworm "Let It Go" from Disney's smash hit *Frozen*. That movie was first released in 2013, a few years before you were born, but as any parent of young children will tell you, Elsa is very powerful!

When you were four years old, some time before Halloween that year, you excitedly told me you were going to dress up like Elsa for Halloween. When I dropped you off in preschool that day, you walked into your classroom and announced to your best friend Taylor and the whole class, "Hey everyone! I'm going to be Elsa for Halloween!" I smiled at the cuteness, as I got back in the car to drive to work.

When I came back to pick you up from school, you ran over into my arms wanting to cuddle. You looked very sad. Your teacher Ms. T told me that you and Taylor had a screaming fight about who could be Elsa. You both argued that there could only be one Elsa for Halloween. I turned to you and said, "Oh, baby girl, anyone can dress up like anyone they want to for Halloween." Your face crumpled and your eyes immediately welled up with tears as you quietly but sternly stated, "No. I want to be Elsa. Taylor cannot be Elsa." I hugged you closer and decided it wasn't worth arguing with you that your scarcity mindset on Halloween was silly. I decided to just love you and comfort you in that moment. Over time you let go of the idea of scarcity over Halloween dress-up.

People can hold their beliefs very tightly, even when they are very wrong. Providing new evidence and logic may not be enough to shift perceptions, especially when there are deep emotions fueling them. This is something I have observed, experienced, and learned many times in my life.

It was a frigid February 2014 evening in Champaign, Illinois, two years before the Supreme Court would revisit *Fisher v. UT Austin*. The Asian American Cultural Center (AACC) at the University of Illinois at Urbana-Champaign (UIUC) had invited me to give a talk about the politics of race, college access, and Asian Americans. Despite the single-digit temperatures and blustery winds across the Illinois prairie that evening, about eighty mostly Asian American undergraduates packed into the AACC's multipurpose room, parkas and backpacks filling all the space between audience members on chairs, tables, and the floor. In my talk I gave a brief history of affirmative action and explained the legal parameters set out by the 2003 US Supreme Court decision in *Grutter v. Bollinger* and its implications for how selective college admissions worked within legal guidelines: that colleges could consider race in limited ways and as one of many factors in creating diverse classes for admission each year.

I ended the talk by explaining that the phenomenon of Linsanity exemplified a contemporary parable for affirmative action. In the winter of 2012, seemingly out of nowhere, Jeremy Lin—a second-generation Taiwanese American New York Knicks fourth-string guard—sparked and led an exciting winning streak for a team struggling mid-season in an arena and space where Asian Americans are not often found. Lin wasn't the first Asian to play in the NBA,[2] but Lin was the first *Asian American* in recent memory to make it to the NBA. In February 2012 Linsanity seemed to be on the minds of every Asian American I knew, across ethnic identities, as people wrote and shared innumerable think pieces about Jeremy Lin's rise to NBA stardom, what Lin represented, and race relations.[3] Linsanity was a media and racial spectacle.

At the height of Linsanity, many were asking how basketball "talent evaluators overlooked his ability."[4] Lin had received accolades as a high school basketball star. He was named first-team All-State in California and Division II Player of the Year in Northern California. As a high school senior, he helped lead Palo Alto High School to a 32–1 record in 2005–6 and a Division II California state championship. Inexplicably, no NCAA Division I college basketball team offered him a scholarship to play for them. Rex Walters, the men's basketball coach at the University of San Francisco between 2008 and 2016, and the last Asian American to play in the NBA, pointed to NCAA rules of recruitment, which limited visits and time college coaches and scouts could watch high school players. "A guy like Jeremy," Walters said, is "that much harder to watch. Most colleges start recruiting a guy in the first five minutes they see him because he runs really fast, jumps really high, does the quick, easy thing to evaluate."[5] In other words, the metrics and testing procedures for evaluating prospective college ball players restricted a broader acknowledgment of diverse talent. They limited coaches from being able to recognize how different players could contribute to the game in unique ways.

Notably, Lin also recognized that racism played another role in creating a barrier along his pathway to the NBA. In a 2013 interview on *60 Minutes*, Charlie Rose asked him, "When it came time to look at colleges, not a single D1 program came calling with a scholarship. Not one PAC-10 team. Not UCLA. Not Stanford, your hometown? What do you think they didn't see?"[6] Lin matter-of-factly explained, "Well, I think the obvious thing in my mind, is that I'm Asian American, which is a whole different issue, but that's . . . I think that was a barrier." In response, Rose prompted Jeremy to elaborate, asking, "When you say because you were Asian American, what is that? Nothing about being Asian American that doesn't give you the ability to play basketball." Lin replied, "Yeah. I mean, it is just—it's a stereotype." Racism and the systems of talent evaluation prevented basketball scouts from recognizing Jeremy Lin's talent, which *looked* different in style and race from many other Division I college basketball players and NBA players, who have historically been predominantly White and now mostly Black.

The practice of holistic race-conscious admission allowed diverse applicants to demonstrate a range of talents in ways that narrow and highly limited measures of merit, such as test scores and high school grade point averages, would always overlook, allowing admission reviewers to gain a more humanized view of individual applicants. Expanding notions of "merit," it allowed students to show who they were and how they could contribute toward a learning community. After all, higher education is about supporting the development of a diversity of talents many people can offer to society.

During the post-talk discussion, an inquisitive young woman hesitantly raised her hand and asked me an earnest question, which led to a thoughtful conversation. She shared that she had recently heard that California was considering legislation to "ban all Asian Americans from enrolling at the University of California" through the reinstatement of affirmative action. Taken aback by this characterization of California's Senate Constitutional Amendment 5 (SCA-5), I watched as an anxious buzz rippled across the room. Having talked with some of the student leaders earlier in the day, I knew that many of these students had long recognized and felt the sting of anti-Asian racism in their hometowns and on campus, but they felt they did not have many opportunities to discuss these concerns, or to have them taken seriously outside of Asian American community spaces. Some told me they wanted to have safe, or brave, spaces to openly discuss and learn more about Asian American stakes and interests in racial issues like affirmative action. They feared that by demonstrating a lack of clarity on race-conscious college admissions and other racial equity issues, and what they meant for Asian Americans and the racism they experienced too, their peers—Asian Americans and others—might judge and dismiss them as being racist themselves.

Because the student's question and concern of an anti-Asian ban in higher education seemed sincere and not intended to undermine my presence and engagement in their cultural center space, I asked the audience how many of them had heard this too. About a dozen students raised their hands. Each said they had heard it through their immigrant parents or other elders. At least one student also said they had seen it in ethnic Chinese American media outlets. Recognizing how real this emotion and confusion was that evening, I explained that what they were hearing through their ethnic social networks were dangerous rumors about SCA-5—a California State Senate initiative to overturn the state ban on affirmative action in public education, which was under consideration during the 2013–14 legislative session.[7] If passed and signed, SCA-5 would have allowed public universities to consider race as one of many factors in admissions,[8] in alignment with federal case law at the time. Just as I had explained in my lecture that night, it would expand how talent and merit were recognized, understood, and valued. From the looks several students gave me, they remained skeptical and afraid of the possibility of outright exclusionary quotas and discrimination against Asian Americans in higher education. After all, anti-Asian discrimination and racism was a very real thing in their experiences. They just weren't sure if race-conscious admissions and affirmative action effectively addressed these problems in their lives, and they wondered if these policies and practices unfairly added to their racial burdens.

At the end of the event, a few students came up to thank me for my presentation. Some said they appreciated my explanation of affirmative action law, and that they felt more informed and prepared to engage in policy debates. A few said they still believed race-conscious admissions produced anti-Asian effects, through an underhanded practice of anti-Asian quotas, echoing the long history of anti-Asian policies. Indeed, anti-Asian laws have included immigration bans, anti-miscegenation laws, and bans on property ownership, and legalized educational exclusion and segregation existed in the previous century.

However, suggesting that affirmative action policies, which are intended to acknowledge social inequities, are akin to explicitly racist laws requires a conflation of anti-racist agendas with racist policies.[9] According to some who believe that affirmative action is anti-Asian in effect, Asian Americans would represent upwards of 25 to 50 percent of selective college campuses without race-conscious admissions practices, even though Asian Americans represented only about 6 percent of US college students in 2019. In the same year, slightly over 16 percent of undergraduates at UIUC were Asian American, not including international Asian students. In Illinois, less than 6 percent of the population was Asian American.

These claims that race-conscious admissions policies are anti-Asian rely on racially biased logics, racial anxieties, and two fallacies. The first myth is that all Asian Americans pursuing college degrees are extraordinarily talented, above and beyond other Americans. The second misconception is that all Asian Americans wish to attend highly selective colleges and universities. The first assumption relies on racial stereotypes of universal Asian American high achievement and negative racial stereotypes of other students of color, measured solely by score averages on unreliable tests.[10] The second represents an idea that is disconnected from reality and empirical evidence regarding the complexities of college pathways and choices. For example, over 40 percent of Asian American college students attend community colleges, and many more attend less selective institutions.[11] Like other college students, Asian American students' enrollment trends are affected by complicated interactions between student and family choices in navigating unequal systems of education.[12] These complex realities and evidence rarely make it into free-flowing debates over narrow assumptions of how selective admissions or college-going structures work.

I have talked with many Asian Americans across the political spectrum who claim to support racial justice and equity. I am troubled in these conversations when people essentially tell me, "You can explain the law and research, but I have my gut. My gut tells me that affirmative action ultimately represents an Asian penalty in practice."[13] In these conversations, both policy supporters and opponents confidently presented falsehoods that affirmative action in admissions was a practice of racial quotas and/ or bonus points for non-Asian applicants of color. They also believed Asian American applicants did not directly benefit from race-conscious admissions processes. Policy opponents believed falsehoods that the goal of affirmative action was to penalize Asian Americans, which was unfair. Many policy supporters also believed similar misinformation that affirmative action was a quota practice that did not benefit Asian Americans, but they supported the policy as a necessity for fairness, given the need to redress historical legacies of racism especially targeting African Americans and other non–Asian American students of color. Supporters argued that Asian Americans needed to think "beyond self-interest"[14] and value the educational and social benefits that Asian Americans derive from racially diverse campus environments. Through my conversations with Asian Americans across the affirmative action divide, I realized that there were shared misunderstandings of what race-conscious admissions was. Do Asian American adversaries in the affirmative action debate even know what they are arguing over?

Only six of the thirty-six Asian Americans I interviewed understood how race-conscious admissions worked. Thirty held myths about race-conscious admissions as quotas or bonus points given to non-Asian applicants of color. I was surprised that so many people, including policy supporters, were misinformed.

When I asked them to tell me what their ideal process was for college admissions, I was even more astonished to learn that almost all the people I talked with, including affirmative action opponents, described principles of how race-conscious holistic admissions worked before the Supreme Court struck down these practices in *SFFA v. Harvard/UNC*. Thirty-three people across the affirmative action divide believed that colleges and universities should consider how race and racism, among other social conditions like economic class and gender, shaped different students' lives and educational opportunities, when deciding which students to admit to selective colleges.

I could have corrected these misinformed beliefs during my interviews, but I didn't. I think I was too bewildered over how badly informed both sides of the affirmative action divide were. It was like everyone was arguing which child could dress up as Elsa for Halloween. But they were all intelligent and civically engaged adults.

As education professor Julie Park explained in *Race on Campus: Debunking Myths with Data*, there are deeply held cognitive biases, or pervasive myths, about race in higher education at play in these debates and discourses. This is especially true for Asian Americans, who are justifiably concerned about racism and discrimination. These worries can manifest into racial anxiety and fears among some, which can feed into an over-reliance on their biases rather than using evidence to help them explain the world around them as they express what they want for the future.[15]

## AFFIRMATIVE ACTION LAW AND ADMISSIONS PRACTICES (1978–2023)

If I could visit with the people I interviewed again, I would try to help them understand how race-conscious admissions worked before the June 2023 Supreme Court ruling in *SFFA v. Harvard/UNC*. I would start by acknowledging that affirmative action and race-conscious admissions practices have evolved over time. They have changed in response to a series of Supreme Court decisions in 1978, 2003, and 2016.[16]

### BAKKE (1978): DIVERSITY OVER RACIAL REPAIR AND JUSTICE

Almost as soon as colleges and universities began implementing affirmative action in the 1960s and '70s, conservative opponents launched attacks on policies seeking to address racial and ethnic inequalities produced by both historic and contemporary systemic racism. Vast amounts of research have demonstrated the legacies and persistence of systemic racism in shaping education and schooling experiences in K–12 and higher education,[17] creating inequalities in educational access by race. In the face of these realities, *Bakke* represented a victory for those who wished to prohibit social institutions and public policies from acknowledging the realities of systemic racial inequalities that limited educational access and opportunities by race.

Justice Lewis Powell's opinion in *Bakke* transformed affirmative action in admissions in two drastic ways. First, it brought in the application of a strict scrutiny legal standard to test the constitutionality of the use of race in college admissions. Strict scrutiny means that there needs to be a compelling state interest to justify the consideration of race; and if there is a compelling interest, then there can be a narrowly tailored use of race. In other words, you must prove that there is a strong government interest that would powerfully validate the use of race in policy and practice. Plus, how race is used needs to be very limited and constrained.

Second, Justice Powell deemed the educational benefits of diversity to be a compelling public interest that justified the inclusion of race as a limited factor in college admissions. The ruling shifted the legal purpose of affirmative action away from redressing racial harms (i.e., the remedial rationale for considering race) to diversity to benefit all students (i.e., the diversity rationale). The shift to strict scrutiny was about concerns that race-conscious admissions would be overly burdensome on White applicants like Allan Bakke, whom the UC Davis Medical School had rejected twice. In the *Bakke* opinion, Justice Powell stated that "preferring members of any one group for no reason other than race or ethnic origin is discrimination for its own sake."[18]

However, the aims of affirmative action were not free of reason. They were to recognize historical wrongs and their contemporary legacies, and to affirmatively act in ways to create a more racially inclusive future. Justice Powell's ruling relied on a false equivalency between a policy intended to address persistent systemic racism and so-called reverse racism against White applicants.[19] Yet eleven other medical schools had also denied Bakke admission to their programs. Allan Bakke's legal complaint against UC Davis Medical School and explanation for his rejections relied on racial assumptions that defined Black, Indigenous, Latinx, and Asian Americans as not academically or intellectually capable of medical school. Bakke argued that he would have been admitted if UCD Medical School did not maintain a set-aside program intended to counter educational and social systems that persistently place extra barriers and burdens on students of color. It seems paradoxical to suggest that the intentional practice of acknowledging that racism has shaped the educational trajectories of students is a "racial preference," when racism has systematically created preferences for White students.[20] To suggest that a limited affirmative action program at the point of medical school admissions is a "racial preference" requires an erasure of how White people, on average, are protected from systemic racism, which subjects people of color in general to poorer healthcare, shorter life spans, higher rates of poverty, and enrollment in less resourced schools than their White peers.[21] The fallacy that the racial status of people of color, and especially of Black and Indigenous people, represents some sort of preferential standing in society was demonstrated by educator Jane Elliott when she prompted a room of White people: "If you as a White person would be happy to receive the same treatment that . . . Black citizens do in this society—please stand," and no one stood up.[22] Or in the case of Gong Lum, when the family recognized that going to school with White children would be a step up from being set aside from Whiteness and attending a segregated Black school. I fail to understand how being targeted by systemic racism for generations but then receiving a limited consideration of this reality at the point of admissions is a "racial preference."

Striking down the remedial rationale—that histories and legacies of racism justify the consideration of race in admissions—the *Bakke* opinion shifted the legal purpose for affirmative action to the diversity rationale. Justice Powell explained that it was acceptable for "race or ethnic background [to] be deemed a 'plus' in a particular applicant's file; [but] not insulate the individual from comparison with all other candidates for the available seats."[23] The *Bakke* ruling shifted the legal goal of affirmative action in admissions, and arguably public attention, away from the policy's historical purpose of addressing persistent and long-standing systemic racism. Since 1978, federal case law and precedent established that the individualized consideration of race can only be employed for the purposes of diversity, or educational pluralism, to benefit *all* students.

The *Bakke* ruling mirrors the nation's general refusal to acknowledge how racism continues to maintain White dominance through systemic dehumanization and oppression of people of color.[24] The decision effectively shifted policy considerations away from confronting and deconstructing persistent systems and norms of White dominance and racism to a racial policy of diversity that benefits everyone, including White students—perhaps the original "all lives matter" argument.[25] Whether one agrees or disagrees with compelling essays like poet Kimberly Reyes's 2018 "Affirmative Action Shouldn't Be about Diversity: It Should Be about Reparations," the *Bakke* precedent restricted race-conscious admissions practices to the goal of achieving the educational benefits of diversity for *all* students.[26]

### *GRATZ* AND *GRUTTER* (2003): AFFIRMING DIVERSITY THROUGH INDIVIDUALIZED REVIEW

In 2003 the Supreme Court further defined and restricted the practices of affirmative action in admissions with the decisions in *Gratz* and *Grutter*. After being denied admission to the University of Michigan, Jennifer Gratz filed and won a lawsuit (*Gratz v. Bollinger*, 2003) challenging the university's undergraduate admissions practice of automatically awarding an extra twenty points to underrepresented minority applicants. The court ruled that this point system created an inflexible preference for students based on race, which deviated from Justice Powell's parameters for race-conscious admissions in *Bakke*. Justice Rehnquist's ruling opinion reinforced the *Bakke* precedent's call for individualized review in admissions: to "consider each particular applicant as an individual, assessing all of the qualities that individual possesses, and in turn, evaluating that individual's ability to contribute to the unique setting of higher education."[27]

In *Grutter v. Bollinger* (2003) Barbara Grutter filed suit against the University of Michigan Law School after being denied admission. Grutter argued that the higher admission rate of minority applicants with similar test scores as White applicants demonstrated a violation of the Equal Protection Clause of the Fourteenth Amendment. The Supreme Court ruled in favor of the Law School, which justified its practice of an individualized admissions process. The Law School included "race as one of many factors" to achieve a compelling interest of educational benefits of diversity for all students. In Justice O'Connor's opinion for the court, "the Law School adequately considered race-neutral alternatives currently capable of producing a critical mass without forcing the Law School to abandon the academic selectivity that is the cornerstone of its educational mission."[28] Therefore, the *Grutter* ruling affirmed the educational benefits of diversity as a compelling interest in using race as one of many factors through holistic review.

For the first time, the terms "holistic review" and "critical mass" were articulated in court opinions. The court recognized that to produce the educational benefits of diversity, colleges and universities could seek to enroll "a 'critical mass' of students of color (i.e., more than a token number, but not a ceiling) to help diminish the impact of stereotypes and racial marginalization."[29] The amorphous nature of "critical mass" would lead to the next lawsuit in the legal saga of affirmative action in admissions: *Fisher v. University of Texas at Austin*, parts I (2013) and II (2016).

### ED BLUM, ABIGAIL FISHER, AND SFFA

The *Gratz* and *Grutter* decisions further limited race-conscious practices at selective colleges and universities that continued to see declines in the enrollments of students of color who are not East or South Asian Americans.[30] Regardless of these outcomes, the conservative attack on the policy continued in the legal arena. In 2008 Edward Blum took up the torch of the campaign against what was left of affirmative action in college admissions. He recruited Abigail Fisher, the daughter of an acquaintance, to be the face of a new lawsuit against race-conscious admissions for diversity at the University of Texas at Austin (UT).[31]

Ed Blum, a White man from Texas, is a conservative political strategist affiliated with the American Enterprise Institute.[32] Prior to his efforts to end race-conscious admissions, he was a central figure in the Supreme Court case *Shelby County v. Holder* (2013), which dismantled a key section of the 1965 Voting Rights Act—a foundational civil rights law won through the sacrifices of civil rights leaders like the late congressman John Lewis. Blum also sought to dismantle immigrant voting rights in the Supreme Court case *Evenwel v. Abbott* (2016), which he lost. Still, Ed Blum claims to be an advocate for "civil rights" in his campaign against race-conscious admissions, which has ironically taken a racially explicit turn in his efforts to recruit Asian American plaintiffs.

In *Fisher v. UT Austin*, Abigail Fisher and Blum specifically attacked the "critical mass" language in previous Supreme Court rulings, taking advantage of the seeming contradiction and tension between unconstitutional racial quotas and desires to create diverse campus environments. They charged that UT was using race-conscious holistic review to achieve some form of racial balancing, in violation of the Equal Protection Clause in the Fourteenth Amendment. However, the legal concept of "critical mass" should not be understood as a rigid number or racial quota. Instead, critical mass is dependent on campus contexts and conditions.[33] After the two *Fisher* cases in 2013 and 2016, the Supreme Court reaffirmed the *Grutter* precedent, ruling that the educational benefits of diversity represented a compelling interest to use race as one of many factors in a holistic and individualized admission process.

Even before the Supreme Court ruled on *Fisher* in 2016, Blum began plotting his next legal moves. As early as 2015 he began creeping around the country visiting Chinese American community events hoping to recruit new plaintiffs. Paradoxically to advance his campaign for a definitive victory against race-conscious policies—and especially ones that seek to increase diversity—Blum engaged in an explicitly racialized strategy in his recruitment to cast plaintiffs for new lawsuits against affirmative action. He even relied on Chinese Americans' sense of racial grievances. In 2015 he announced at a meeting of the Houston Chinese Alliance, "I need Asian plaintiffs."[34] Prior to that documented 2015 meeting, his organization Students for Fair Admissions, Inc. (SFFA) had already filed federal lawsuits against Harvard (*SFFA v. Harvard*), featuring an anonymous Chinese American student, and the University of North Carolina at Chapel Hill (*SFFA v. UNC–Chapel Hill*), featuring anonymous White students, in November 2014. In these new legal attacks his explicit goal was "a declaratory judgement . . . from the Court that any use of race or ethnicity in the educational setting violates the Fourteenth Amendment and Title VI of the Civil Rights Act of 1964."[35]

The Harvard trial started on October 15, 2018, and lasted three weeks in the US District Court for the District of Massachusetts. Despite Blum's recruitment efforts, no Asian American testified to substantiate the claim that Harvard's practices harmed Asian American applicants.[36] On the other side, several Asian American students and alumni testified in defense of diversity and race-conscious admissions. Along with other students of color, Asian Americans testified that race-conscious admissions directly benefited them.

In November 2020 the US Court of Appeals for the First Circuit sided with Harvard and affirmed the district court's ruling—that SFFA's claims of anti-Asian discrimination lacked evidence. SFFA appealed the case to the US Supreme Court, which heard oral arguments in both the Harvard and UNC cases on October 31, 2022.[37] On June 29, 2023, the majority of the Supreme Court justices ruled to end the limited consideration of race in admissions.

At the same time, Chief Justice Roberts's ruling opinion reaffirmed the importance of diversity to the country's well-being, exempting the military academies (e.g., West Point, Annapolis, etc.) from the ruling. He stated in a footnote that "no military academy is a party to these cases," convinced by the US government's contention that diversity is needed for national security.[38] If diversity is essential to the US military, why are other postsecondary institutions not allowed to leverage diversity in their educational missions? Don't all other sectors of life in the US also benefit from racial diversity? As Justices Sotomayor, Kagan, and Jackson pointed out in their dissents, there are significant contradictions in the majority's opinion, which also relies on a deep denial of US history. As Justice Jackson powerfully asserted, "The Court has come to rest on the bottom-line conclusion that racial diversity in higher education is only worth potentially preserving insofar as it might be needed to prepare Black Americans and other underrepresented minorities for success in the bunker, not the boardroom (a particularly awkward place to land, in light of the history the majority opts to ignore)."[39] Awkward is a diplomatic way to characterize the majority opinion in this case.

Chief Justice Roberts ended his opinion by explaining that even though colleges and universities can no longer consider race, "nothing in this opinion should be construed as prohibiting universities from considering an applicant's discussion of how race affected his or her life, be it through discrimination, inspiration, or otherwise."[40] Confusing, right? Perhaps the stirring up of confusion and uncertainty is the point. The contradictions and confusion in the opinion feed into voluntary overreactions and rollbacks of what colleges and universities can still do for diversity.[41] Unfortunately, many colleges and universities would rather avoid risking litigation altogether, doing too much in rolling back diversity and equity initiatives, than creatively come up with new ways to advance equity.[42] In some ways, the Roberts opinion reflects how race-conscious holistic admissions had already been operating.

### ASIAN AMERICAN MISCONCEPTIONS OF AFFIRMATIVE ACTION

Seven years before the SFFA ruling, in 2016, when my research team and I started interviewing Asian Americans who were actively engaged in the public debates over race-conscious college admissions, I thought that Asian American activists who were actively fighting for and against affirmative action would articulate generally accurate understandings of how race-conscious admissions work post-*Grutter*. I was very wrong.

These interviews revealed unanticipated commonalities across the Asian American affirmative action divide. Most of the people I interviewed shared false understandings of how race-conscious admissions worked. It was like there was a common belief that there could only be one Elsa on Halloween. In answering, "What is affirmative action in college admissions?" thirty of the thirty-six interview participants—both policy supporters and opponents—offered inaccurate definitions about the mechanics of race-conscious admissions.

Many policy opponents and supporters shared a belief in the myth that affirmative action produces an "Asian American penalty" in selective admissions processes.[43] Buying into this falsehood requires a disregard of the legal parameters around race-conscious admissions practices before 2023. It also draws on an assumption that intelligence can only be measured through narrow (and problematic) standardized tests and high school GPA. Furthermore, it relies on deeply entrenched, conscious and unconscious, racial stereotypes of intelligence among Asian Americans and lack of intelligence among non-Asian people of color.

### THE ASIAN AMERICAN PENALTY MYTH AMONG AFFIRMATIVE ACTION OPPONENTS

All the policy opponents I interviewed believed postsecondary institutions practicing affirmative action used racial quotas, point systems, or automatic preferences for non-Asian students of color that created a system of anti-Asian discrimination in admissions. For example, Richard believed affirmative action to be race-based preferences for non-Asian students of color and the practice of racial quotas. "It's the idea that there is a certain natural number of people of a certain race, or a percentage of a certain race that should be at this university as compared to other metrics. We need to really try to reach this goal. That's basically what it is." Richard believed that affirmative action was a set-aside program to ensure a particular racial demographic mix on campus. Similarly, Jake believed that affirmative action was essentially "a determinative race preference program" that harmed presumably hardworking Asian Americans with higher academic performance scores.

Others, like Jian, were more explicit in asserting that affirmative action was "a quota system" that reserved slots for Black people. Interestingly, Jian began by mentioning "minorities" and followed by specifying "African minority" in stating whom he thought benefited from the policy. Most of the anti–affirmative action interview participants believed that affirmative action was a racial preference for non–Asian American students of color. For example, Ruth defined affirmative action as a policy "where a certain group of people, based on color, ethnicity or other, receive bonus points or special consideration to get them past the front door where other groups are not allowed." When I asked her which groups were receiving bonuses, she named "Blacks and Hispanics, or Latinos if you want to call them 'Latinos.'"

Integrated into the belief that affirmative action is a quota or unfair preference targeting and benefiting African Americans and Latinx students were racist ideologies and the notion that the policy lowered academic standards for college entrance. Thomas, for example, defined affirmative action through explicitly anti-Black terms:

> They [college admissions] don't care how good of a grade you do. You have to get that percentage of [racial minority] kids in your school. Even though they have 1.0 GPA, I don't care. Get them in. Think about it. If all Black people had 1.0 GPA, first of all, I don't think they can graduate, but let's just say that, and we have 4.0s, but with SCA-5 they take away

30 percent of all spots [from Asian Americans], and they give to those people with 1.0 GPA. How are they going to graduate? They're not.

There is no evidence that students with a 1.0, or failing GPA, who cannot even graduate from high school, are being let into colleges with high academic standards. Still, Thomas believes that affirmative action allows unprepared Black students entry. Many other affirmative action opponents also believed that the policy allowed for unqualified students to be admitted, echoing a long-debunked "mismatch" theory.[44] While most interview participants mentioned and presumed that African American and Latinx students were less qualified than Asian American students, George, who identifies as Chinese American, specifically named Vietnamese Americans—another Asian American ethnic population—as less academically qualified. When I asked him if he thought affirmative action allowed unqualified students to go to college, George responded, "Absolutely. I told you a couple of my daughter's friends, they're close friends, they come to my home. I always talk with them. One is a Vietnamese here. They dropped out [of college]." By naming his daughter's Vietnamese friend as academically unqualified for selective colleges, George revealed that he believed affirmative action programs targeted Asian American groups as policy beneficiaries. The comment also suggested a sentiment that betrays the use of the panethnic term "Asian American" among some Chinese American policy opponents.

As a result of a presumption that affirmative action directly targeted and benefited (less academically qualified) African Americans, Latinx, and some Asian Americans, some policy opponents also asserted beliefs that race-conscious admissions practices harmed Asian Americans, particularly East Asians. Sheng's view relied heavily on SAT score differentials. "Asian students would have to score hundreds of points more than other racial groups of students. Even if you control for similar extracurricular activities. The gaps in terms of the SAT scores [are] staggering. We feel that it's really unfair." Central to Sheng's opinion that affirmative action was in effect anti-Asian was a misinterpretation of Thomas Espenshade's work. However, test scores are just *one* (very flawed) factor in the complex, holistic admissions process. There are many considerations in a multifaceted and holistic evaluation system that result in admission decision variations; a test score should not be a determining factor of "merit" or admission, according to the Supreme Court in *Fisher II*. Notably, while some anti–affirmative action Asian Americans pointed to a so-called Asian test score penalty for admission, they never acknowledged that those same studies also found that low-income Asian American applicants with lower SAT scores benefited from race-conscious admissions programs.[45]

### MYTHS AMONG AFFIRMATIVE ACTION SUPPORTERS

Like anti–affirmative action Asian Americans, some pro–affirmative action Asian Americans in the study also held misconceptions of race-conscious admissions. For example, Tina thought that affirmative action meant that Asian Americans who have "done all the right things . . . [gotten] great grades" are less likely to get into selective colleges than other applicants. She justified this false understanding of how affirmative action worked by reminding me that college access was not a problem for Asian Americans. Tina held a misconception that affirmative action was a leg up for non-Asian people of color that she believed limited the admission chances of Asian Americans. Still, she supported the policy, she explained, because she politically identified as a person of color and believed it necessary to be in solidarity with other communities of color that faced deep disparities in college access. Interestingly, Tina identified as Cambodian American, which is a segment of the Asian American population that has very low rates of college access and attainment.[46]

When asked how they defined affirmative action, many policy supporters called on the historical spirit and intention of affirmative action: to redress historical racial wrongs. For example, Helen felt a connection to the historical justification for affirmative action in admissions. She pointed to a long legacy of racist policies and institutions that oppressed "folks of color" with barriers to advancement in leadership, employment, and education. For her, affirmative action was "one of the direct ways of trying to neutralize those policies, so that folks are given an opportunity, kind of like for the lost time, when all those really messed-up policies were in place." Helen understood persistent racial and socioeconomic disparities as products of a long history of racism and intersectional racial barriers that privileged White men. Like other policy supporters, she believed that affirmative action was a way to account for past wrongs. Yet this justification, or legal rationale, was no longer allowed by the *Bakke* precedent.

Most affirmative action supporters referenced ideas from the original intent of affirmative action, articulated by President Lyndon Johnson in a 1965 commencement address at Howard University:

> Freedom is not enough. You do not wipe away the scars of centuries by saying: Now you are free to go where you want, and do as you desire, and choose the leaders you please. You do not take a person who, for years, has been hobbled by chains and liberate him, bring him up to the starting line of a race and then say, "you are free to compete with all others," and still justly believe that you have been completely fair. Thus it is not enough just to open the gates of opportunity. All our citizens must have the ability to walk through those gates.[47]

Unfortunately, federal court rulings after this speech shifted the legal rationale for the consideration of race in admissions away from directly intervening in the systemic reproduction of racial inequalities.

Still, there was a fine line between acknowledging the historical motivation for affirmative action and understanding contemporary legal parameters and practices in selective admissions. Six of the pro–affirmative action interview participants more correctly defined affirmative action in admissions. For example, Melissa believed that affirmative action was a practice of giving "additional consideration" and not making race an overly determinative factor in admission decisions. Interestingly, this description of race-conscious admissions was not far off from how nearly all thirty-six interview participants described their ideal admission system.

### (RACE-CONSCIOUS) HOLISTIC REVIEW IS IDEAL

Despite the variations in misconceptions of race-conscious admissions, there was surprising, general agreement across the participants that the ideal process for college admissions was a holistic one. When I asked, "What is your ideal system of college admissions?" thirty-three of the thirty-six participants fundamentally described race-conscious holistic admissions. They described a system in which admissions offices recognized that diverse socioeconomic contexts (e.g., families, home environments, schools, communities, etc.) shaped individual students' opportunities and accomplishments. For example, Evan, an anti–affirmative action activist, believed that if "kids that grew up really dirt poor, but have succeeded decently well, that [show] their potential to go and do [the work], I'm absolutely fine with that. There's nothing wrong with [evaluating them highly]. Some people might call it affirmative action." Evan was essentially in agreement with admissions practices that evaluated student accomplishments within the context of their opportunities. Although his comment suggests a focus on economic class inequality, his use of the term "affirmative action" might indicate an acknowledgment of the difficulties of separating class and race in unequal educational experiences and contexts.

Eric, another anti–affirmative action activist, felt that evaluating students for academic merit required a recognition of student accomplishments within their unequal contexts of K–12 opportunity.[48] When asked specifically to name example criteria for admissions, Eric listed things like a passion to learn, leadership, and a "strong cultural awareness . . . because that allows you to have an open mind to explore new educational opportunities . . . to do what's good for the world in the future." When asked to explain why these characteristics were important to him, he said he believed that the educational goal of elite postsecondary institutions was "to train future global leaders" who would "need to be culturally aware." Therefore, according to Eric, admissions to such colleges should be a process to identify students ready to engage analytically and critically with complex materials and learning. Notably, these are things that cannot be determined easily through standardized tests, which Eric admitted are not designed to assess such competencies or readiness. "Obviously, you can't say just because someone has high SAT scores that means they're smart. You can get a high score on it as long as you can figure out the system of it." Throughout my interview with Eric, I was baffled over why he was such an adamant affirmative action opponent, when he articulated fundamental values of a race-conscious holistic review system.[49]

I felt similarly confused as I interviewed Bingwen on a sunny Saturday afternoon in California on a restaurant patio after we had eaten lunch together. In responding to my question of what an ideal admission system was, he stated that universities should "evaluate students based on the opportunity they were given when they grew up. So, you need to benchmark against the relative success for an individual compared to the opportunity they had access to." Bingwen did not believe it was fair to directly compare the grades of a wealthy student from a private high school to a student of lesser means. "If the rich kid does not even take the hardest course offered by his very famous private school, then that's a dead giveaway that this is not a motivated student, but if the poor kids show initiative of going long distance, they should be rewarded."

Eric, Bingwen, and other anti–affirmative action interview participants recognized the importance of evaluating college applicants within the contexts of their opportunities. Although they spoke in terms of class stratification and recognized that class inequalities reproduced educational inequalities, they still recognized that admissions offices should evaluate student talents within the contexts of their individual socioeconomic circumstances. The lack of direct acknowledgment of systemic racism in producing these unequal contexts of opportunity and achievement reflected the central Asian American affirmative action divide. Still, their descriptions of context-informed admissions aligned with parameters for race-conscious admissions before 2023.

Asian American affirmative action supporters, on the other hand, were more direct in naming race and racism as key factors that shaped educational opportunities. For example, Asha believed that affirmative action was fundamentally about "ensuring that the system moves away from treating people like numbers and finding the humanity within a collection of data." She argued that racism and other systems of oppression were foundational forces that shaped people's divergent experiences: "You cannot fully understand a person, if you don't also consider their race, or their gender, or their economic background, or whatever." Similarly, Mya believed that affirmative action expanded notions of "merit" in evaluating students for selective college admissions, to recognize how different students with varying experiences and perspectives can enrich educational environments in higher education. These ideas were actually a key part of how race-conscious admissions worked.

## INSIDE THE BLACK BOX: HOW DID RACE-CONSCIOUS HOLISTIC ADMISSIONS WORK (2003–2023)?

Many falsely believe that race-conscious admissions, between 2003 and 2023, was the practice of racial quotas and/or automatic point preferences and systems, or worse, a racist ban against Asian Americans in US higher education. For example, in a lengthy 2019 *New York Times Magazine* essay, writer Jay Caspian Kang repeatedly equates race-conscious admissions to a system of minuses and pluses, or a generally automatic practice of racial preferences—a process the Supreme Court had already deemed unconstitutional in the 2003 *Gratz* case. He opens the long-form essay describing Alex Chen, who graduated from a selective New York City public high school and was a first-year Yale undergraduate when the article was published, as "a first-generation[50] (considered a plus), middle-class (minus) Chinese American (minus, arguably) with two college-educated parents (minus) from a major American city (minus) with aspirations to study either computer science (minus, given all the Asians who want to go into STEM disciplines) or political science (plus)."[51] This description reveals a poor understanding of how race-conscious holistic admissions operated within the legal guidelines of *Bakke* (1978), *Gratz* (2003), *Grutter* (2003), *Fisher I* (2013), and *Fisher II* (2016).

It was frustrating to see Kang, a generally respected writer, talk about race-conscious admissions with little connection to how admissions actually worked. Throughout the essay, Kang presents rich profiles of several Asian American students and their perspectives on affirmative action. He presents a diversity of individual Asian American stories, experiences, and perspectives on race, racism, and affirmative action, ironically demonstrating a practice of individualized assessment that higher education professionals use in race-conscious admissions. Unfortunately, Kang ends the essay reinforcing a myth that Asian American students, like the ones he profiled for the story, should hide their personal experiences and stories.

The inaccurate representation of how admissions actually works in Mr. Kang's essay is rather common in news articles and popular essays. Admittedly, I held similar views of admissions work until 2003, when I became an admissions reader at UC Davis. Given the lack of accurate explanations and descriptions of contemporary race-conscious admissions in the news media and the highly litigious environment and defensive cloak surrounding the admissions profession, the process of holistic college admissions—especially how race-conscious admissions worked—remains a mystery to the public.

Plus, research has only recently started to catch up to the changes in admissions practices since the 1990s. Some of the most discussed works on affirmative action in college admissions present analysis and data from a bygone era in admissions that predates post-*Grutter* and *Gratz* (2003) holistic admissions processes. For example, sociologists Thomas Espenshade, Alexandra Radford, and Chang Chung engaged in statistical modeling of admissions outcomes, using data from the admissions cycle in 1997. They designed their model, which accounted for eleven variables in student characteristics, in an effort to model admissions outcomes at seven institutions. In a 2005 article, Espenshade and Chung open with a stunning statement, suggesting that the removal of affirmative action would lead to big Asian American wins in acceptance letters through significantly reduced admission rates for Black and Latinx applicants.[52] In their article they present data showing that admitted Asian Americans students collectively had a much higher SAT average than admitted students identifying as White (140 point difference), or as Black or Latinx (450 point difference).

Before anyone stops reading here and decides this must mean that SFFA and Ed Blum are somehow the Asian American champions we've been waiting for, the Espenshade research is not "smoking gun" evidence that affirmative action is the same as anti-Asian discrimination. Don't believe me? Then maybe you'll listen to Dr. Espenshade himself. In a 2010 interview he explained that a major flaw in his research was that he didn't actually know how admissions worked, having never sat in on an admissions committee. He went on to say, "People may read [my research] and want to say, 'Oh, because I'm Asian American, my SAT scores have been downgraded.' That is not really the way to interpret these data. Many times people will ask me, 'Do your results prove that there is discrimination against Asian applicants?' And I say, 'No, they don't.'"[53] The process of how applicants are evaluated for admission generally remains unaccounted for, in research and in public discourse.

Espenshade's research is not evidence that race-conscious admissions was anti-Asian discrimination because these studies' procedures did not attempt to model holistic review practices and processes, nor did they acknowledge college-going variations by race, class, and structural inequalities—the complexities and patterns in the types of colleges to which different students apply. They were also based on outdated models and data from 1997, several years prior to the 2003 *Grutter* ruling. Using data from 1997—an era when holistic review was just beginning to take shape—means that analytical implications for a post–*Grutter/Gratz/Fisher* world of holistic admissions are very limited.

So how exactly do selective colleges and universities practice race-conscious holistic admissions? To answer this question, we must recognize that holistic admissions has been an evolving professional practice of evaluating and selecting from among an abundance of unique applicants, brought on by legal developments.[54] Unlike historically antisemitic and discriminatory practices of accounting for a vague notion of "character" among applicants in the 1920s, contemporary holistic review plans are intended to achieve a more equitable evaluation of talent among students from diverse contexts of academic development and socioeconomic opportunities. In a 2001 speech to the American Council of Education (ACE), former University of California president Richard Atkinson explained the UC's move to expand to comprehensive assessments of applicant files, allowing universities to recognize a wider array of evidence of a student's qualifications beyond a four-hour high-stakes exam score.[55]

Atkinson was leading a public university working under the constraints of a statewide affirmative action ban (Proposition 209) that had experienced a precipitous decline in enrollments of African Americans, American Indians, Latinx, Pacific Islanders, and Southeast Asian American students,[56] at a time when the *Grutter* and *Gratz* cases worked their way toward the Supreme Court. He knew from research on standardized tests and college admissions that the SAT was extremely limited in its utility for predicting individual students' academic potential, and a key concern for public universities remained predicting and supporting academic persistence and timely graduation rates. Saul Geiser, a research professor at UC Berkeley's Center for Studies in Higher Education, had long empirically demonstrated that the SAT was not very good at predicting how well students would do in college. In other words, the usefulness of the SAT, on its own, to evaluate students' academic talent was extremely limited. In alignment with such research, the Supreme Court stated in *Fisher II* that single measures of academic talent and potential, such as test scores or class rank, "will capture certain types of people and miss others" and that valuing one piece of information about applicants "is in deep tension with the goal of educational diversity as this Court's cases have defined it."[57] To be clear, no one piece of data on students can ever provide a full picture of who a student is, their learning dispositions, and what they are capable of. There are established limitations in the SAT's capacity to measure student academic potential, not to mention how the design of the SAT is set to reproduce and maintain a racial test score gap.[58]

Holistic processes accounting for a range of student characteristics in admission review are necessary to consider applicants' whole stories, experiences, and accomplishments within their specific contexts of opportunity (e.g., families, schools, communities, etc.). It's an assessment approach that includes a range of data points, seeking to imagine what kind of student an individual applicant would be on that specific campus and gain a more reliable prediction of an individual student's academic and other potential.[59]

As many admissions officers have explained to me, race-conscious holistic admissions practices allow individual students to give context about who they are and how best to understand their educational journeys.[60] They invite students to bring their whole selves to the table, to tell their stories of who they are. Admissions professionals I interviewed wanted to respect how students told their own personal stories. One admissions professional in the field for twenty-seven years gave the example of an African American applicant whose application materials talked a lot about being a figure skater: "That was the most prevalent thing in their life. And maybe they have some story to tell about being Black and a figure skater. But that wasn't the story they chose to tell. And so I think we have to respect what the student is telling us." There was a professional respect for how the student's central identity had to do with figure skating. I appreciated that they did not reduce the student to a racial demographic number, as some often presume admissions officers do. They went well beyond checkmarks in the optional racial demographic section of the application to receive how applicants described themselves.

When applicants of varying ethnic and racial backgrounds identified and explained how their backgrounds shaped who they were as students—their experiences, perspectives, leadership, accomplishments, and so on—admissions professionals I've interviewed were better able to gain a deeper understanding of the individual's academic qualifications and how the student might contribute toward the various dimensions of life in their specific campus environment. Reviewing the voluminous files and data for each applicant, admissions professionals construct detailed understandings of each applicant, including guesses as to how they might engage as learners and contribute in different ways on their particular campuses. Context matters greatly in this process, and they recognize that for some students, race and racism played impactful roles in shaping who they were and how they engaged in educational spaces in and outside of classrooms.

However, it is important to note that race was never *the* reason any student was admitted or denied entry in holistic evaluation of individual applicants. Evaluating individual students within their unique contexts allowed admissions reviewers to recognize the diversity between students with shared identities. Admissions readers were able to recognize an Asian American student as a unique individual and different from the next Asian American student, if these students discussed and shared these experiences in their application materials as significant to who they were as individual students. Another admissions professional in the field for sixteen years explained, "I think we train pretty well to say, one, don't assume that a race equals a certain experience. Two, don't ignore that race as lived experience is not a powerful piece of the puzzle in terms of how a student's thinking about themselves."

In my conversation with this same person, we discussed their frustration in seeing Asian American applicants not discuss or indicate their racial or ethnic identity, as a misguided strategy hoping to improve their admission odds.[61] Further explaining how they worked to honor how students chose to present the stories of who they are, they told me that when faced with files from applicants who limit the information they shared about their racial or ethnic identity, "We try really hard to make what is in the file drive the decision. It doesn't mean you can't impute [information], but you shouldn't be imputing all the way to the admit bin." In other words, decisions to admit students were driven by the vast information provided by applicants, with racial identity representing just one part of an applicant's story. As a follow-up, I asked about applicants who chose to hide their ethnic or racial identities over fears of negative biases. They explained that they had noticed this particularly among Asian American applicants and felt sad, because they "have not been given guidance and they've read in one little post in social media that [being Asian American] is harming you. They just make these decisions, which seems so counterintuitive to their best interest." Several admissions professionals explained that applicants that withheld information about themselves were not doing any favors for their cases. On the contrary, they felt these students were hindering a stronger case and review of their application materials.

With incomplete information, admissions professionals explained that they were unable to provide a more detailed and corroborated evaluation of individual students, because these details and points of context information helped set individual students apart from the crowded field of applicants. As I learned from interviews of admissions professionals and enrollment management leaders at selective institutions, context was everything. In evaluating students, they wanted to understand student accomplishments and potential contributions within the context of the individual applicant's home, school, and community settings, which could all shape the contours of educational challenges. They also wanted to establish a sense of how individual applicants might engage in the particular college's campus contexts.

The holistic admissions process is a complicated, multilayered, and time-consuming matchmaking process, with admissions officers playing the matchmaker role between prospective students and the many stakeholders (e.g., trustees, administrators across campus, faculty across disciplines, students) and their varied priorities and interests. As Justice Kennedy affirmed in the *Fisher II* (2016) opinion, "Considerable deference is owed to a university in defining those intangible characteristics, like student body diversity, that are central to its identity and educational mission."[62] As my interviews with admissions officers revealed, each postsecondary institution's mission is multifaceted, representing a multitude of institutional priorities and demands.[63]

Although the admissions professionals I interviewed articulated a personal investment in advancing diversity as a goal for their institutions, they also acknowledged that competing institutional priorities often placed structural constraints on their ability to increase diversity. As one admissions officer stated early in our interview, "The institutional priorities that take precedent at these institutions, I mean, they're all about privilege. So it is about legacy status, it is about donor abilities, and about geographic location." The educational mission is complex and multilayered, including maintaining fiscal solvency. As some in the enrollment management field have explained to me, "No money, no mission." These institutional realities result in admissions decision-making processes that cannot simply rely on one or two academic variables or race. Instead, a complex holistic process has developed to evaluate applicants for academic strengths, first and foremost, and then many other student characteristics that can fit into an institution's specific organizational mission and goals.

Now that the Supreme Court has ended the consideration of race as one of many factors in admissions, the mix of institutional priorities (e.g., financial need, geography, athletic talents, etc.) will likely diminish the number of students of color admitted. This includes Asian American students and especially those who are low-income and among the first generation in their families to attend college, in favor of White and wealthier applicants.[64] As one study published shortly after the June 2023 Supreme Court ruling found, preferences for legacy students and geographic diversity in rejective admissions have lowered the chances of Asian American applicants in favor of similarly qualified White applicants.[65] These racial disparities have nothing to do with race-conscious admissions and implicate ongoing systemic racial biases that privilege White students. Without race-conscious admissions practices, I worry that White-Asian racial disparities identified in this study may be exacerbated in the admissions calculations between competing institutional priorities.

It can be difficult to understand how the holistic admissions review process works. As such, I don't fault people for misunderstanding these opaque systems and processes. In fact, I could not fully grasp how holistic review worked until I became an admissions reader myself. To help readers better conceptualize a race-conscious holistic review process, I have included an interactive activity in appendix A (found online at beacon.org /PoonAppendix), for teachers, students, and anyone with an interest in better understanding the process. In the group activity, participants pretend to be an admissions office for a specific university and review application materials for five academically qualified students.

## WHY THE MAJORITY OF ASIAN AMERICANS SUPPORT AFFIRMATIVE ACTION

At the end of the day, most Asian Americans on all sides of the affirmative action divide understand the importance of holistic admissions processes that evaluate individual students within their unique contexts of educational opportunity. Both supporters and opponents accurately drew from various historical iterations of affirmative action practices in admissions, even when operating from outdated legal constructs. A healthy policy debate over affirmative action requires a more accurate understanding of the policy and how it was practiced in admissions. Although affirmative action opponents and supporters in this study articulated widely divergent racial ideologies, most of them held shared misconceptions about the law and about race-conscious admissions practices, like the UIUC students I had met in 2014. Most of them also agreed that holistic review practices accounting for unequal socioeconomic circumstances and contexts of educational opportunity were ideal for evaluating individual student accomplishments and potential.

They fundamentally agreed with Sally Chen, an undergraduate student who testified in defense of race-conscious admissions during the 2018 *SFFA v. Harvard* legal hearings. Sally said, "There are complex stories in Asian America that need to be told and they can't be separated from the impacts of racism in this country." Race-conscious holistic admissions processes and practices represented systemic ways to recognize and appropriately value individual student experiences, contexts, achievements, and potential, which may have been affected by race and racism, including Asian American students. This may be why the majority of Asian Americans remain supportive of affirmative action.[66]

When I was completing these interviews in 2016, I was surprised to learn that many policy opponents and supporters held misinformed understandings of race-conscious admissions. It was also unexpected to hear both opponents and supporters describing key elements of holistic review as their ideal process for selective admissions. I wondered whether anti–affirmative action Asian Americans' views could be changed if they gained a clearer understanding of how contemporary race-conscious admissions worked. I just wasn't sure if offering factual information to both groups would help enrich the debate.

Dear Té Té,

The great Elsa battle of 2019 between you and your preschool best friend Taylor would not get settled with the correction of assumptions. Telling you and Taylor that you were both wrong to think there could only be one child that could dress up as Elsa for Halloween would not help bring about a reconciliation. Emotions were high. Information alone would not cut through the quarrel. Still, you remained each other's best friends through pre-K.

The people I interviewed for this book expressed many emotions across the affirmative action divide. However, unlike you and Taylor, I'm not so sure they could ever be best friends, given the deep ideological differences between affirmative action opponents and supporters.

# CHAPTER 3

# COMMUNITY DIVIDES

*Theories of Change, Social Media, and Identities*

Dear Té Té,

In December 2022 the temperatures had dropped below zero degrees Fahrenheit in Chicago. On Christmas Eve morning after a night of howling bitter cold winds, you said, "Mama, I got a question for you."

I knew this was your preamble to hard questions, which were coming fast and furious by the time you were in the second grade. You noticed a lot of things in the world around us. For example, living in Chicago, we often saw people panhandling in busy intersections and by expressway exit ramps on a regular basis.

I was glad I had a cup of coffee in my hand to wake me up. Readying for your question, I said, "What's your question?" as I brought my mug to my lips.

"Are unhoused people OK right now? It's so cold outside."

I was so proud that you were growing up into a caring and thoughtful young person. We sat down on our couch and cozied up with warm blankets. I told you that the city government had opened a handful of warming centers across Chicago and that public libraries were open to receive people needing warmth. However, I told you, we live in a big city that doesn't have enough warming centers and shelters to make sure everyone's needs were met. I asked you what you thought we should do.

You told me that everyone should have warm shelter and healthy food, and I agreed with you. I asked you my routine question: "How do you think we can learn more about this problem, so we can figure out how to make things better?" You rolled your eyes at me, because I was yet again answering your questions with another question. But then, after a few moments of thought, with a deep sincerity and earnestness you said, "Why don't we give the next unhoused person we see all our money?"

"OK," I replied, "but then how would we pay for our house and food?"

"Why does anyone need money to get a house and food anyway?" you retorted.

It was a great question, I told you. Instead of getting into a theoretical discussion about the problems of capitalism—an economic system of extraction, few haves, and many have-nots—I decided to talk with you about the upcoming city election. There were a growing number of candidates for mayor and city council that we needed to learn about. The local election would have significant consequences on the welfare of our city and how problems like poverty and homelessness would be addressed.

The election in February 2023 narrowed the field of mayoral candidates to two Democrats, Brandon Johnson and Paul Vallas, for a run-off election scheduled for April 4, 2023. Public safety and education were two key issues in the election. Cook County Commissioner Johnson, a former Chicago Public Schools (CPS) teacher and Chicago Teachers Union organizer, called for increasing investments to schools, mental health facilities, and public services to "address the root causes of violence and poverty."[1] Paul Vallas, the former CEO of CPS who had ushered in an era of public school privatization starting in the 1990s in Chicago and other urban school districts, called for more policing.[2] The two candidates offered vastly different approaches to addressing these problems.

In many ways, the disagreements over affirmative action between Asian Americans represented different approaches to addressing the problem of racism. Unlike most affirmative action opponents, Asian Americans who disagreed with the policy still recognized that racism was a problem.[3] They just held very different views of how to go about confronting and solving anti-Asian racism.

On March 16, 2021, a White gunman in the metro Atlanta area traveled to two Asian-owned spas—Gold Spa and Young's Asian Massage—and killed eight people, including six Asian women. Their names and ages were Daoyou Feng (44), Delaina Ashley Yaun Gonzalez (33), Hyun Jung Grant (51), Suncha Kim (69), Paul Andre Michels (54), Soon Chung Park (74), Xiaojie Tan (49), and Yong Ae Yue (63). This mass shooting set off a national reckoning with anti-Asian violence, and public attention fixed onto what appeared to be increasing reports of violence against Asian Americans, who present as East Asian, Southeast Asian, and Filipino.[4]

Some reports indicated drastic increases in racially motivated attacks on Asian Americans.[5] Adding nuance to the claim that incidents targeting Asian Americans are increasing, other research has suggested that mostly what has changed is the level of fear among Asian Americans.[6] More specifically, there seems to be an increased consciousness among Asian Americans and others about anti-Asian racism and violence, and especially racist misogyny, which have been endemic throughout US history. It has been a drastic shift from how Asian Americans often feel absent from or even pushed out of discussions about race and racism. There is a feeling of urgency to step into this moment of visibility to shape it in a way that maintains space for Asian American voices. Amid an elevated consciousness, how Asian Americans and others define and articulate what is anti-Asian violence and racism will shape both what is seen as the problem and what solutions are possible and necessary. How they articulate their theories of change to invest in problem-solving will bear consequences for Asian America and beyond.

Although there is an increase in the reporting of anti-Asian racism and violence, racial scapegoating, verbal and physical attacks, and being targeted by racist policies are not new to Asian Americans. One only needs to turn to the field of Asian American studies to learn about systemic racism and the dehumanization and barring of Asian Americans from the full rights of US citizenship. For example, in 1854 the California Supreme Court ruled in *People v. Hall* that the testimony of a Chinese American witness to a murder by a White man was inadmissible, because like African Americans and Native Americans, Chinese Americans were not eligible to participate "in administering the affairs of our Government." The court stated that the Chinese were "a race of people whom nature has marked as inferior, and who are incapable of progress or intellectual development beyond a certain point." White supremacy and the possession or lack of Whiteness defined who could participate in US civic life. White patriarchal ideologies of US citizenry can also be traced to the 1871 mass lynching of eighteen Chinese Americans in Los Angeles, the racist and misogynist 1875 Page Act that banned Chinese women from immigrating to the US, the 1882 Chinese Exclusion Act, numerous "Alien Land Laws" that barred Asian Americans from purchasing and owning property, anti-miscegenation laws outlawing interracial marriage between Asians and Whites, and the mass incarceration of Japanese Americans in concentration camps during World War II. The COVID-19 era of anti-Asian racism stems from long-standing historical roots.

Starting at the end of the nineteenth century, the US began waging war in Asia—in the Philippines, Japan, Korea, Vietnam, and elsewhere in Southeast Asia. It has continued to maintain a military presence and occupation throughout Asia and the Pacific. In the aftermath of September 11, 2001, the US has waged a continuous war and program of military aggressions in Afghanistan and West Asia. For more than a century, Asians have been racialized as enemies and threats, hypersexualized and dehumanized in the US imagination.

These racialized sentiments have led to tragic violence. In 1989 a White gunman, who had expressed a hatred toward Vietnamese people, killed five children (Sokhim An, 6; Ram Chun, 8; Oeun Lim, 8; Raphanar Or, 9; and Thuy Tran, 6) and wounded thirty others in the schoolyard at Stockton, California's Cleveland Elementary School, which enrolled many Southeast Asian American children from the community. Also in the 1980s, a group calling themselves the "Dotbusters" targeted South Asian Americans in New Jersey with violent assaults. After 9/11, people who were or appeared "Arab" or "Muslim," including South Asian Americans, have suffered racist attacks that grow from xenophobic racism and Islamophobia.[7] Such violence included the 2012 mass shooting at a Sikh gurdwara in Oak Creek, Wisconsin, that killed seven Sikh Americans: Paramjit Kaur (41), Satwant Singh Kaleka (65), Prakash Singh (39), Sita Singh (41), Ranjit Singh (49), Suveg Singh (84), and Baba Punjab Singh (72). Additionally, trade wars starting in the 1980s with Japan, and later with the People's Republic of China, have also driven racial hostilities and violence against

Asian Americans. The decline of the US auto industry in competition with Japanese automobiles served as backdrop to the 1982 murder of Vincent Chin in Detroit. These violent incidents, along with countless others with which the public is even less familiar, are acute outgrowths of the larger realities of US global empire and systemic anti-Asian racism.

Despite centuries of systemic racism, violence, and sentiments, anti-Asian racism and marginalization are sometimes questioned.[8] Widespread social dismissal of Asian American racialization can lead to what Cathy Park Hong called minor feelings, which "occur when American optimism is enforced upon you, which contradicts your own racialized reality, thereby creating a static of cognitive dissonance."[9] When Trump and other Republican politicians began scapegoating China and "the Chinese" for the pandemic in early 2020, many Asian Americans began to fear racial backlash.[10] In light of reports about several instances of anti-Asian violence across the country—including the March 2020 stabbing of the Cung family including three- and six-year-old children at a Sam's Club in Texas, the January 2021 murder of eighty-four-year-old Vicha Ratanapakdee, and the February 2021 slashing of Noel Quintana's face on a New York City subway—Asian Americans began decrying increasingly reported violence.[11] However, collective cries over fears of anti-Asian COVID violence seemed to go unnoticed outside of Asian American community spaces and social media for a full year, until the Atlanta Asian spa killing. It's a kind of racial gaslighting and a powerless feeling.

As more Asians and non-Asians continue to consider and problematize racial violence connected to scapegoating in response to the pandemic, we need to recognize that frames of anti-Asian violence as "new" or "increasing" are incomplete and ahistorical. Anti-Asian racial scapegoating also does not represent or offer a comprehensive defining framework for a deep understanding of and solutions for anti-Asian violence and racism. For instance, on the day before the Atlanta shooting, US immigration enforcement deported thirty-three Vietnamese Americans, tearing loved ones away from their families and communities. This too is anti-Asian violence.[12] Less than a month after Atlanta, on April 15, 2021, a White gunman entered an Indianapolis FedEx warehouse, where about 90 percent of workers identified as Sikh, and murdered eight people: Amarjeet

Johal (66), Jaswinder Singh, Amarjit Sekhon, Jaswinder Kaur, Samaria Blackwell (19), John Weisert (74), Karli Smith (19), and Matthew Alexander (32), taking them away from their families and communities.[13] An overemphasis on COVID-related anti-Asian racial violence can render invisible the problems of racist misogyny central to the Atlanta shooting and racist xenophobia in immigration and deportation policies and the Indianapolis shooting.[14] Varying racial worldviews, or defining frames, of who Asian Americans are and about what constitutes the problem of anti-Asian racism and violence provide distinctly different soil and seed that grow divergent strategies and solutions for change.

Not only is anti-Asian racism not new, but neither are Asian American projects of resistance and activism, despite all-too-common quips in 2021 that it's good to see Asian Americans finally stand up for themselves, or calls on Asian Americans to stand up and speak out.[15] As Asian American folk musician Chris Iijima sang in 1973, "We're still here, and we're going strong; and we're getting tired of proving we belong."[16] This is the shared chorus from Iijima's "Asian Song" sampled by Asian American hip-hop group Magnetic North, Taiyo Na, Ann One, and Chucky Kim in their 2010 song "We Belong," which was remixed in 2021.[17] In these songs the artists from different generations offer Asian American stories of struggle, which differ in time and names of protagonists, but share a central hook—the common heart of the two Asian American anthems—written by Iijima:

Because these hands have washed the clothes;
These hands have served the food, heaven knows.
My neck has felt the mob's rope and it's been behind barbed wire.
My arms have laid down railroad track. My back has been for hire.
And these hands have fought injustice. And this soul is still on fire.

Although the faces, names, and contexts of Asian American experiences have changed, what remains the same is that Asian Americans continue to face intersectional systemic oppressions *and* they have also long fought against them. The amnesia and un/intentional marginalization of Asian American histories of oppression and resistance serve to maintain White supremacy. When there is a hyperfocus on moments of crisis, it can produce analyses that frame news spectacles like Atlanta and Indianapolis as isolated instances or individual acts rather than as logical outcomes of persistent oppressive systems, leading to solutions that cannot get at the root of the problem.

Divergent positions on affirmative action among Asian Americans represent differences in their analysis of racism—how they define racism as a problem—and their agenda for addressing the problem of racism. Asian Americans across the affirmative action divide generally share a recognition of racism, and particularly anti-Asian racism and violence, as a real problem. However, significant differences existed between the people I interviewed for this book and how they understood the problem and nature of racism, and therefore what to do about it. They had divergent theories of change in tackling anti-Asian racism. Other differences, including their preferred engagements in social media, immigrant generation, and ethnicity and gender identities, seemed to inform their divergent racial worldviews and theories of change.

### "WHAT IS RACISM AND WHAT IS IT NOT?": DIFFERING THEORIES OF CHANGE

Across the affirmative action divide, Asian Americans shared a recognition that racism, and especially anti-Asian racism, is a problem. When asked to tell me about themselves at the start of each interview, many participants in this study shared stories about their early life exposures to anti-Asian racism. For example, Ligaya, a second-generation Filipina affirmative action supporter, described moving as a child from a racially diverse working-class city to a predominantly White suburb in California and encountering racial violence. When they first moved to their new town, her sister was biking to school with a Chinese American friend, and some kids threw objects at them, calling her "a Jap and [telling] her to 'go home.'" Ligaya described these violent experiences as a "big part of our growing up."

Racial isolation and exposure to violence in childhood were also common among affirmative action opponents. When Thomas left China for Singapore and later Australia as a child, he recalled being physically harassed and assaulted by classmates in both countries. So when he arrived in the United States, he thought, "Wow. People might call me a 'Chink' or make fun of me, but they don't beat me anymore. Wow, this is heaven." He gladly accepted verbal assaults over physical violence.

When I interviewed Min-Ji, a 1.5-generation[18] Korean American policy supporter, she did not directly talk about her early experiences with racism when I asked her to tell me about herself. It wasn't until I asked her to tell me about her thoughts on race and racism that she shared with me: "You asked me [what my experiences with racism have been], it's so much about where was I in my understanding of racism, in my own experience. But also like, what is racism and what is it not?" As Min-Ji pointed out, the concepts of racism held by Asian Americans can change over time.

Still, I was surprised in my research that even among Asian Americans who oppose race-conscious admissions, there is a recognition that racism is a problem, unlike many White affirmative action opponents.[19] However, their definition and understanding of racism is limited to individualized notions of racism. By situating the problem of racism in individuals, they tend to dismiss systemic analyses of racism that connect and draw linkages between anti-Asian racism with other forms of racism that target other people of color (e.g., anti-Black racism). Without a systemic view on racism, many affirmative action opponents can view race-conscious programs for equity as anachronistic, as Wilson did. Although he said he supported affirmative action, "because racism actually exists," he went on to explain, "the definition of affirmative action is . . . it's a remedy for addressing the historical discrimination." He opposed what he believed affirmative action had become—in his words, a "racial preference" for people of color who are unqualified for admission to prestigious universities. He believed that racial barriers to education opportunity were in the past and gave credit to mid-twentieth-century civil rights leaders for dismantling segregationist laws. In the 1950s and 1960s, he explained, Chinese Americans and other Asian Americans were not allowed to buy houses, but because of African American–led civil rights victories, "we have rights now."

Those days of systemic injustices were over now, according to Wilson, and upward mobility in the twenty-first century is really just a product of how much work an individual or family is willing to do. He offered Chinese families as a model of work ethic and socioeconomic rewards.

Chinese families, he said, encourage and discipline their children to study hard and pursue educational achievements: "If you want to change your social status, your economic status, the most effective way is study, you get a degree, you get a good job." Chinese Americans who were affiliated with anti–affirmative action organizations, like Wilson, believed that the way to end racial inequalities was through sheer individual grit found in what he deemed to be Chinese cultural and family values. They disagreed that inequalities are produced by contemporary structural conditions aside from interpersonal disrespect. Instead, they believe that the problem of racial inequalities and disparities lies with individual behaviors among people of color. It's an assimilationist perspective that avoids questioning social, political, and economic systems and norms.

On the other hand, Asian American policy supporters recognize racism as a systemic problem that requires systemic solutions for change. Like the policy opponents I talked with, many affirmative action supporters recounted personal experiences with anti-Asian racism and violence. Unlike their adversaries, affirmative action proponents shared stories of their personal journeys in making sense of their individual experiences and contextualizing them within larger systems of racism. They often recognized and made connections between anti-Asian racism with other forms of racism (e.g., anti-Black racism, anti-Latinx racism, etc.) and systemic oppressions (e.g., settler colonialism, xenophobia, patriarchy, militarism, etc.). For example, when I asked Jimmy why he was motivated to engage in the affirmative action debate, his answer demonstrated a view of Asian Americans having linked fates with other communities of color. He didn't think of himself as "separate from African Americans and Latinos." It was why he thought it was important for Asian Americans to "show up and not just for our own community and different aspects of own community but to stand in solidarity" with other people who are working for a more just society. Jimmy was concerned about building anti-racist coalitions for cross-racial solidarity and was deeply invested in organizing Asian Americans to show up to support other communities of color. His analysis was common among other Asian American interview participants who were affiliated with pro–affirmative action organizations. They understood that racism is systemic and to fight it requires cross-racial solidarity.

## FOUR WORLDVIEWS DEFINING ANTI-ASIAN RACISM
## AND SOLUTIONS TO THE PROBLEM

To understand the complex and multiple deviations among Asian Americans in how they frame the problem of racism and offer agendas for change, I offer a model to further discern the diversity between and among Asian American supporters and opponents of race-conscious admissions. At the heart of the affirmative action divide is a moral disagreement informed by differences in racial ideology.[20] On one hand, policy supporters believe that the state and social institutions have a moral obligation to intervene in racial inequalities produced by historical and contemporary injustices and unequal laws, policies, and norms. On the other hand, opponents assert that affirmative action is "pernicious to individual liberty" and that public institutions have no right to intervene in the reproduction of inequalities, which are outcomes of individual efforts. How we learn and evolve in our understandings of race and racism also plays into determining these differences.[21]

What people believe about the nature of a given problem informs the solutions they choose to address it. In the debate over race-conscious admissions, the central question is: How should colleges and universities determine who receives invitations to enroll in their degree-granting programs? Underlying this question is the problem of inequalities in college access (i.e., who goes to college and where), and particularly their materially unequal consequences along racial and ethnic lines. Although Asian Americans generally agree that racism is a problem, how do racial inequalities in college access animate their theories of change? Do Asian Americans see racial disparities in college admissions as a problem? And if so, how do they define this problem, and what solutions are they invested in promulgating?

To answer these questions, I start by offering a theoretical model (figure 1) to illustrate four distinct racial worldviews and theories of change followed by the Asian Americans I interviewed across the affirmative action divide.[22] The most significant difference between affirmative action supporters and opponents was whether they recognized racism as a systemic problem. Policy supporters are found on the left side of this model (fig. 1). They recognized social inequalities as systemic problems. Policy opponents are represented on the right side of the figure. Systemic analyses on

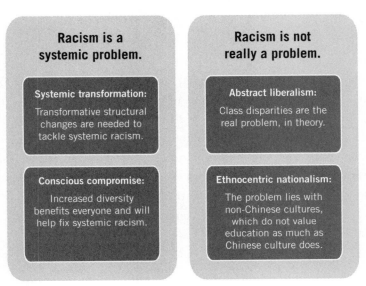

FIGURE I. *Four racial worldviews*

racism were lacking in their assessments of social inequalities. Worldviews represented at the top of this model included a belief that solving social inequalities would benefit the general public. Those on the bottom of the figure were motivated by a view that social policies and institutional practices should be driven by individual gains and benefits.

Policy opponents articulated the two frames on the right side of the model of abstract liberalism[23] and ethnocentric nationalism, and supporters expressed both conscious compromise and systemic transformation frames on the left side. Although the people I interviewed didn't express views representing frames on the left and right sides of the model, I believe that people are constantly learning, which can lead to changes in perspectives over time.[24] This model accounts for how Asian Americans' complex and divergent understandings of both racism and whether there is a shared public obligation to disrupt racial inequalities inform their political activism and advocacy on affirmative action. Each of the four frames, created at the intersection of the two axes, represent a distinct theory of change—both an analysis of the problem (i.e., racial inequalities in college access) and a preferred solution.

### SYSTEMIC TRANSFORMATION

Among affirmative action supporters, interviewees expressed an investment in systemic transformation (top left in figure 1), centering keen insights into the need for more fundamental structural change, and positioning affirmative action as a limited, but necessary, policy tool toward those ends. For example, Jacob expressed that affirmative action was about taking action because the status quo was unacceptable, "whether it's our work on immigrant rights, or queer justice, or gender equity, to me, they're all affirmative action programs, and we're not just relying, or putting our faith into either the markets, or faith that things will improve." In this worldview, affirmative action is about acting to transform status quo systems for a more just society.

### CONSCIOUS COMPROMISE

Other policy supporters articulated support for race-conscious admissions through a frame of conscious compromise (bottom left in figure 1). They argued that the policy benefited people of all racial backgrounds. They also believed that the policy helped address systemic inequalities. Charles, for example, explained that affirmative action in college admissions is about promoting diversity in higher education, which he viewed as essential for students to get "ready for a career and having experiences with other people in other backgrounds and cultures." Charles's response strongly aligned with the legal precedent that defined the purpose of race-conscious admissions as intended for cultivating the educational benefits of diversity.[25]

### ABSTRACT LIBERALISM

While supporters recognized racism as a structural problem, opponents viewed racism through an interpersonal lens. Some policy opponents suggested the need to address economic class inequalities in schooling but did not see the connection between racism and class disparities (top right in figure 1). For example, William explained that he was supportive of a class-based affirmative action: "To me, the purpose is to care about disadvantaged groups so they can have a better chance, because they don't have a good chance in reality so we need to consider the difference." He proceeded to explain inequities through the metaphor of a classroom of students being asked to compete in a game of trash ball: "Some kids in the front row and some kids in the last row, and the teacher just put a trash bin in the front and give every student two balls. 'OK, so whoever throws your ball into the trash bin, you will get a prize.'" He acknowledged that this setup wasn't fair to the people in the last row: "They are disadvantaged. That's why I'm for socioeconomic-based affirmative action." In this worldview, racism plays no role in creating inequities.

### ETHNOCENTRIC NATIONALISM

Other opponents articulated an ethnocentric nationalism that positioned Chinese culture as superior to those of others (bottom right in figure 1), especially Black and Latinx cultures. Through this frame, participants used both biological and cultural claims to explain away ethnic and racial inequalities in education and opposed any state or public interventions in racially unequal experiences or outcomes in education. For example, Ruth explained her opposition to improving racial diversity in selective high schools and colleges as unfair to Black and Latinx students, whom she presumed to be "less qualified to attend these schools." To her, entry into these institutions was a reward for those who have worked the hardest and scored highest on designated exams. Ruth believed that cultural differences helped explain ethnic and racial differences in who attended these schools. "I think there's a little Chinese influence there because in ancient Chinese culture, to do well you had to write exams. You had to do a very rigorous program to become part of the Chinese government." In contrast, she said that Black and Latinx families didn't possess the values for hard work and education. "Is it home life, culture, absent father, economics? What are those issues? Let's try to get to the root of the problem." The theory of change that Ruth and others with an ethnocentric nationalist worldview articulated relied on stereotypes of Black, Latinx, and Chinese cultures and values. The underlying contention was that to change inequalities in Black and Latinx representation in selective educational institutions, interventions would need to be enacted within Black and Latinx families, cultures, and communities.[26]

## INTERCONNECTED EXPLANATIONS: SOCIAL MEDIA AND IDENTITY

At the heart of the Asian American affirmative action divide is a difference in theories of change. What led Asian Americans to invest themselves in these various frames and theories of change? Differences in social media practices, immigration contexts, and ethnic and gender identity generally coincided with how interview participants articulated different frames, and thus, theories of change to address racial inequalities. Although patterns in social media practices and immigrant, ethnic, and gender identities did not fully explain and predict whether an individual would be a policy supporter or opponent, these differences were notable enough to warrant a discussion.[27] There are critical differences within the Asian American population, which is rarely recognized for its diversity.

### DIFFERENCES IN SOCIAL MEDIA CULTURES

At the start of this study, I learned that differences in social media practices among Asian Americans shaped the contours of the affirmative action divide. Early in 2016 I created lists of Asian American organizations that had either supported or opposed affirmative action in the debate over SCA-5 in California and through amicus briefs submitted to the Supreme Court in both the 2013 and 2016 *Fisher v. UT Austin* cases. I quickly found publicly posted email and web or social media sites for almost all of the more than 160 Asian American organizations that supported the policy. Conversely, although I had compiled a list of 156 organizations that identified as representing Asian Americans opposed to the policy, I found it very difficult to locate contact information or any Internet or social media presence for any of them. This was my first clue about the key differences in communications cultures defining the Asian American affirmative action divide.

Within a few weeks of starting this research project in spring 2016, I had secured and scheduled interviews with twenty-six of thirty-six interviewee participants: nineteen policy supporters, two individuals with mixed opinions on the policy, and five policy opponents. These interviews took place in person or via Zoom between May and July 2016. It was relatively easy to find and communicate with these participants using email addresses found on their websites and via Facebook, Twitter, and LinkedIn. By May 2016 I had secured twenty interviews with individuals affiliated with pro–affirmative action Asian American organizations, but I had still only been able to schedule two interviews with policy opponents.

I started getting worried about how difficult it was to recruit and secure interviews with people from anti–affirmative action Asian American organizations and turned to friends on Facebook, where I openly pondered why it was so hard for me to find and communicate with Asian Americans affiliated with anti–affirmative action organizations. In response, my friend Cat suggested I connect with Y., one of her Chinese immigrant friends, who had just talked with her about concerns over noticing a lot of other Chinese immigrants actively opposing affirmative action. Through Facebook messages, Y. asked me, "Have you tried WeChat?" This simple question unexpectedly introduced me to Chinese diasporic social media.

In February 2021, WeChat was the fifth most utilized social media app in the world with over 1.17 billion users.[28] Most people in the United States, unless they have social connections to people in mainland China, have never heard of it. Because Facebook and other social media platforms common in the US are banned in China, Chinese Americans and others who wish to stay connected via social media to people in China have increasingly adopted WeChat. As some research and observations have demonstrated, many Chinese American immigrants rely on WeChat for news and information, creating influential ethnic Chinese social media echo chambers that can also create social isolation and segregation from a diversity of perspectives.[29] Through WeChat I was able to quickly secure ten interviews with key Chinese American immigrant anti–affirmative action actors and one interview with a policy supporter. I scheduled an additional three interviews with participants affiliated with anti–affirmative action organizations through referrals (i.e., snowball recruitment). Although these organizations claimed to represent Asian Americans, all of the study participants from these groups identified as Chinese American.

The activist mobilization of Chinese Americans against affirmative action between 2013 and 2020 seems to contradict, or at least add a new wrinkle to, scholarship and documentation of Asian American civic and political engagement. Particularly among immigrant populations, there have been long-standing barriers to civic engagement.[30] With this in mind, I asked interview participants to share stories with me about how and why they became politically active. During one of my interviews in California, Thomas, a self-proclaimed leader of Chinese Americans, a WeChat influencer, and a policy opponent, explained his journey of political engagement by offering a lengthy explanation for how Chinese American mobilization against affirmative action has grown as a movement more generally. I present Thomas's explanation of the growth of contemporary Chinese American activism mostly intact in appendix B (found online at beacon.org/PoonAppendix). Even though I believe there are some exaggerations in his narration (please read with a grain of salt!), his story animates the centrality of WeChat in the rise of anti–affirmative action activism and conservativism among contemporary Chinese Americans more generally.

Before WeChat, Thomas told me, he had been participating and leading small-scale demonstrations with no more than fifty people, starting in 2005. Thomas and his compatriots protested in support of China's international political declarations. For example, they showed up to support China's claims in territory disputes with the Philippines and Japan. He explained that it was hard to mobilize people to these direct actions over international politics.

However, the combination of WeChat and claims of anti-Chinese maltreatment sparked rage-motivated activism among Chinese diasporic communities. According to Thomas, he became a central figure and leader in organizing a cycle of protests leading to wins that propelled more direct actions and activism on a range of issues. In this narrative, Thomas situated himself and WeChat activists as "forerunners," or pioneers in starting a Chinese American movement in 2013. Throughout his storytelling, I sensed that he was either unaware of, or didn't care about, other historical and contemporary Chinese American and Asian American activism.

Dramatically, during our interview in a booth at a McDonald's in his Southern California neighborhood, Thomas told me that in 2013, "There was this guy named Jimmy Kimmel who had a show on TV called 'Kids Table.'" In a Kids Table segment on ABC's late-night show *Jimmy Kimmel Live*, one child responded that the United States should "kill everyone in China" in order to handle the nation's financial debts to China. Audience laughter ensued, and Kimmel responded by saying, "OK. That's an interesting idea."

"That enraged a lot of people," Thomas explained. Motivated by anger and humiliation within his WeChat social circles, Thomas shared that he organized rallies outside of ABC Studios in New York and Los Angeles, in addition to a petition to cancel Jimmy Kimmel's show. As a result, Kimmel issued an apology. The Obama administration, in response to the petition signed by over a hundred thousand people, stated that the comments on the TV show did not reflect the perspectives of the US government and that it would be a First Amendment violation for the administration to demand an end to the Kimmel show.[31]

Thomas claimed the victory and told me that over the next few months, in early 2014, "Everybody was telling me, 'Hey dude, we should do something.'" His networks on WeChat were hungry for more direct action protests. Thomas recognized that "you only protest if there's something worth protesting. If there's nothing, you really can't do anything." Some in his networks called for protests against the use of the slur "Chinaman" by Bob Beckel. "He's, I think, an NBC or FOX News anchor," Thomas explained.

During one of the rallies, he met Mei Mei Huff, the wife of a Republican state senator in California, who told him about SCA-5, framing it as a law proposed to exclude Chinese and other Asian Americans from the University of California in favor of "undeserving" other people of color. Aligned with the grievance politics in both the Kimmel and Beckel media incidents, Thomas said he "told everybody how [SCA-5] is very bad for us because it uses skin color to limit the admissions based on race, which is not fair."[32]

After a series of wins, including the defeat of SCA-5, Thomas said he and his networks were looking for the next issue to protest. In the meantime, he realized that voter registration and mobilization was an important path to power. Thomas saw that the Jimmy Kimmel incident "awakened a lot of people into a big group to protest against inequality. SCA-5 made these people realize that we can influence politicians with grassroot efforts." Each win led to another win in their movement for political power.

Then came the multicity protest in support of a Chinese American former New York City police officer, Peter Liang, who was convicted of manslaughter in shooting and killing Akai Gurley, an unarmed Black man, in the stairwell of a public housing building. Liang was a twenty-seven-year-old rookie police officer in November 2014. He and his partner were patrolling the Pink Houses—a public housing building in Brooklyn. Akai Gurley was a twenty-eight-year-old Black man and father of a little girl. Because the elevator was often out of order, Gurley was entering the stairwell to exit the building. Reportedly, when Officer Liang heard the door open to the poorly lit stairwell, he was frightened and shot a bullet from his gun, which ricocheted and hit Gurley.

Rather than immediately call for an ambulance and medical attention, Liang called his supervisor. His actions and inactions led to Gurley's death. I remember being shocked to see thousands of Chinese Americans across the country mobilize in 2015 and 2016 to protest the indictment of Liang, who was found guilty of second-degree manslaughter but only sentenced to probation. Why was this case such a galvanizing event for so many Chinese American immigrants? Was it a frustrating reminder that Chinese Americans were treated differently than White Americans? The protesters claimed that it was unfair that White police officers, such as the ones who had killed Eric Garner in Staten Island the year before, had not been indicted. Although there were large numbers of Asian Americans who supported Peter Liang, there were also Asian Americans organizing in support of Akai Gurley's family, led by CAAAV Organizing Asian Communities in New York City.[33]

Thomas's story of WeChat's role in the growth and development of contemporary Chinese American racial grievance activism illustrated basic elements of social movements. Political sociologists have explained that social movements are composed of informal social networks premised on shared values, which mobilize for direct action protest motivated by central galvanizing themes, with communication serving a key role in keeping things together and moving forward.[34]

While Chinese American affirmative action opponents rallied and mobilized in visible numbers starting in 2014, creating spectacles for media attention, Asian American policy supporters have not been as visibly active in public advocacy for race-conscious admissions. Aside from the intergenerational, cross-racial, and cross-ethnic rally to #DefendDiversity in Harvard Square on the eve of the *SFFA v. Harvard* US District Court hearings, there have been relatively few direct action events to support the policy in comparison to the opposition. This direct action asymmetry in the affirmative action divide parallels the differences in the amount of discussion centering race-conscious admissions found in WeChat compared to other mainstream social media spaces, where those who are not fluent in Chinese are more likely to be found. According to communications scholar Chi Zhang, there is a considerable amount of unsubstantiated information exchange about affirmative action on WeChat, where the topic is one of the top two most discussed subjects.[35] In comparison, over the same scope of time affirmative action was not as commonly discussed in mainstream news sources and social media platforms. If Chinese American immigrants are more likely to be found on WeChat, where affirmative action is framed as an urgent problem, it can explain their urgency in activism around this issue. In contrast, other Asian Americans, including US-born Chinese Americans, are mostly engaged in communications exchange on mainstream US social media platforms, where affirmative action is not as commonly a hot topic and therefore less of an urgent issue. Varying social media modes of practice highlight the existence of different echo chambers and channels for the spread of information, including fake news, that can shape divergent theories of change.[36] Moreover, recognizing variations in ethnicity, immigration pathways, and gender among the participants in this study may help explain differences in social media practices and their preferred theories of change.

### DIFFERENCES IN IDENTITY: ETHNICITY, IMMIGRATION PATHWAYS, AND GENDER

Interview participants who were affiliated with pro–affirmative action organizations were more diverse along gender and ethnic identities than those affiliated with the anti–affirmative action cause. Among the twenty-one who were affiliated with pro–affirmative action groups, the majority identified as women (thirteen). They also represented a range of ethnic identities (see the Interview Participants table). Notably, two of the Chinese-identified individuals (one woman and one man) affiliated with pro–affirmative action organizations expressed skepticism and uncertainties about the policy. I include these two individuals and their thoughts in chapter 4, along with other policy opponents.

All fifteen people affiliated with anti–affirmative action organizations identified as Chinese American, and fourteen of them identified as men while only one identified as a woman. Although not all anti–affirmative action Asian Americans identify as Chinese American men, my research team and I were unable to make contact and secure interviews with Asian American individuals who did not identify as Chinese but were affiliated with these organizations. Despite persistent and extended efforts into fall 2016, we were also only able to secure one interview with an anti–affirmative action Asian American who identified as a woman.

Though I can confidently state that there are non-Chinese Asian Americans opposed to affirmative action, I am also fairly certain based on opinion polling and research from AAPI Data, observations of rallies against affirmative action, and my research experiences that the majority of Asian Americans who actively organize against it are Chinese Americans.[37] This general demographic contour of the Asian American affirmative action opposition may have contributed toward challenges in securing interviews with non-Chinese leaders of Asian American organizations opposed to race-conscious admissions. I continue to ponder why it was difficult to secure more than the one interview with a woman opposed to affirmative action. Perhaps a future study can explore the gender dynamics that seem part of this story.

Another resonant demographic difference I noticed between Asian American policy supporters and opponents in my study was the difference in contexts and pathways of immigration. Among the twenty-one participants affiliated with pro–affirmative action organizations, few (seven) identified as immigrants, all of whom arrived in the US between 1965 and 1987 through family reunification and refugee pathways. On the other hand, most of the fifteen policy opponent interviewees (eleven) were immigrants. Of these immigrants, most (seven) had arrived in the US after 1990, and mostly on graduate student visas. One of the other four opponents also immigrated as an international student, but before 1965, while the other three immigrated as children or young people with their families in the 1970s and 1980s.

Interestingly, most of the immigrant policy opponents had arrived in the US during immigration eras when there were stricter immigration policies that privileged highly educated and professional class immigrants, while immigrants affiliated with pro–affirmative action organizations arrived in the US during a more liberal era of immigration after 1965 but before increased restrictions in 1990. Perhaps this pattern suggests that people who have benefited from restrictive policies remain supportive of manufactured restrictions, and that those who have benefited from more inclusive policies remain supportive of expansive and inclusive policy positions.

US-born participants in this study were also more likely to be affiliated with pro–affirmative action organizations. This aligns with other research that has found a conflict in affirmative action perspectives between Chinese Americans ages eighteen to twenty-four and older Chinese Americans.[38]

## CHOOSING WHO WE WANT TO BE

Asian Americans generally agree that racism is a problem. They do not, however, agree about what to do about this problem. They bring divergent theories of change, as reflected in the affirmative action debate, shaped by diverse experiences of immigration histories, ethnic backgrounds, gender, and social media practices. These striking differences beg the question: What is an Asian American agenda? Can there ever be a unified agenda with such vast diversity among this population?

Some participants in my study, like Albert and Grace, expressed a frustration over the Asian American divide and the lack of an Asian American agenda. Both were members and leaders of pro–affirmative action Asian American organizations, even though they personally did not agree with affirmative action policies. Both also suggested that traditional Asian American civil rights organizations and leaders seemed to prioritize the political agenda of organizations that represented other communities of color over the interests of Asian Americans. According to Albert, "The progressive Asians are siding with what I think is [the agenda of] Blacks and Hispanics." He was also concerned that "the conservative Asians are in some ways siding with the Whites. You know what I mean? Well, they're helping that White agenda, unwittingly I think," in their opposition to race-conscious admissions. Grace offered a generational explanation for the ideological divide among Asian Americans. Referring to long-standing traditional Asian American civil rights organizations, she observed that a lot of Asian advocacy organizations say things like, "Oh, we got to support the undocumented people." Grace pointed out that less than 10 percent of undocumented immigrants were Asian. She didn't feel like advocating for policies that supported undocumented immigrants was a central issue for Asian Americans. She didn't believe affirmative action was an Asian American policy issue.

Both Albert and Grace expressed an interest in working with other communities of color for civil rights, but they believed that Asian American interests were distinct from and sometimes at odds with the agendas of other people of color. Their ideas contradicted Jimmy's belief that there was a linked fate and shared agenda between Asian Americans and other people of color. When asked what they believed were key issues in an Asian American agenda, neither Albert nor Grace offered clear recommendations. Albert explained that Asian Americans across the political spectrum should get together and talk with each other. Beyond offering that it was "very important to have a voice on immigration," Grace also felt a need "to hear more from our own advocates." However, Grace would likely find that the answers on what issues should be central to an Asian American agenda would depend on the advocates she asked.

Among the people I interviewed, interconnected differences in social media practices, immigration pathways, and ethnic and gender identities were associated with differences in affirmative action perspectives. Divergent theories of change in what to do about racism are at the heart of explaining the conflict between Asian Americans in the affirmative action divide. Just as in the affirmative action divide, divergent theories of change characterize and animate community divides that have been found in broader Asian American community racial politics before and since COVID-19. Although some Asian Americans have further invested in the police state to combat anti-Asian violence, especially in the COVID era, others refuse to rely on policing.[39]

Some Asian American organizations and leaders have offered and led campaigns and projects guided by expansive views of justice long before Atlanta. For example, Vigilant Love is a community-based organization founded by Muslim American and Japanese American leaders, forged through solidarity programs since 2001, after September 11.[40] Its mission is to create "spaces for connection and grassroots movement to protect the safety and justice of communities impacted by Islamophobia and violence in the greater Los Angeles Area." Vigilant Love's leaders draw direct connections between Japanese American experiences of racism (most palpably through the US concentration camps of Japanese Americans during World War II) and the Islamophobic racism faced by Muslim Americans (e.g., the Trump Muslim ban). Community leaders in organizations, such as AAPI Women Lead and New Breath Foundation, have advanced explicitly abolitionist theories of change.[41] In their analysis, anti-Asian violence and racism grow from the roots of US imperialism, the prison industrial complex, and the carceral state. Therefore, combatting anti-Asian violence requires deep intersectional and cross-racial solidarity work.[42] What these organizations have in common is an agenda that centers solidarity with other marginalized communities that face systemic racism and violence. At the core of their work is a recognition of linked fates. As the late Chinese American Detroit activist Grace Lee Boggs stated, "The only way to survive is by taking care of one another, by recreating our relationships to one another."[43] Boggs also reminds us that when we pursue self-interest, we devolve as human beings.[44]

Centering one's self-interests and the refusal to recognize the interconnectedness of how racism impacts various communities of color differently characterize how others have reacted to Asian American racial grievances in 2021. Following the February 2021 viral spread of a video showing an elderly person in Oakland's Chinatown being violently shoved and knocked down, some well-intentioned Asian American celebrities put up funds for reward money to encourage people to share information with the police. In doing so, they encouraged and enabled the furtherance of anti-Black and anti-Latinx policing. Although the same celebrities have asserted in their social media that Black Lives Matter (BLM) in solidarity, their actions unintentionally served to augment the very police state the BLM movement has decried. Moreover, in this case, it turned out that the elder was Latinx. Still, the underlying public narrative that persists is that violence against elders is specifically an anti-Asian problem that can be solved with more policing and criminalization.[45] Other Asian Americans have also allied themselves with conservative ideologues such as Senator Ted Cruz and Nikki Haley, who identifies as Indian American, in responding to anti-Asian violence by attacking critical race theory (CRT) and race-conscious admissions and affirmative action in higher education.[46] They claim that developing and articulating critical analyses of racism—that is, problematizing systemic racism—to illuminate possible strategies against racism is somehow anti-Asian.

Té Té,

Leading up to the 2023 Chicago run-off election between Brandon Johnson and Paul Vallas, you were disappointed that kids weren't eligible to register and vote in the election. It seemed unfair to you that voting laws had determined that children were not allowed to participate in deciding who would lead and shape our city's future. Between the divergent ideas and strategies for change presented by the two candidates, you felt Johnson's made more sense to you. Although you weren't allowed to vote, I told you that we could volunteer for the Johnson campaign to knock on doors in our community, share with our neighbors why we agreed with Johnson's vision for Chicago, and encourage them to vote. I told you, participating in get-out-the-vote efforts was just as powerful of a civic activity.

Two days before the election, on an unusually warm Chicago day in early April, we joined your classmate Bruce and his mom and volunteered for the Johnson campaign. For three hours, we knocked on about a hundred doors. You and Bruce raced each other to each door. When we were done, we rewarded ourselves with some playground time and ice cream.

Brandon Johnson was elected Chicago's fifty-seventh mayor.

Grace Lee Boggs pointed out, "You don't choose the times you live in, but you do choose who you want to be, and you do choose how you want to think." How will Asian Americans choose to be, think, and, I would add, act when confronting racism that targets Asian Americans and other people of color? In the next two chapters, I offer narratives of how affirmative action opponents and supporters have chosen who they want to be, and how they want to think *and* act, as Asian Americans.

# CHAPTER 4

# "IF NOT ME THEN WHO?"

*Chinese Americans Reacting to Racial Erasure*

Dear Té Té,

On the school day right before Lunar New Year in 2023, you told me you were going to wear your red satin and gold floral-accented Chinese cheongsam dress to school and bring your storybooks about Asian diasporic New Year celebrations to share with your second-grade class. "I want to share our culture with my friends," you said. It triggered mixed emotions for me. I felt gratified that you felt proud of our cultural heritage. I also felt some apprehension, likely due to lingering traumas from my childhood. Would your mostly Latinx classmates receive your sharing as exotic or odd? Would they unintentionally or intentionally say something to cut down your confidence and self-worth?

Just a month or two before, you had come home telling me that the kids in school were talking about their different "cultures," which I took to mean ethnic identities. You giggled when you told me, "No one could guess my cultures." In your nearly 90 percent Latinx urban public school, the Puerto Rican kids guessed you were Puerto Rican and the Mexican American kids guessed you were Mexican like them. I felt happy and interpreted this story as children expressing an acceptance of you. As I explained to you that there were indeed Puerto Rican and Mexican people who looked like us, but that we weren't part of that diaspora, you interrupted me and excitedly told me, "They didn't know that I'm Chinese and Thai, kinda like Toribio is both Mexican and Puerto Rican!" I could tell you were brushing me off, as I imagine a lot of kids of academics and professors do when we try to offer more information. You were too enthusiastic about the interaction with your friends to hear your boring race scholar mom share additional information. You ran off to your bookshelf to pick out a few of your numerous books you would bring to school, as you continued to tell me that you couldn't wait to share about Lunar New Year and Songkran—Thai New Year—with your class.

It was astounding to me how you reveled in conversations about cultures with your classmates as a fun and positive experience. You didn't see these dialogues with your classmates marginalizing your identities or rendering them invisible. You chose to enthusiastically share your cultures with your teachers and classmates. Getting to bring pictures and stories from our family and communities to contribute to your class's learning and conversations made you beam with excitement and pride.

This, however, was very different than the stories you had brought home from a predominantly White summer camp in 2022, when some White children asked you if you were Chinese and if you liked noodles. You told me you were confused about why they had asked you these questions and why it suddenly made you feel "funny" about liking noodles. Your instincts in both cases told you something different about the nature and intentions behind the interactions.

With your schoolmates you felt seen and valued. In the summer scenario you wondered if and why our culture was being seen as an object of abnormality for anyone. Besides, you said, "Why wouldn't I like noodles? Noodles are delicious!" I sighed to myself, "Baby's first microaggression." I explained to you that a lot of the kids in your summer camp came from schools that were mostly White like them, where meeting someone different from them was new. You thought about it for a minute and shared a realization with me: "Oh . . . they're missing out! I feel bad for them." You just brushed it off and went along with your day.

I am often surprised by your reactions. You have always been so self-possessed in responding to the world around you. My growing-up years were more like your uncomfortable summer camp experiences of being seen as an object of ridicule and feeling marginalized. Instead of feeling compassion or just brushing it off, I often felt shame and anger. I responded differently, but I also grew up in a different era than you—what you call the "olden days" of the 1980s and '90s.

Growing up in an era of deep narrative scarcity[1] about Asian Americans made me feel invisible and unimportant. Whenever I noticed images of people who looked like me on TV, film, or anywhere else, it often felt shocking and out of the norm. One time in the early 1990s, when I was in high school, I went with my mom to the grocery store and wandered off into the books and magazines section to pass the time. My eyes quickly ran past the usual tabloid covers and headlines:

TOM [CRUISE] AND NICOLE'S [KIDMAN] ENDLESS HONEYMOON

PLASTIC SURGERY OF THE STARS: DO THEY OR DON'T THEY?

HILLARY AND TIPPER: WINNING WOMEN

PRINCESS DI AND PRINCE CHARLES: IT'S OVER![2]

A glossy magazine cover with smiling Asian American teens looking out at me stopped me cold in my tracks. Stunned, I looked around to see if anyone else was in the aisle and if they too saw the anomaly on the shelves. If they had, what did they think? What would they think seeing an Asian American teen looking at a magazine with Asian American faces on it? Would it look peculiar to them as much as it felt excitingly unusual to me? My heart racing, I picked up the news magazine with happy-looking teens carrying books and wearing the latest fashions—overalls, neon colors, floppy hats—and looked down at it in my hands, allowing my long hair to curtain and conceal my face from anyone who happened to push their cart through the aisle. I don't remember the magazine or the exact title of the cover story, but I do remember that it felt electric to see a mainstream magazine acknowledging the existence of kids who looked like me.

What did the periodical have to say about us? The short story inside the glossy publication pointed to the high academic achievement among (some East) Asian Americans and posed questions about whether brand-name colleges—Harvard, Stanford, Princeton, and so on—were discriminating against them . . . us. Were these famous colleges so inundated with Asian American college hopefuls that it made it harder for someone like me to be admitted? The short cover story left me unsatisfied and wondering whether the most famous American colleges and universities were just perpetuating another form of the racist bullying I experienced in school. It all left me feeling unsettled over how to make sense of my experiences in school and how places of enlightened higher learning could also be places of racism.[3]

The story raised questions about racial discrimination against Asian Americans, but the way it framed racism against Asian Americans was foreign to me, because it inherently suggested that Black students were favored over students like me. It was confusing to see pictures of youth like me accompany a story about racism that bore no resemblance to the anti-Asian racism, which served to uphold White dominance, I had witnessed and experienced throughout my young lifetime. I supposed, like the youth in the featured narrative, I was a striving high achiever in my school, encouraged and supported by my teachers, perhaps propped up by a racialized stereotype promise of Asian high achievement.[4] Until I saw that magazine in the grocery store, I had no idea that Asian Americans were viewed as high achievers.

Starting in pre-K, I regularly experienced racist and xenophobic bullying. When I punched a fellow four-year-old for calling me a monkey, the White teachers taught me "sticks and stones may break your bones, but names will never hurt me." The lesson was clear—ignore and accept the racist hurt. The physical pain dissipated much more quickly than the lingering damage to my spirit. From pre-K through twelfth grade, I endured being the target of racial harassment perpetrated by my Portuguese and Polish classmates, some of whom were recent immigrants. However, whenever I would hit, kick, or punch my harassers, my White teachers never reported or punished me beyond giving me a lecture about the importance of nonviolence.[5] It was just never talked about again.

In school we were taught not to talk about or deeply problematize racism. I also chose not to ask my parents for help. They were often busy working multiple jobs in construction, engineering, restaurants, retail, and sewing,[6] and were stressed out about making the mortgage and paying the bills. When I was in elementary school, my dad would go to his salaried engineering job from 8:00 a.m. until 6:00 p.m., come home to eat dinner, and drive an hour to my uncle's busy Chinese restaurant in Connecticut to help, often coming home to sleep after midnight. When I was in junior high my parents started a small party supplies store, which depleted their savings year after year. During those difficult years, my mom ran the store six days a week, coming home to cook dinner, clean, get three kids ready for the next day, and sew some piecework for local dry cleaners before going to bed. My dad was so busy by the time I was in high school that he wasn't able to come to my high school graduation. The last thing I wanted to do was bother them with "kid" problems. I figured I could find ways to endure my circumstances, as my parents persevered through theirs.

I never really felt seen in the complexities of my experiences. There were few stories that affirmed my experiences and struggles to make sense of the world. However, that didn't mean I had no lessons on how to make sense of race and the racial harassment I experienced growing up. I turned to pop culture and library books.

Although my struggle was not the same as African American experiences of racism, I felt an affinity and admiration for Black civil rights movements and cultural projects. In the early 1990s I religiously watched *The Cosby Show*, *A Different World*, *Living Single*, *Fresh Prince of Bel Air*, and *In Living Color*. On the radio, my musical tastes shifted from New Kids on the Block to New Edition, Janet Jackson, Mary J. Blige, SWV, TLC, De La Soul, Tribe Called Quest, Tupac Shakur, Dr. Dre, Snoop Dogg, and the Notorious B.I.G.

To be sure, I wasn't only consuming Black pop culture. I enjoyed the occasional episode of *Cheers*, mostly because it depicted a very different aspect of Boston than I knew through my grandparents who lived in Boston Chinatown. Nirvana, Pearl Jam, The Cranberries, INXS, New Order, Erasure, and The Cure were also spinning in my CD player. Like many Asian Americans of my generation, New Wave music was part of the soundtrack of my youth.[7] As an Asian American teen in the 1980s and '90s, I almost never saw or heard myself reflected in the culture I was consuming, emulating, and playing with. Of course, there was pop music in Asia, and my mom would play cassette tapes of Cantopop artists like Anita Mui and Andy Lau, but they were foreign cultural representations to me. In between Black and White pop culture, I felt a deeper emotional resonance with Black cultural representations. They offered me something

I needed: encouraging models of possibilities to thrive and forge identities in a predominantly White world with self-dignity and worth.

During my junior year of high school, I started receiving college recruitment mailers that vividly depicted racial acceptance as a reality in higher education.[8] They fueled my dreams of college as a multicultural utopia—the perfectly landscaped quads populated by faces of all different colors smiling at each other, concentrating on lab experiments, engaging in the debates of the day with world-renowned professors who cared about what they thought, together in diverse cultural artistic performances. All these scenes of harmonious racial diversity seemed like heaven to me—a place where it wouldn't matter anymore that I wasn't White. I longed to go someplace where my Asian American experiences wouldn't be invisible and dismissed anymore.

College represented *the* way out of my hostile hometown and out of racial marginalization. I thought if I could get into a highly rejective college that none of my White classmates could get into, I would finally prove my human dignity and worth (to White people) and earn my way to a sense of belonging in a White-dominated society. I spent endless hours in my bedroom, pouring over a well-worn copy of the 1993 edition of *Barron's Profiles of American Colleges* while surrounded by college brochures on the floor. I mistakenly presumed that the few colleges Barron's categorized as "most competitive" would be where I could escape racial hostilities.

Perhaps concerned and a bit confused about my obsession with college acceptance, my parents didn't explicitly discourage me from applying to Ivy League institutions, but they braced me for disappointment, explaining that I should apply to more "realistic" and affordable colleges than Harvard and the University of Pennsylvania. Even though I was among the top of my graduating class, they recognized the limitations of my educational circumstances and opportunity structures better than I did at the time. My high school did not offer the most rigorous academic curriculum or resources to support my dreams of becoming an Ivy League student. I also did not take the most rigorous curriculum available in my high school. Instead, I chose to only take three years of science classes, partly taking myself out of the honors track at school.

When Harvard and Penn rejected me, I was devastated. After a lifetime of being told I didn't belong in America because I wasn't White, I naively thought an Ivy League acceptance could represent a stamp of approval, more official than my US-born citizenship and passport, that I belonged. I thought it could be a well-deserved reward and validation of my parents' constant struggle, exhaustion, and stress. Some girls daydreamed about their teen idols; I fantasized about flaunting an Ivy League acceptance letter in every racist White kid's face—a major mic drop, saying without words, "You thought you could keep me down? You thought you were better than me? Peace! I'm out!" as the gates of an exclusive Ivy institution opened for me and not them. I just needed to work harder and earn my way into acceptance in America, out of being targeted with racist violence. Now, without that paper, I wondered if my bullies had been right all along—I would never be accepted because I was inferior.

I thought maybe that news magazine I had seen in the grocery store was right. Maybe the only reason I didn't get in was because of anti-Asian discrimination due to this thing called affirmative action that supposedly only benefited Black and Latinx people, never mind that the Ivies are in the business of rejecting nearly all their applicants each year. Never mind that I hadn't taken the most rigorous courses available to me at an underfunded public school, where most graduates went on to the military, community colleges, or local and more open-access universities. I was angry that I had been told that if I worked hard, I would be rewarded, but when I worked hard and endured a hostile schooling environment, I was not given the reward I had decided I deserved. I registered to vote for the first time as a Republican, buying into their messages of honoring individual grit and hard work while dismissing calls to change structural conditions as unrealistic.

Still, I had acceptance letters from other great colleges and universities. So when my rejection letters had come from a couple colleges that rejected almost everyone, across racial identities, I wasn't convinced that Harvard had racially discriminated against me in their decision.[9] After all, they did turn away over 90 percent of their applicants. I figured I must be in good company, but being turned away by rejective colleges stung on an existential level. Just like my bullies, teachers, and popular media, these colleges seemed to convey to me how invisible and unimportant I was. News stories suggesting anti-Asian discrimination in colleges represented one of the first times I had seen national outlets acknowledge Asian American existence. The narratives they pushed didn't feel quite right to me, but I yearned for any affirmation of my racial realities. I wanted to be seen and break out of the racial erasure of my experiences.

Debates over race-conscious college admissions policies have represented one of the few public discourses that have included mainstream acknowledgment of Asian Americans. Asian Americans were not central to these policy debates until Ed Blum and Students for Fair Admissions (SFFA) put us center stage when they filed their lawsuits against Harvard and Yale starting in 2014. The dress rehearsals for co-opting Asian Americans in this moment, however, began in the 1980s, when Asian American college students began raising concerns that rejective colleges and universities seemed to be limiting admissions to Asian Americans *in favor of White applicants*.[10]

The Reagan administration launched federal investigations into allegations of anti-Asian quotas in favor of White applicants. Some politicians went a step further and suggested that affirmative action policies favored other students of color, namely, Black students, at the expense of Asian Americans. This additional claim came from White conservative pundits who recognized an opportunity for them to create a wedge between people of color—a divide-and-conquer strategy to maintain power in a hierarchy of racial inequalities. It was one of the earliest cases of White anti-equity conservative activists using Asian Americans as "racial mascots" for their anti–affirmative action campaign. According to law professor Sumi Cho, White anti–affirmative action actors were using racist stereotypes of Asian American academic achievement to deflect claims that their attacks on affirmative action were racist. They could pretend to care about Asian Americans—a minority group—while seeking to end racial equity policies.

About thirty years later, in the mid-2010s, when Ed Blum, the founder of SFFA, suspected he would lose in the *Fisher v. UT Austin* case, he traveled the country on a mission to cast an Asian American in the SFFA lawsuit against Harvard, UNC, and other universities.[11] He never found any Asian Americans who would step up publicly and serve as the name and face of his next legal complaints which included *SFFA v. Harvard* and *SFFA v. UNC*. You could say he failed to find a willing racial mascot for his anti-equity cause, but consent is unnecessary in the casting and creation of a racial mascot.[12]

At the same time, as I learned from my interviews for this book, there are indeed Asian Americans willing to support and ally themselves with Ed Blum's efforts against race-conscious admissions, and they are not unwitting mascots.[13] In 2016 I spoke with seventeen people who opposed race-conscious admissions practices. As I listened to them, I realized they were not unthinking racial props for White affirmative action opponents. They were thoughtful and deeply invested in their efforts to advocate for what they understood to be Asian American rights.

The inspiration for these interviews came from Professor Peter Kiang. During a conversation in 2013, in which I was bemoaning Asian Americans in California protesting SCA-5 and race-conscious admissions, Peter matter-of-factly asked, "Have you ever talked with them to learn why they feel and act the way they do?" That simple question got me curious. Peter challenged me to remember that these policy opponents were people who identified as Asian American like us, and that I might learn a lot by listening to them.[14] He was right; finding out why they felt the way they did about affirmative action was illuminating and added complexity to my understanding and analysis. Inviting these individuals to speak with me and listening to them was different than it would have been had I invited just anyone with different policy views than me. For example, I would not have felt safe recruiting and spending time with most people who supported Donald Trump, a political figure who advocated for and endorsed racist views and violence.

Even though I know that anti–affirmative action perspectives among Asian Americans are not limited only to Chinese Americans, I was unable to secure interviews with Asian American policy opponents who didn't identify as Chinese. My research team and I had identified over 150 civic groups and organizations that claimed an Asian American or ethnic Asian (i.e., Chinese, Indian, or Korean) identity and demonstrated their opposition to race-conscious admissions policies through their participation in litigation, petitions, and organized protests. Over 70 percent of these organizations were led by Chinese Americans and had missions and activities that centered Chinese American interests.[15] For some context, fewer than 25 percent of Asian Americans in the US identify as Chinese.

Because the people in this chapter are all Chinese Americans, the stories in this chapter overall cannot be understood as Asian American stories, although they claimed to represent Asian American interests. At the same time, some of the narrative threads may feel familiar to other Asian Americans or people holding other ethnic and racial identities. Still, I do not consider their stories to be reflective of Asian American perspectives more broadly. I also do not suggest that the pro–affirmative action narratives in this book represent the totality of Asian American views, even though the interview participants featured in the next chapter are more ethnically diverse. Through these two chapters I want to contribute toward a fuller picture of Asian American narratives, which are wide-ranging and always evolving.

When I met with the Chinese Americans I interviewed for this chapter and deeply listened to what they shared with me, I couldn't help but feel a sense of familiarity. Many of them reminded me a lot of my parents, uncles, and aunties—deeply human and imperfect elders whom I love. In these moments of familiarity, I also wondered: How did we arrive at such different positions on race-conscious admissions, and what would it take to overcome the problem of racism? In each interview I found myself asking genuine questions to learn about each person's experiences and stories and how they arrived at their policy stance.

To be upfront, I hold serious disagreements with these people's ideas about race-conscious admissions policies and about Black and Latinx people, but I acknowledge their humanity and appreciate the candid thoughts and personal stories they shared with me. They viewed race-conscious admissions as an unfair punishment of Asian Americans' (and especially Chinese Americans') hard work and achievement in favor of other people of color and, in some cases, White people. In general, they were invested in improving the social status of Asian Americans, and they resented the ways policy debates about race and education felt dismissive of their struggles and experiences. No Twitter exchange or news media clip could fully represent the complexities of their thinking. I learned that our differences live and evolve in how we have come to view the world's social problems and our divergent political investments.

### REJECTING ERASURE

I first met Eric at a national conference that brought together Chinese Americans for civic engagement and community building in fall 2016. He was a senior at a highly exclusive and rejective[16] liberal arts college. Before meeting him, I had heard of him. Eric was a young activist who was central to efforts to dismantle race-conscious admissions. At the conference he attended a workshop I facilitated to walk participants through a mock admissions activity intended to demonstrate key principles of race-conscious holistic admissions at selective institutions.[17]

At the start of the activity, I asked people to raise their hands to indicate whether they were opposed to, supportive of, or unsure of how they felt about race-conscious admissions practices. Most of the room, including Eric, raised their hands in opposition to the policy. By the end of the activity, Eric shared that he was no longer certain about how he felt about where he stood in the policy debates. I found him to be thoughtful, engaged, curious, and open to learning. Before leaving the conference, I invited him to schedule a time for me to interview him, and he immediately agreed to participate.

Growing up in California, Eric had attended a predominantly Asian American and Latinx public high school, where most of the Asian Americans identified as Filipino and only about 10 percent of the students were White or Black. He told me that he had first learned about race and racism through his debate team. His African American debate team coach, he said, helped him understand "racial tensions throughout the United States." Through debate team, they considered issues of anti-Black police brutality and "watched a lot of Malcolm X, Martin Luther King, and a lot of other African American activists during that time."

His debate team coach also exposed Eric and his classmates to some Asian American history in this extracurricular space. Eric pointed out that his history teachers never taught them about Asian American history, "but our coach included a lot of Asian American history" to explain that racism affected all racialized groups.

It struck me that in a high school where the largest racial group was Asian American, learning about race, Black history, and Asian American history was relegated to extracurricular spaces. Notably, Eric never discussed learning about Latinx or Native histories either, even though the second-largest racial group in his high school was Latinx. Most of his friends, he said, were Chinese American because "a lot of people in our AP courses tend to be Chinese, so naturally I tended to be friends with more Chinese people." Like most of the people in this chapter, his close social circles and consciousness of people around him were predominantly East Asian and White. I was struck by his characterization of his friend group as "naturally" more Chinese. He explained it as a natural occurrence, rather than an outcome of systemic designs. As sociologist Eduardo Bonilla-Silva has explained, "racism without racists" relies on people explaining away racial inequalities as natural.[18]

As someone who was in an almost all-White high school on the East Coast twenty years before Eric, I was surprised to learn that even in a well-resourced public high school that was predominantly populated by people of color, US history remained whitewashed in the 2010s.[19] It was also disappointing but perhaps not surprising to hear about the ethnic segregation occurring within the school through tracking.[20] This marginalization of Asian Americans and other people of color in schools and society, which in cases like in Eric's high school seemed paradoxical, came up throughout my conversations with Chinese Americans seeking to end race-conscious admissions.

About five years before our interview, I had met Richard through mutual Asian American pop culture and identity blogging networks. He was an Ivy League–educated, second-generation Chinese American who had grown up in the 1980s and 1990s. When we reconnected for our virtual interview in 2016, he was living in a suburban community in the Pacific Northwest. Richard had attended predominantly White private schools on both the East and West Coasts, where he was the target of racial bullying. He could not recall any teachers intervening in these instances.

Richard noted how ironic it was that these same teachers, who turned the other way when he was being racially bullied, assigned readings by Maya Angelou and Langston Hughes. His teachers, he said, "couldn't see the discrepancy between reading and sometimes crying over a Maya Angelou poem and tolerating racism in their own school. To them, racism's just anti-Black."

Like me, Richard was also exposed to books outside of the formal high school curriculum. For me, reading Malcolm X and Ron Takaki's books during high school, even though my teachers discouraged me from doing so, was formative in helping me think about Asian Americans in relationship to racial power dynamics and systemic racism. For him, the lone Asian American teacher in his high school encouraged him to read Frank Chin. Reading works by Chin was profoundly formative for him, helping him think of himself as "worthy." Engaging with Chin's writings helped Richard view himself differently from how his bullies had made him feel.

Though I did not share this with him during our interview, I noted to myself that it made sense that Richard, an affirmative action opponent, had his first encounters with Asian American identity through the writings of Frank Chin. A pioneering Chinese American playwright and author, Chin infamously dueled with fellow pathbreaking Chinese American writer Maxine Hong Kingston, starting in the 1970s.[21] Among Asian American literary circles, Chin is known as much for his brilliant pen as he is for advocating for ethnocentric and sexist ideas of Asian American identity that center Chinese American men.

While listening to Richard during our virtual interview, with his well-appointed kitchen in the background, I sensed from him an undercurrent of resentment over how public discourses about racism often centered anti-Black racism at the expense of others. He believed that White people could recognize anti-Black racism but could not do the same for Asian Americans, Latinx, and Native Americans. It was as if White attention to different forms of racism was a prize in a zero-sum game, and it seemed to him that White awareness was what validated a form of oppression. "I think if there were a Black kid at that time who was getting beaten up, they would have that imagery from all the poetry that they had been reading and they would put an end to it immediately."

Richard assumed that anti-Black racism was central in his White teachers' consciousness, above any other form of racism. Because Richard described his schools as predominantly White and never mentioned peers who identified as Black, I am uncertain that his mostly White teachers would have responded more proactively to counter anti-Black racism and harassment. Perhaps the teachers would have responded differently to anti-Black racism, but research suggests that few teachers are prepared or supported to serve as anti-racist educators.[22]

Richard seemed to believe that (White) educators, and perhaps White-dominated society in general, cared more about countering racial animosities targeting African Americans than the hardships of anyone else. I am unconvinced by this assumption, especially as anti-Black racism continues to be ever-present and undeniable. For example, police departments continue to enact extrajudicial and state-sanctioned violence targeting Black communities, and state governments are rejecting the inclusion of African American studies in K–12 schools.[23] Although I understood Richard's concern over the lack of public attention focused on Asian American concerns, I do not believe that caring about the problem of anti-Black racism had to be mutually exclusive from being concerned with anti-Asian racism.

Returning to my conversation with Eric, I asked him to explain his concerns when it came to Asian Americans and why he was so invested in actively opposing affirmative action. Like Richard, he expressed a desire to counter the erasure of Asian Americans in political advocacy. More than once in our conversation, he mentioned that he believed that Asian Americans "tend to be shafted a lot when it comes to political complaints."

Eric believed that the complaints he filed with the federal government to investigate anti-Asian discrimination in admissions pushed White politicians to be "more aware that Asian Americans finally have a voice and they're standing up." Animatedly, he expressed his frustration over what he perceived as "White American articles that were like 'Why are Asian Americans standing up and complaining all of the sudden? Can they just stay quiet?'"

When I asked Eric what it was that was upsetting him, he leaned into stereotypes of "Asian American culture" as a hindrance to "speaking out and complaining." To him, the pushback he got in response to his federal complaints represented White Americans silencing Asian Americans. "Aren't we allowed to have our own say in this country?" he asked.

I held myself back in the interview from challenging Eric's internalized stereotypes that Asian cultures valued obedient submissiveness in contradiction to (White) American cultural values of free speech. Some of the earliest news media images I remembered from the 1980s were of the Gwangju uprising in South Korea and the People Power Revolution in the Philippines that overthrew the government of Ferdinand Marcos. In the years leading up to my meeting with Eric, I closely followed the news and social media feeds of young people in Hong Kong who started the Umbrella Revolution in 2014. Surrounded by White Western views on Asia and Asians, Asian Americans can easily unconsciously, or consciously, buy into sweeping generalizations of what "Asian culture" is, as Eric had. When political resistance, activism, and movements are common throughout Asian history and contemporary events, the claim that Asian culture is not about complaining or speaking out lacks evidence.

I noticed that both Richard and Eric centered White views on Asians and Asian Americans and political dynamics between White and Asian Americans in the social and political views they expressed, like many others in this chapter. There seemed to be an implicit desire to be treated with respect by, and just like, White people, without an acknowledgment of the problems with a racial hierarchy. At the same time, they were different than White affirmative action opponents in that they recognized racism as a problem in the world. We agreed on that point, despite our other disagreements.

### "TELL PEOPLE THAT WE, THE CHINESE AMERICANS, WE ARE NOT AGAINST AFFIRMATIVE ACTION"

On a sunny summer afternoon in 2016, I drove my rental car into an industrial area in the East Bay in the San Francisco metro area to interview Wilson at his small business. He wore a light blue striped button-down collared shirt with the sleeves rolled up, a pen in the shirt pocket, and a pair of dark slacks—like a politician trying to make constituents feel he would get business taken care of but was still relatable to the people. Unlike most of the anti–affirmative action interview participants, Wilson had immigrated from Hong Kong. Like my immigrant family, he also held reservations about the political tactics and WeChat echo chambers of mis- and disinformation that other, more recent Chinese immigrants from mainland China used. Given the history of British colonization and tensions between Beijing and Hong Kong, the former British colony and its people have developed their own distinct hybrid cultures and politics. Knowing that I could speak Cantonese, he interspersed Cantonese words and sayings in his comments and reflections throughout our interview. He reminded me so much of my own father and uncles, who were part of the mass migration from Guangzhou, China, for refuge and asylum in Hong Kong right after World War II, and then to the US in the 1960s and '70s when US immigration policies opened up to Asian immigration. Like my dad, Wilson had struggled to make ends meet while in college, and like some of my elders, he was a small business owner.

At the end of our ninety-minute interview, I asked Wilson, "Do you have any last thoughts that you would like to share about [affirmative action]?" Since that day, I have continued to reflect on what he said in response:

> You're a scholar, you have a lot of influence [on] your students, society, the media. If you can, help tell people that we, the Chinese Americans, we are not against affirmative action which is so important. If you tell the news, "Chinese Americans are against affirmative [action]," others might not treat us good. And anyway, we are not that powerful. You have to listen. We still need affirmative action to break many barriers restricting us or discriminating against us, and [it's] also important we cannot fight alone.

I remember hearing the traffic and a train speed by outside of the window as I listened to Wilson's plea. I wondered, "Wait! Is he an affirmative action supporter?" Did I mistake what side he was on when I scheduled this meeting? It was such a reminder of how we are all walking contradictions at times.

Wilson did not want me to say to my audiences that Chinese Americans were against affirmative action. He even said that Chinese Americans still need affirmative action as an oppressed minority group. He believed that what higher education called "affirmative action" was not actually affirmative action. Instead he believed race-conscious admissions required Chinese Americans to sacrifice college opportunity for other students of color.

Throughout the interview, Wilson's understanding of race-conscious admissions was that it was a practice of matching up the racial demographics of selective college enrollments with state racial demographics. Following this perception, he believed that in California's case, where about 15 percent of the population was Asian American, state universities would keep Asian American enrollment shares at about the same proportion. He suggested that the increasing Latinx enrollment shares in the University of California would soon mean a cap, or quota, on their admission to the university, if the population were to exceed their shares of the state population in campus enrollments.[24]

Wilson also shared that he was disappointed by long-established Asian American civil rights groups. To him, they were just telling Asian Americans to unquestioningly support affirmative action, which he believed required them to "give up our fair opportunity in higher education." He wanted national civil rights organizations to "come up with something so we can explain" affirmative action better, to "lead the people so we have one voice."

As Wilson explained everything he thought was wrong with Asian American civil rights organizations, my head felt like it was spinning as I tried to fully understand what he was sharing with me. In my mind, he wasn't wrong. I too had long been frustrated by many of the Asian American civil rights organizations for not pursuing deeper engagement and popular education with everyday Asian Americans. It triggered a memory of something my father had said to me in the late 1990s when I first started learning about organizations like the Asian Pacific American Legal Consortium (now called Asian Americans Advance Justice), OCA, and the Asian Pacific American Institute for Congressional Studies. I had asked my dad whether he'd heard of these organizations and what he thought of them.

My father believed that the worth of these organizations was only as good as what "regular Asian Americans think of them, and if they have even heard of them." He challenged me to go to any Asian ethnic enclave like Chinatown and ask people if they'd heard of these organizations. I remember him asking me, "What good are they if the people have never heard of them?"

Unlike national civil rights organizations, my father said, people know local, direct service organizations like South Cove.[25] He wished there was even one national Asian American civil rights organization respected, trusted, and known by Asian Americans. Wilson's critiques of the Asian American civil rights community and earnest request to listen echoed in my head, weaving into memories of my own father's observations.

Wilson and others in this chapter believed that the reinstatement of race-conscious admissions practices would mean that California universities would decrease the numbers of Asian Americans admitted and enrolled to more proportionately and closely match their representation in the state. In his mind, if representation was not the central concern, then why use terms like "under-represented minority" or "over-represented"?[26] Although he was careful to distinguish between this supposed quota practice and affirmative action, which he asserted was a good and necessary policy, he adamantly opposed SCA-5, which would have partially repealed Proposition 209—California's affirmative action ban. This narrow and winding logic seemed disconnected from legal facts at the time.

It would be simple to dismiss Wilson and others as wrongheaded. It would also be too easy to believe that presenting them with history and facts would solve the Asian American affirmative action divide. And every time I slip into a desire to write off Chinese and other Asian Americans opposing affirmative action, I remember him insisting, "You have to listen!"

I listened to others like Jake, via Zoom, who sat comfortably on a plush white sofa in a sunny room in his Southern California home when we spoke virtually. Occasionally his elementary school–age daughter with long, straight hair would hop into view and give Jake an affectionate snuggle. At one point in our time together when his children went outside to play, he signaled to me that he wanted me to listen very carefully: "Just to be completely clear, I hope this isn't a point that you drop. I support affirmative action. I support diversity."

It was surprising to hear this from Jake—someone who had been countering race-conscious diversity policies for decades. As I continued to listen, I wondered, "What's the catch?"

"It's very rational to me to want to put in programs that help people who are disadvantaged succeed so that hidden talents and initiative can be used to benefit society," Jake said. I found myself agreeing with much of what he had to say next:

> Racism is actually kind of irrational. So is sexism. It's pretty irrational. If you don't take advantage of the talents of your society, your society is probably going to fail, or have a lesser chance of succeeding. Anyway, so I support affirmative action. Diversity makes a lot of sense to me.

I remember nodding in agreement with Jake, until he leaned forward toward the screen and proceeded with sarcasm in his voice, "I support being conscious. You shouldn't be unconscious. You can't be. That's just stupid, to be unconscious and to deny that somebody's of a different gender, a different race." Jake shifted in his chair as he launched into a lecture about the law:

> But then the question is under law, and as a matter of fundamental equity and fairness, should you and can you assume that somebody is either advantaged or disadvantaged just because of the color of their skin or their gender? And the answer is no. There is no such thing as reverse discrimination or reverse racism. Those are euphemisms coined to justify racism.

Jake believed race-conscious admissions practices were simply about assumptions of advantage or disadvantage based on demographic boxes applicants checked off, and that the checkboxes were *the* thing that got any student admitted or rejected—an inaccurate assumption.

Somewhat like Jake, Eric believed that affirmative action was a policy gone wrong in practice, even though he had never witnessed the inner workings of admissions cycles. He was also open to the idea of collective redress: "I like [affirmative action] in theory. I don't like it in practicality. In theory it is good—that we ought to address the systemic discrimination that exists in our society and ameliorate that by helping minorities achieve their dreams just as much."

Eric believed "that the Asian American minority is being disadvantaged for another minority" through affirmative action. His position was premised on zero-sum perceptions, which are often found among high-status groups who believe that gains for one group will always be at the expense of another.[27] That said, he expressed to me that he was fine if affirmative action in practice resulted in a preference for minorities over White applicants, telling me that's "how it should have been." To him, college admissions would always produce winners at the expense of losers. He falsely presumed that Asian Americans were losers in race-conscious admissions, benefiting Black students. However, he was hypothetically amenable to White students losing to Black and other students of color. There was no collective uplift possible in his mind, and in this twisty logic, he could claim he supported affirmative action and actively oppose it.

Albert, a leader of a pro–affirmative action organization, also believed that education policies seeking to ameliorate racial inequalities disadvantaged Asian Americans in favor of other students of color. We met in his modern artist loft in a gentrifying urban neighborhood. Even though he lived in Southern California, Albert was very familiar with selective public magnet high school admissions policies in New York City, and he spoke without acknowledging the differences between such policies and those in college admissions. He animatedly explained that his main concern was that policies for educational diversity placed an especially heavy burden on Asian Americans in New York City, whom he believed had "the highest poverty rate" in the city.

Although a 2021 report found increasing poverty among Asian New Yorkers,[28] they were not the group with the highest rates of poverty. The Latinx population, followed by Black New Yorkers, had the highest rates of poverty.[29] Notably, the majority of Asian Americans enrolled at New York City magnet high schools, like Stuyvesant and Bronx Science, are low-income Asian Americans, and proposed reforms to admissions practices would offer increased opportunities for this population.[30]

Asian New Yorkers are "just struggling to get ahead," Albert said. According to him, there were "escape hatches" for everyone but Asian Americans from the New York City Public Schools. Expressing some resentment, he pointed out that it was unfair that "Blacks and Hispanics" in the city had more opportunity and "access to certain prep programs like Prep for Prep or Better Chance." These are programs that give talented low-income students of color scholarships to elite private boarding schools, which offer pipelines to the most prestigious colleges and universities. White families, he believed, also had "an out, because of income and other social capital."

The perceived structural inequality left low-income Asian Americans to fend for themselves in what Albert called the "really, frankly, crappy" urban public schools. "The poor Asians who are working in restaurants, taxicab drivers, construction, working as seamstresses, they don't have any outlet." It was logical to him, then, that Asian New Yorkers "put everything they have into their kids' education to get out. They're struggling just as much as the Black families." I could see where Albert was coming from, especially thinking back to how painful it was to watch my own parents struggling to support me and my brothers. Throughout our conversation, Albert and I shared stories from our childhood experiences in our families' Chinese restaurants. We disagreed, however, on how we understood different forms of racism.

Albert equated the race and class exploitation experiences of low-income Asian American families with those of Black families, glossing over the differences between anti-Asian and anti-Black racism.[31] The resentment over systemic neglect of low-income Asian American struggles spilled over into false assumptions that race-conscious admissions in higher education did not acknowledge or account for the differences in economic class status and other identities at the intersection of race.[32] Countering these suppositions, researchers have found that without race-conscious admissions practices, White students would be the biggest winners, while Asian American students would see insignificant changes.[33] This evidence countered the logic presented by Albert and others who claimed to support diversity and oppose affirmative action. Through my conversations with Albert and others, I sensed undercurrents of anti-Black ideologies, which psychologists have found to be highly correlated with Asian American opposition to affirmative action.[34]

While sitting in her well-furnished and tastefully decorated suburban Chicago home, I listened to Grace reference her (mis)understanding of the Espenshade and Chung study, which I explained in chapter 2, to argue that she supported affirmative action in limited ways but disagreed with a supposed "Asian penalty": "A lot of Asians feel that they have been bypassed [by affirmative action]. I think it was this Princeton research or something saying that Asian scores have to be so much higher, not only higher than Black and Hispanic, even higher than Whites."[35]

Grace wondered, "Why can't we challenge the Whites? Actually, to me, the struggle is not with the Hispanics or Blacks. Why do we have to be performing better than Whites?" She wanted to be clear that White dominance was the problem for her. I noted that she didn't see anti-Black or anti-Latinx racism as an issue connected to her agenda. Acknowledging that systems of education remain White-dominated, Grace suggested that Asian Americans against affirmative action should challenge quotas against Asian Americans in favor of White applicants. She weaved a fine line between expressing support for affirmative action and her opposition to contemporary race-conscious holistic admissions practices.

Much like Wilson, Grace wanted to see more Asian American public interest, civic leaders, and organizations engage in popular education projects to help Asian Americans better understand that affirmative action was not "hurting Asian Americans." She wanted them to encourage Asian Americans to recognize the need to collectively advocate for a "bigger pie" with other people of color.

But then, within the next minutes of our interview, Grace vented a frustration she had over Asian American organizations' expressions of racial solidarity against anti-Black racism. To her, Asian American organizations were quick to express solidarity with Black civil rights organizations. In essence, she wondered: What about our own? Why do Asian American organizations decenter Asian American interests?

Grace wanted to see these organizations also speak up and support Asian American businesses destroyed in urban uprisings in response to police murders of Black people, such as the one in Baltimore after police killed Freddie Gray in 2015. "If [Asian American] organizations don't speak up for our own people, when are we going to speak up?" Grace seemed especially bothered that a popular Asian American blogger and author, Phil Yu,[36] would speak out in support of the Movement for Black Lives during the Ferguson uprising, but he "didn't report anything about Asian businesses being destroyed!"

In the 2015 Baltimore uprising, fifty Asian-owned businesses were damaged or destroyed. What Grace did not acknowledge was that more than 350 Black-owned and "other community" businesses were also wrecked.[37] Because Asian Americans are not exceptional in the harms we experience and endure, we can and should invest in cross-racial solidarity as a solution to uplift what Heather McGhee called the "sum of us" to cultivate "solidarity dividends."[38] For example, the practice of advancing solidarity dividends among Asian Americans can be seen in the example of David Choi, a restaurant owner whose restaurant Seoul Taco was damaged during the 2020 anti-Black racism uprisings in Chicago after the police murder of George Floyd in Minneapolis. Choi posted on his Facebook, "EVERYTHING IN MY STORE WILL BE REPLACEABLE . . . while lives are being senselessly lost, on a way too regular basis."[39]

The people in this chapter believed there was a zero-sum game in public (White) attention paid to minority interests. They resented that mainstream Asian American civil rights advocacy organizations and leaders did not seem to speak up (only) for Asian American interests. At the same time, they also wanted African American organizations and leaders to engage in solidarity with Asian Americans. Albert even expressed some resentment toward mostly Black education equity leaders in New York City who were calling for fairer admissions processes in the city's public magnet high schools. He exclaimed, "They were villainizing Asians! I just think that's wrong because instead of seeing these poor Asians as their allies, they saw them as the enemy."

Notably, both Albert and Grace had been leaders in Asian American organizations that explicitly supported affirmative action. However, both explained that they were individual members of larger organizational leadership structures. They were much more on board with calls for more careful, detailed collection of data along ethnic and class lines to reveal educational and other socioeconomic disparities among Asian Americans. In advocating for the diversity of Asian American interests, they echoed Eric's concern with pushing admissions offices and other public institutions to acknowledge economic and ethnic differences among Asian Americans. This perspective was a key distinction between these three individuals and many others in this chapter. Explaining the need for recognizing differences among Asian Americans, Eric felt that the lack of detailed data on Asian Americans made it easier for politicians and "White America just to say, 'Oh, Asians are doing fine right now because they're all going to good colleges. They're not all in poverty.'"

Eric recognized that there was a diversity of ethnic identities and "cultures" among Asians and disliked how this diversity was often rendered invisible. With regard to the varying patterns of economic class among Asian American groups, he noted that "Indians and Koreans and Chinese people, they tend to be more middle-class and some even upper-class," and he pointed out that "Southeast Asian or even Pacific Islander[s,] more of them tend to be in poverty. You can't say that all Asians are doing fine when there's so many Southeast Asian people in poverty."

I wondered if he thought Southeast Asian or Pacific Islander cultures and identities, rather than long-standing systemic inequalities, were to blame for the socioeconomic disparities many among these populations faced. Generally, Eric conflated culture, ethnic identities, and socioeconomic status and disparities. He also engaged in what Indigenous scholar Eve Tuck called "damage-centered" politics: playing into the idea that Indigenous people and people of color and communities only deserve attention and investment when people and institutions in power recognize the harms they experience as legitimate.[40]

Grace also leaned into cultural explanations for employment disparities among Asian Americans, compared to others. She believed that employment data pointed out a "ratio of three to one" between Asian American professionals to managers, "but for other groups, White, Hispanic, Black, one to one. If you have one professional, you actually have one manager. The reason Asians don't advance as well as others is because of culture differences. It may be language; it may be this and that. We got to be networking better."

Counter to Grace's beliefs that White, Latinx, and Black employees did not see the kinds of disparities between rank-and-file workers and organizational leaders that Asian Americans did, among Fortune 500 corporations there were twelve Asian American CEOs and only three Black CEOs.[41] There are, unfortunately, plenty of racial and ethnic disparities to go around.

Questions about the status of the glass ceiling faced by Asian Americans aside, Grace framed Asian Americans as lacking the kinds of cultures valued by American employers. Like Eric, she wielded Asian cultural stereotypes to offer rationalizations for racial and ethnic disparities that situated the problem with individuals and cultures rather than organizational or systemic biases. At the same time, Grace and others characterized non-Chinese Asian Americans and other people of color as culturally deficient in pursuing formal education. They assumed that other people lacked cultures that valued education and hard work, placing the problem to be solved with people's cultures and not social-political systems and systemic conditions.

### PERSONAL RESPONSIBILITY: "IT'S A CULTURAL THING"

Most of the people represented in this chapter believed that systems of educational pathways and socioeconomic mobility were fair. They used stereotypes of East (and South) Asian people as having the right cultural attitudes toward work and schooling to explain their higher-than-average educational attainment levels. Conversely, they shamelessly drew on stereotypes of other people of color in their assumptions that they were not hardworking and thus undeserving of educational rewards.

Like eight of the other people I interviewed in this chapter, George had come to the US from China for graduate school in the 1990s, after growing up in a modest middle-class home in Shanghai and Beijing. I met him at a Corner Bakery in Orange County, California, near his home. George was a proud dad to two adult children who had attended prestigious universities. His daughter, he was happy to share, was doing quite well at an Ivy League law school. Sharing his thoughts on socioeconomic disadvantage with me, he suggested that differences in educational achievement were natural but also related to personal responsibility—whether someone took the initiative to pull themselves up with hard work or not. He firmly believed that there was a fair set of rules that facilitated participation in social institutions like higher education that distributed gains. "Some people can do big things; some people can do small things. But the reward is based on what you put in there."

George viewed affirmative action as the antithesis to what he believed was a fair and "colorblind" reward system. At the same time, he also supported having "some kind of safety net for the country, to have safety net for those people that are really suffering . . . to bring the stability to the country, to the society."

When I asked George to explain what he meant by "disadvantage," he listed physical and mental disadvantages, suggesting that disadvantages are inherently natural and not socially constructed. He went on to argue that cultural differences should not be considered disadvantages: "I would be very cautious about cultural difference. For example, you have two families. One family, they encourage their kids to work hard, get a good education. The other family, they don't care. What they have is what they deserve. That's their choice. Believing that poor personal choices produced socioeconomic inequalities, George disagreed with social institutions or policy that sought to disrupt inequities. Yet plenty of research points out how strongly Black and Latinx communities value education and have heroically struggled for education despite racial barriers.[42]

To George, some cultures support hard work and others do not. In his view, culture was also a personal choice to be responsible or not: "Are they responsible for themselves? Personal responsibility."

Similarly, in offering an explanation for Black and Latinx educational disparities in San Francisco's public schools, Ruth drew on anti-Black and anti-Latinx stereotypes. "Is it a cultural thing? I don't know. Is it because the fathers are absent from the home? Is it an economic thing because the kids have to go to work at a very early age?"

Whatever the reason for the general persistence of racially unequal educational outcomes, Ruth asserted that it was "not helpful to give [Black and Latinx students] who are not prepared for a rigorous education and have them attend an elite university where they're unlikely to succeed." Drawing on a debunked theory of college mismatch,[43] she held deeply stereotypical views of Black and Latinx communities, never acknowledging that there are indeed academically excellent Black and Latinx students.[44]

Additionally, many like William believed that Chinese people were just culturally more hardworking than other people and punished for educational achievements. I asked him, "Are Chinese Americans a minority?" and he responded, "Chinese Americans are minorities. Yeah, in the number of them, there's, I think, totally, I think it's less than five million in the States. Yeah, they definitely are a minority. Yes." To further comprehend how he understood what it meant to be a minority, I asked, "In college admissions are they a minority?"

William responded that Chinese Americans are not a minority in college admissions, because, he explained, "the culture of Chinese culture, kids study very hard. Parents pay more attention to schools. Simply, they just spend more time, starting with the family, parents spend a lot of time teaching their kids growing up in an environment knowing they need to do well academically." According to him, this culture of hard work removed Chinese Americans from being considered for programmatic supports, such as affirmative action, that target minorities.

Ruth also believed that Asian Americans were not considered to be beneficiaries of affirmative action programs. She assumed that affirmative action programs served White women and African Americans. Although she noticed she was one of few Asian Americans in the company that employed her, Ruth quickly refused the notion that Asian Americans like her had been or could be affirmative action beneficiaries in employment. For her, affirmative action was unfair to hardworking people like her. Given what she had told me about her employer's affirmative action program, I found it hard to believe that she had never been a beneficiary of the policy. Still, she and William adamantly believed that affirmative action programs excluded Asian Americans.[45]

## BLACK PEOPLE AND AFFIRMATIVE ACTION
## AS SOURCES OF ANTI-ASIAN RACISM

Generally, the people featured in this chapter held narrow views of what constituted anti-Asian racism. Most of them defined affirmative action as anti-Asian discrimination. Some suggested that anti-Asian racism came from the animosities that Black people targeted at Asian Americans.

Jun was born in Shanghai, grew up in Beijing, came to the US for grad school in the 1990s, and resided in a suburb of Philadelphia at the time of our interview. When asked to share any experiences or observations of racism, he shared a story about hardworking Chinese immigrant friends—a husband and wife with two children—who experienced getting "beat up every once a month" in their small Chinese takeout restaurant. These friends, he said, reluctantly purchased a gun and outfitted their restaurant with bulletproof glass.

According to Jun, while the wife was pregnant, a "very tall Black guy just beat her on the ground. You ask me do I see discriminations [against Asians]. My friends have [experienced it]. The majority of that discrimination comes from Black [people]."

It was disheartening that Jun believed that African Americans were the primary source of anti-Asian racism and violence. Contrary to his belief and common media and public assumptions, the majority of attacks targeting Asian Americans are perpetrated by White people.[46] Unlike Jun, others were more obtuse and careful in expressing their racial resentments. They positioned affirmative action as a policy of anti-Asian discrimination that concurrently benefited Indigenous people and people of color. To them, their concerns were over whether their children would get into the nation's most rejective colleges and universities and why they were, like other students, often among the great majority of applicants who were denied entry at the most exclusive institutions.

Sheng immigrated to the US from China for a graduate degree in sociology in the late 1990s. He later completed a law degree in New York and stayed in the Northeast and started a family. Sheng was different from most of the other immigrant participants in this chapter who had completed science or engineering graduate degrees. Interestingly, despite his sociological training, he did not believe he had ever directly experienced racism. However, he did worry that his children would experience anti-Asian racism in the form of race-conscious college admissions. He believed that Chinese American commitments and concerns over their children's well-being motivated the ethnic community to create the civic organization he led and support the filing of federal complaints accusing Ivy League institutions of anti-Asian discrimination.[47] "I think this issue is [important] for a lot of Chinese parents," he told me. "Specifically, on the affirmative action issue, a lot of [us] feel that this policy is harming the chances of our children to come into the elite universities. We don't feel it's fair."

Stanley also believed race-conscious admissions discriminated against Asian Americans in favor of other people. Based on a misreading of the Espenshade and Chung study, he believed affirmative action created anti-Asian constraints in a zero-sum admissions scenario with decisions based on test score differences and benefiting all non-Asian applicants. "There is clear discrimination against Asian American students. You know the Espenshade study?: 140 points to White students. 270 points to Hispanics. 450 points out of 1600 SAT system to Blacks in order to gain equal access to Ivy League schools." It was strange to me how he framed these SAT test score points in relationship to Ivy League admissions, as if these points were taken away from Asian American students.

Stanley was especially incensed by the idea that Asian American students should "yield to White students in an affirmative action program." As if to argue that he was more enlightened than other Asian Americans, he pointed out that "most Asian Americans are unhappy about yielding to Hispanics and to Blacks. I am not. I think diversity has its advantages." Curiously, Stanley asserted that his organization, which submitted an anti–affirmative action amicus brief in *Fisher v. UT Austin*, "embraced diversity."

Throughout his interview Stanley was worked up and argumentative. Born in Shanghai during Japan's colonial occupation, he was a retired college professor and former politician with an activist streak on the East Coast. His family left China right before the People's Republic of China took control of Shanghai in 1949. Stanley spent his formative years being educated in Hong Kong. He was able to complete his education in the US before the 1965 Immigration and Nationality Act, first in Kentucky and then in Washington, DC. When asked whether he had experienced any culture shock when he first arrived in Kentucky in the 1950s, he said, "No culture shock because I wasn't into the community. All I did was study, study, study." But he went on to also share:

> One time, I went downtown to mail something to home. Nature called. These are the small southern towns that you have the old people sitting on the bench. For the first time, I went to the public facilities. There were two. One is for White and the other one for the "colored." I thought, "Naturally, I'm colored." I pushed the door and I'm about to enter colored. The White folks sitting there, "He don't belong there. Go to the White." I thought about it. I still say, "But, I'm colored," so I went into that side.

When asked to share more about his experiences with racism, he responded by saying he encountered "very little" racism and did not respond to the prompt to reflect on what he saw around him. He went on to say that the only time he had experienced racism was during his time in electoral politics, citing how some political opponents in the 1980s had accused him of "wanting to sell America" to China. It was striking to hear from Stanley that he had spent little time thinking about his experience in relationship to the segregated bathroom in the 1950s and what it meant to him, and to observe him quickly respond by centering his experiences with little acknowledgment of African Americans or other people of color.

Despite his age, Stanley was very energized to talk about affirmative action and even gave combative monologues about the policy during the interview. He asked, "What's the definition of affirmative action?" Before a response could be offered to him, he almost shouted, "The original words were, 'Owing to historic reasons, the advantage given to White, the Whites will yield to the minorities.'"

Stanley, who expressly identified as a Democrat, resented what he saw was an affirmative action program that required Asian American "suffering" for the benefits of White people. "Given the long history of the clear discrimination against Asian American students, why should Asian Americans yield so many points to Whites? That's clear discrimination. In the words of the three dissenting Supreme Court Justices plus those on the Fifth Circuit Court said that the discrimination suffered by Asian

Americans is shameless. Those words exist. You should quote it." Those words do not in fact exist. None of the rulings he referred to in the *Fisher* case found that race-conscious admissions harmed or discriminated against Asian Americans.[48] Additionally, the lower courts in the SFFA cases found no evidence of anti-Asian discrimination. Regardless of evidence, in June 2023 the Supreme Court ruled against Harvard and UNC's limited consideration of race in their admissions practices.

It may be an understatement to say that my views on anti-Asian racism and discrimination differ from those of the people represented in this chapter. At times I found it hard to follow their claims. To be clear, my difficulty was not due to language barriers. The logic flow was sometimes disconnected from facts and evidence. Nonetheless, we all still agreed that anti-Asian racism was a problem needing to be solved.

### TWO INTERRELATED STRATEGIES FOR COMBATTING ANTI-ASIAN RACISM

Another thing that surprised me during my conversations with the seventeen people in this chapter was that—with the exception of one person—many were generally supportive of the Democratic Party. Given the timing of these interviews (summer and fall 2016), the 2016 presidential and general election was on a lot of people's minds.

I met Jian in Silicon Valley on a sunny June day in a suburban strip mall near his home. After driving through the well-manicured planned community and finding parking, I bought an overpriced latte, with that leaf design all quality baristas know how to make in the steamed milk, and got comfortable in a corner of the sunny café as I waited for Jian to arrive. Emerging from a shiny BMW, he was almost six feet tall with an athletic build. He had some gray hair around the temples and wore a navy polo shirt and khakis. I would learn that he was an avid soccer player on a team in a local league.

Before we kicked off the interview, Jian said to me with a smirk on his face, "I can tell by your surname and how you talk that you're probably 'Chinatown Chinese.' Am I right?" I asked him what he meant by Chinatown Chinese. He explained, "You know what I mean. You probably have family who work in restaurants and sewing factories, low-class immigrants who came decades ago."

I tried to keep calm. As I sipped my hot drink, Jian continued, "My generation of Chinese immigrants is different than yours. We're highly educated professionals. We don't need handouts. Your generation of immigrants gave us [Chinese Americans] a bad reputation in America, relying on government handouts."

He was right, I told him. My immigrant elders had worked in restaurants and garment factories. I also said to him that he forgot about the casino workers. As he smirked, I told him I was proud and grateful to my elders, who were also lucky to benefit from a more robust public safety net, which allowed them to raise children who now have advanced degrees. My reminder that he could call me "Dr. Poon" seemed to reset the dynamics of our meeting, as he recognized I wasn't going to just roll over and allow him to disparage my family.

In my Hong Konger immigrant family, my elders would sometimes talk negatively about newer immigrants from mainland China, saying they were the "low-class Chinese." To experience the tensions between different Chinese Americans with Jian, who arrived in the US in the 1980s, made me pause and remember the vast diversity, disparate experiences, and tensions within the Chinese diaspora, along with the different legal conditions under which we migrated.[49]

Because of the foreboding start to our conversation, I was surprised to learn that Jian was an active Democrat. The aggressive way he opened our conversation led me to expect him to be aligned with Thomas, who was active in the Trump campaign. As Jian warmed up to me, he explained, "I became a [US] citizen in '92. In my early days I was pretty solid Democratic. I supported the Democratic Party. I'm an active donor every year. I donate maximum, then, it was $700 or something." He had chosen to register as a Democrat in 1992 after watching the Republican National Convention, where Pat Buchanan made "this big speech on the cultural war, saying that he's against immigration, saying in the US you can only have one religion, you cannot have other religions."

Jian did not like the anti-immigrant sentiment and theocratic vibes from the Republican Party. However, during our interview before the 2016 election, he remained undecided. "I voted Clinton for the last two times, twice. For Trump, I really . . . yeah, I don't know. I probably am not going to vote for Trump now, although sometimes I thought about that. My conscience cannot do that."

It was good to hear that his conscience would not allow him to support Trump, but I found his temporary consideration of voting for Trump to be surprising given his disdain of the Buchanan speech in 1992. I also noted that he did not mention President Barack Obama at all and wondered if this Democrat had voted for John McCain and Mitt Romney over the first Black president.

Jian spent a lot of time helping new immigrants from China learn about California and US politics and civic engagement. He wanted to help his fellow immigrants think more about broader public interests, beyond the self-interests of Chinese Americans. At the same time, he expressed disappointment over recent legislation in California (Assembly Bill 1726-AHEAD Act: Accounting for Health and Education in Asian and Pacific Islander Demographics), spearheaded and supported by Asian American and Pacific Islander community leaders and community-based organizations, seeking to improve the collection of ethnically disaggregated data. He worried that the collection of ethnically disaggregated data would make it more difficult for his kids "to get into UC Berkeley or something, because there could be a quota system."

There could not, however, be a quota system, given the US Supreme Court ruling in the 1978 *Bakke* case. Plus, Proposition 209 in California had banned affirmative action in the state going back to 1998. AB 1726, which took effect in 2022, directed the State Department of Public Health to expand Asian American and Pacific Islander ethnic demographic categories available in public health data, to better inform public health services supporting the diverse AAPI communities in the state. It did what Eric had discussed earlier in the chapter: address a desire for the state to recognize the different social service needs and interests among AAPIs. Before final passage in Sacramento, however, policymakers had removed education data from the bill to appease Chinese American protesters.[50]

California AB 1726 was sponsored by Assemblymember Rob Bonta, a Filipino American politician from Northern California. It was not the first time a bill calling for ethnic data disaggregation for AAPI populations had been introduced or passed in the state legislature. Just like previous versions of the bill, it represented the product of sustained long-term AAPI policy advocacy.[51] Still, some Chinese Americans launched vicious disinformation campaigns against the bill, underscoring bad assumptions that having more data to diagnose inequalities would lead to anti-Chinese discrimination.[52]

In discussing how he was trying to help new Chinese immigrants understand the need to care about more than Chinese American interests and to form a panethnic coalition, Jian seemed unconvinced that policy advances for the diversity of AAPIs could be mutually beneficial to people like him, especially in college admissions. He explained that his fellow Chinese immigrants worried that AB 1726, if it included education data, would mean that "the University of California could accept more other minorities than Chinese American. And, that's actually true, right?" But it wasn't true. AB 1726 did not overturn Proposition 209, the state's ban on affirmative action. Moreover, race-conscious admissions would not mean quotas or a culling of Chinese Americans or Asian Americans from colleges. Although he believed bad information that the availability of ethnically disaggregated demographic data could lead to Chinese exclusionary practices, he advocated for panethnic politics: "You want to stand up as a minority to work with other minority people, among people, or the people from Indonesia or whatever, from Vietnam or whatever. You need to have more solid correlation to think about it."

Jian believed that Chinese Americans should also think about other Asians, contending that "you don't have to focus on yourself. This is not China anymore. You need to be united, then you have more experience." In what he shared, he seemed to frame "minority people" as Asian diasporic populations. It seemed ironic that this person who was advocating for panethnic coalition had started our meeting by insulting my immigrant Chinese family.

Seeing through the complex contradictions, I felt that Jian articulated tensions between two key strategies for confronting anti-Asian racism that were expressed by the people in this chapter. First, they believed the best way to end racism was by not engaging in critical examinations of the problem. To examine, surface, design, and enact solutions to the problem of racial inequalities were racist acts. They believed that racism is simply a problem of individual attitudes and feelings, as I discussed in chapter 3.

Therefore, systemic changes like collecting and analyzing ethnically disaggregated data—AB 1726—were anathema to them. Second, they were deeply invested in growing Asian American political power, mostly through their involvement in Chinese American civic organizations. Paradoxically, they valued panethnic and ethnic organizing and civic engagement but did not agree with race-conscious policies aimed at racial and ethnic equity.

### "DISAPPEAR INTO THE WHITENESS"

I first met Bingwen in 2015 when we were both on a panel at a conference of journalists. During my trip to Southern California, he agreed to meet up with me at his local Souplantation for lunch and an interview. It was my first visit to the storied, now defunct, chain of casual soup and sandwich restaurants that some of my Asian American friends in California raved about.[53] Like Jian, Bingwen had a lot to say about AB 1726. "I prefer you either [disaggregate by ethnicity in demographic data collection] for all races, not just Asian American, or you don't do it. You cannot say Asian American is very bad, therefore we need to separate [disaggregate]."

Bingwen explained, "If you look at the historical precedence, the Jewish people did not achieve equality until they disappeared into the White. They used to be singled out." According to him, Jews overcame significant discrimination in the early 1900s through the dint of their hard work, "and finally they disappeared into the White. It's no longer a census category. Jews are treated the same as other Whites." He did not seem to recognize the persistence of antisemitism and antisemitic violence. In 2023 antisemitic attacks were at an all-time high.[54]

I didn't want to misconstrue what he was saying, so I asked him if he thought that without ethnic or racial demographic data, people would start being treated as individuals, like Whites. Bingwen answered:

If you treat everything from a racial perspective, everything would be racial of course, because that's the way you look at it. The only way you can really get over the hurdle of giving the people who need help the help, is to just look at their background directly as an individual. I dislike the argument that some people make that says, if we use socioeconomic basis and saying there'd be too many Whites and Asians being helped. What's wrong with poor White and Asian people getting help?

I agreed that without a critical race lens I would not be able to explain both why there were racial disparities and suggest ways to dismantle them. I wondered why we wouldn't want to name and solve the problem of systemic racism and its production of racial disparities. I also agreed in principle with him that each person should have their individual circumstances recognized by social institutions and be offered support as needed. However, treating people as individuals and recognizing systemic inequalities need not be mutually exclusive. How this society works to reproduce intersectional inequalities is the product of centuries of historical foundations centered in principles of systemic oppression—settler colonialism, chattel slavery, the exploitation of immigrants, dispossession, war, patriarchy, and capitalism. When this is the case, how can we work toward continually improving our society if we cannot use demographic tools to check the status of change?

Proceeding with our interview, I asked Bingwen, "With Jews becoming White, is that the ideal model you think people of color should follow?"

Yeah and especially if you look at the race. It's getting more and more diffused, the concept with all the interracial marriage and other things. What do you . . . Who can define race? For Elizabeth Warren who claimed to have either 1/16, or 1/32% of a . . . a fraction of Native American and is she a minority? It's just not very meaningful. What if an Asian married a Hispanic? Is the kid supposed to receive more favorable treatment, or more harsh treatment, depending on how you count that? I think the concept of race is becoming harder and harder to define as the time goes. I think it's the right time to just put a focus on the real issue. Typically, real problems are harder to solve. That's why people want to avoid talking about it. In fact, they may not even be politically correct to talk about it.

Bingwen was suggesting that the real problem was in Black and Latinx communities not possessing the right cultures and grit, as other less "politically correct" interviewees had expressed. It was also disturbing for me to hear Bingwen suggest that society wouldn't know whether to treat someone who identified as both Asian and Latinx positively or negatively. It seemed to go against his call to treat each person as an individual with unique circumstances.

At the same time, Bingwen claimed he was not calling on Asian Americans to become White. "I think we can keep our identity at an individual level. For example, I'm Chinese American. I'm pretty proud of my heritage." That said, Bingwen believed cultural pride was "different than asking for government assistance and saying, because I'm Chinese American, therefore I need to be favored, or disfavored. That's just flatly wrong." To him, affirmative action was a handout program based simply on cultural identity rather than an approach to contend with long-standing structural inequalities.

Reflecting back to him what I thought I heard, I asked if he wanted all people to be treated as individuals, just like White people. "Yeah," Bingwen said, "just treat people on the same basis." To him, social policies seeking to hold institutions accountable to, and inclusive of, a diverse populace was too similar to communism. "If everything needs to be partitioned by population, then what's the difference between that ideology and communism? That's exactly what communism is asking for. That's what I was brought up in [in] a society like that and we know it all failed." In this hyperbolic view, efforts for equity were "essentially communism in disguise."

Like many in this chapter, Bingwen had immigrated to the US from China for graduate school and stayed, preferring life here. What I realized in listening to him and others was that campaigns for equity, even those led by Asian Americans, reminded them of the authoritarian regime in the People's Republic of China. I wondered, though, why someone as thoughtful as him—a trained scientist who also enjoyed studying history—refused to recognize how the US had historically created systems, norms, and processes in laws and policies that were designed to make it easier for many straight White men to reap the rewards of society. Why didn't he acknowledge that immigration and institutional policies that opened doors of opportunity for him and his peers had set them and their children up for comfortable middle-class lives, when they had not for many other people?

Perhaps given his adolescent experiences under the authoritarian rule of the Chinese Communist Party, he latched deeply onto ideas of rugged American individualism. He didn't want to relinquish his ethnic identity. He just wanted the rights and privileges afforded White people in US society. He and others recognized they would need to grow their political power to offer leadership and representation for what they believed to be Asian American interests.

## "STANDING UP FOR COMMUNITIES THAT NEED TO BE HEARD"

Toward the end of my time with Eric, I asked him what motivated him in his activism. He wanted to provide Asian American youth, he said, with "a platform to speak out." He was concerned that Asian Americans were often an afterthought in US civil society and among White power players. He wondered, "Why is no politician ever reaching out to the Asian American population?" as they presumably did with Black voters. He viewed his filing of a federal complaint over race-conscious admissions as something to politically mobilize fellow Asian Americans. Like other anti–affirmative action activists, he felt he was an exceptional leader, one of the first who was fighting on behalf of fellow Asian Americans to have a "voice." It was not lost on me that he, and several others in this chapter, did not seem to recognize past and contemporary political movements by Asian Americans and how advances of these historical efforts relied on cross-racial solidarity with Black, Latinx, and Native community movements.[55]

Thomas, as mentioned in chapter 3, believed that his organizing to mobilize Chinese diasporic communities in the US and elsewhere was exceptional. "The Peter Liang protest," he said, was "the biggest Chinese American protest in the history of the United States currently—ever since the dinosaurs." He was glad he was able to lend his communications gifts to the cause, because had someone else led the efforts, "it might not be that big" of a protest and showing. In his high self-assessment, he alone had the ability to communicate across Chinese American communities.

I told Thomas that it sounded like he was very motivated by a sense of right and wrong and a desire for fairness. He lamented to me about the strains of being such a unique leader of the community and of all the sacrifices he had made for the Chinese diaspora. "I don't want to do this. I don't want to see inequality happen. I don't want to go in the street and protest. Why would anybody want to take their day off from fishing and go protest? Somebody in my Trump group said 'Thomas, Peter's up to you.' Exact words, and I feel fucked." Thomas dramatically explained to me that he was obligated to lead his community. "My people who fought on my side on [the] protest, they look up to me, and they want me to do the right thing, even though by sacrificing myself. I do it for the people."

Less dramatic in how he expressed similar lonely leadership sentiments, Evan—an attorney and longtime activist against race-conscious education policies—quietly and somberly responded to my question about what motivated him to advocate against these policies with a rhetorical question: "If not me, then who?"

There was a spirit and personal dedication to be singular leaders for Asian Americans, as the exceptional "voice for the voiceless," as Eric described. The (ahistorical) assumption here was that Asian Americans could not, or did not have a desire to, speak for themselves.[56] Therefore, extraordinary individuals like those in this chapter need to step up to give them a voice.

Although these sentiments were well intentioned, they could also feel patronizing. For example, throughout Stanley's interview he would go off track in his responses to questions about his experiences with or observations of racism. Although it was difficult to follow Stanley's tangents, it was clear he was very passionate about electoral politics and the organization he founded and continued to lead. In his stories and responses to interview questions, he positioned himself and his organization as central to the political empowerment of Asian Americans. He was nonplussed when he learned that my former research assistant, Dr. Megan Segoshi, who interviewed him, was unaware of his organization. Perhaps by simply stating that she had not seen the organization's website or received their emails before, her answers challenged the actual importance and impact of the organization, his feelings of sacrifice, and his self-importance to Asian Americans—a community that he believed needed to build political power to support their well-being.

In the aftermath of the 1996 campaign finance scandal that framed Asian American political donors as suspicious foreign agents,[57] Stanley described establishing his organization in fits and starts. He wanted to guide Asian Americans toward developing national political power. The problem in his mind was that "Asian Americans are politically immature."

Stanley felt very strongly that "Asian Americans have got to be politically much stronger to get the government to get behind us." To achieve this, he was very concerned about raising money for his organization to advocate against anti-Asian discrimination. Prompted in the interview to say what he was hoping to accomplish through his work, he launched into explaining the project he was working on at the time. It was a major fundraising campaign to get Asian Americans to donate to his organization to fight affirmative action, but not diversity. "We are not against diversity. We embrace diversity."

## ANTI-AFFIRMATIVE ACTION DESIRES

My biggest takeaway from listening to these seventeen people was that they deeply worried about their children, grandchildren, and fellow Chinese Americans and our chances in a society with few social safety nets. Some shared stories with me about experiencing poverty and concerns over narrow pathways for upward mobility for low-income Asian Americans. These worries seemed to mirror past research suggesting that some Asian Americans felt compelled to grasp onto educational opportunities, especially in STEM fields, that have been demonstrated as one of the few reliable pathways to economic stability and mobility.[58]

I can empathize with these anxieties as someone who grew up in an economically unstable family with parents who often told me my career aspirations were unrealistic. Each time I got excited about an idea for my future—journalist, professional dancer, astronaut—I would hear something to the effect of, "That would be terribly hard for an Asian American girl." Once these statements were coupled with the very real racial harassment I experienced in school, I had no doubt there would be racial and gendered barriers to confront in my life.

I did not realize until my interviews with the seventeen people featured in this chapter that we shared similar experiences with racial harassment in our lives. These people believed stridently that they are exceptional and singular leaders standing up and fighting for Asian Americans to have a "voice" in American civil society. Curiously, some took time to explicitly tell me they were not opposed to affirmative action or diversity. However, they viewed race-conscious admissions as discrimination against Asian American minorities; as a policy of handing out prizes to those (mainly other people of color) who have presumably not worked as hard as (East and South) Asian Americans have, and therefore are undeserving of such rewards. Most of all, they wanted to be recognized, through a color-evasive perspective, as hardworking Americans deserving of all the rights and privileges that they see unquestioningly afforded to White Americans. Some conveyed beliefs that Asian Americans, especially Chinese Americans, revere a culture of hard work and academic achievement that sets them apart from other people of color, whose educational disparities resulted from their own poor choices and culture. These sentiments churned my stomach.

Nonetheless, I was simultaneously struck by moments in the interviews where we took time to connect outside of our policy disagreements, on things like parenthood and our love for our kids. For example, amid a tense virtual back-and-forth with Jake, when I was presenting probing follow-up questions to clarify if he actually supported affirmative action as he said, his daughter, who appeared to be in second or third grade, walked into view of the camera. Jake said, "I understand the remedial rationale . . ." then referring to his daughter, he stated lovingly, "This is one of the concrete reasons that I continue to do what I do. Say hi." He muted the audio and I observed father and daughter share a moment, maybe chatting about plans for a playdate or dinner. I looked at his daughter, imagining my own future meetings when Té Té would join me on screen, when she was older. After his daughter left the room, Jake went back to his point without skipping a beat: "So I understand and I think I would support remedial rationale, if there's a very concrete tie, not just some sort of fluffy, generic, 'everybody who's Black or Hispanic or Asian is disadvantaged' kind of crap."

There were other moments I found surprising. For example, several of the interviewees—Jake, Evan, Stanley, Wilson, Grace, and Eric—asserted that they supported affirmative action. They presented varying logics behind their proclaimed policy support. For the most part, though, we didn't agree on the solutions to the problem of (anti-Asian) racism. Although we agreed that anti-Asian racism and the erasure of Asian American narratives and interests from the political sphere are problems that need solutions, we disagreed on the nature and contours of these problems. They sought to advance an out-of-sight-out-of-mind approach to solving racism as a problem. Ironically, though, they were also actively involved in organizations that claimed a racialized Asian American identity and singular leadership in advancing Asian American interests, not just anyone's interests.

I am still shocked every time I see Asian Americans vehemently protesting affirmative action and policies for diversity or education equity, like they did in Washington State alongside White supremacist Proud Boys, or when some Chinese Americans heckled Congresswoman Alexandria Ocasio-Cortez in 2019 with signs reading "Equity is a code word for anti-Asian."[59] Their worldviews are so fundamentally different from mine and those of many Asian Americans in my family and social circles. However, having met some of these people in person, I cannot simply and easily dismiss them. Their voices are loud and, for better or worse, they grab a disproportionate amount of media attention and coverage.

Dear Té Té,

I have deep and passionate disagreements with the folks in this chapter. That said, I cannot deny my proximity to them. Like them, I am part of the Chinese diaspora. Many of them are immigrants like my family elders who raised me with love. I cannot deny that their narratives also represent who we are. I also learned from listening to them that some of them may be open to learning and evolving their views.

For example, I continued to follow what Eric has been doing in the world, especially with regard to the SFFA lawsuits. In fall 2022 Eric gave an interview in which he voiced his regret that Ed Blum has taken his federal complaint against Harvard too far and reiterated that he does not support efforts to dismantle affirmative action. It was a nice reminder that we are always learning and changing. I noticed that how Eric articulated his views had evolved a bit since I had last talked with him in 2016, though I still disagreed with many of the points he presented.

However, we don't need a unified voice for Asian Americans. We have many voices that come from our various journeys through a complex world.[60] All of these stories and people just want to be heard and seen.

# CHAPTER 5

# "K(NO)W HISTORY, K(NO)W SELF"

*Asian Americans in Solidarity for Justice*

When you were in the first grade, Té Té, you asked me for the first time but not the last time, "How did you and Papa meet and how did you know you were going to get married?" You were wondering about your origin story.

Your father and I met a month after I moved to Chicago in 2012. We dated for about three months before we knew we would eventually get married. I knew he was the one for me about two months after we met, one night when we were riding the L train in Chicago. I can't remember where we were going, but I do remember we were bundled up for the cold weather, which didn't bother me as I was warmed by the butterflies this new boyfriend gave me. We held hands while sitting shoulder to shoulder, bumping back and forth to the rhythms of the Red Line train.

Our conversation was always comfortable and easy. When we met in our mid-thirties, we realized we had about a dozen friends in common. We also shared an understanding of what it meant to be Asian American. At our different colleges, some of our most life-changing learning experiences happened outside of the classes we took for our respective majors in college—engineering and business management. Both of us had taken a few classes in Asian American studies and sociology and were involved in service-learning programs, leadership activities, and Asian American student organizations.[1] These experiences helped us develop a critical sense of how social systems reproduced injustices. They encouraged us to connect with community efforts aimed at dismantling systemic inequalities, and to pursue the public interest career paths we both followed that eventually brought us together.

For all these similarities, we were also very different. He grew up solidly middle class in a rural community in southern Illinois, the son of a medical doctor and nurse recruited from Thailand to fill a shortage of health professionals serving rural America. Despite growing up in a sundown town, he has mostly pleasant memories from his childhood in a quintessentially "Midwestern nice" community.[2] I grew up in a financially unstable home with parents who often worried about how to make ends meet. I have few happy memories from my childhood, faced with economic anxieties, isolation, and racial hostilities in western Massachusetts.

Our differences and shared values made for an exciting chemistry. That evening on the L, our flirtatious banter got a bit serious and turned toward what we envisioned for the future. I asked my then boyfriend, "Where do you see yourself living in the future?"

We both agreed we loved cities and would want to live out our lives in a city, rich with public transit, public parks, cultural institutions, and great food. I then worked up the nerve to ask him, "If we had kids," I hesitated, "where would you want them to go to school?"

Without hesitation, he answered the question. "They would go to the public school in the neighborhood." To my delight the underlying premise of *us having kids together* in my question didn't trip him up.

I was giddy that he so naturally envisioned having a family together and that we would raise our family in a city. Keeping my cool, I followed up on his assumption of enrolling in the urban neighborhood school and asked, "You're OK with any public neighborhood school in the city?" Without skipping a beat, he said, "If we are going to make a life in a neighborhood, of course we would go to the neighborhood school in whatever neighborhood we landed in."

I was surprised by his confidence that any public urban neighborhood school would be fine. So I asked him, "What if the neighborhood school we're zoned into is very troubled? What if our child has learning needs the school can't meet? What if there's evidence of high teacher turnover in the school? What about safety?" Most importantly, I didn't want my kid to feel racially isolated as the only Asian kid, like I was when I was growing up.

I continued to pepper him with more questions: "What if the climate of the school makes it hard for children to learn? Would we be setting up our kid to not get into a good college and make their way in a harshly unequal world?"

Your father said he thought that if we are really committed to social justice and we chose to purchase a home in a neighborhood—any neighborhood—there's just no question where our kid would go. If you live in the city, it just makes sense to go to your neighborhood school, he said, pointing out that being invested in a city, a community, means that you participate in the local public school. Going elsewhere was an act of community divestment to him. Besides, he asked, "what's the worry? That our kid would go to a school that was predominantly Black or Latinx? What's wrong with that? Isn't that different than going to White schools like the ones you and I did when we were growing up?"

Your father pushed back. He reminded me that I had recently shared with him that education research has found that it doesn't really matter what school a kid goes to; it's really a kid's parents' educational levels that matter in predicting the kid's educational and economic future. "Wouldn't we just exacerbate inequalities and segregation by not going to our local school?" he asked.

And there it was. Your father—a Chicago urban planner, the man I was dreaming about marrying and making a life with—was calling out the anti-Black and anti-Latinx racist ideologies underlying what I had said in our private conversation. I had so many feelings in that moment—excitement, shock, and introspection. Was this man really holding me accountable to our stated shared values *and* recalling research I had told him about?

I must confess that I was hesitant about committing my hypothetical child to a predominantly Black or Latinx school, because city powers often divest from these schools, leaving them without needed resources. I presumed that such schools—Black and Latinx spaces of schooling—wouldn't be good enough or safe for my child, and you weren't even here yet! To top it all off, as a race and education scholar, I knew better. The evidence and research, which I knew well, told me I had nothing to worry about, especially since this future husband and I were both highly educated and possessed significant amounts of social capital to help us navigate any situation. Nevertheless, mainstream racist ideologies shaped what I felt. That night I was especially in awe over your father's ability to question my perspectives about our hypothetical kids and where they would go to school one day.

When some people first meet your father, they mistakenly think he's just a quiet and easygoing guy who will just go along with whatever his much louder wife wants, but he is one of the most strongly principled and naturally diplomatic people I have ever met. These qualities were fully present that cold evening and made me flush in the cheeks. He was pointing out the inconsistencies between what I had said were my values and what I was saying, but he didn't make me feel shame. Instead, he was lovingly challenging me to interrogate what I really stood for. It was in that moment I realized I wanted to spend the rest of my life with him. We would be partners that would hold each other accountable to our shared values and continue learning together.

The values your father and I share were rooted in teachings from our respective families, but they were cultivated by learning opportunities we had in college classes about race and racism. They were nurtured through the relationships we built in student and community-based organizations, many of which emerged from the ethnic studies movement of the 1960s and 1970s, working for equity. These programs did not indoctrinate us into a singular view of the world. Instead, they offered a broad ethical grounding from which to engage in our discussions and exchanges of ideas. In many ways, our educational opportunities, how we have pursued our careers, made political choices, and lived our respective lives are deeply connected to the legacy of student-led campaigns to transform higher education and community conditions.

In the 1990s, at his midwestern college, your father and his friends protested and petitioned for their university to create an Asian American studies program with an academic minor and major. Around the same time in the Northeast, I was taking my first Asian American studies class and having my mind blown, learning new language to help me make sense of the racial hostilities I witnessed and experienced in my young life.

When you were in kindergarten in 2021, Governor Pritzker signed into state law a requirement for public schools to include one unit of Asian American history across the state of Illinois. I could have never predicted this policy development. Two years later, the state legislature would pass a law to require the same of Native American history. Although there are growing efforts to codify ethnic studies into public school curriculum standards, this kind of education remains contested.[3] These new laws expanded existing Illinois state standards, which already included teaching about Black history and about the Holocaust and other cases of genocide. For most people, however, opportunities to engage in learning from the ethnic studies tradition remain rare. Even though these courses and academic departments are in a growing number of colleges and universities, they remain nonexistent at most postsecondary institutions.


Motivated by curiosity, the people in this chapter engaged in social justice ideas in their families, through their involvements in community-based organizations, on their college campuses, and in their professional experiences. How did these Asian Americans arrive at their values and political engagements for social justice? What does it mean to be Asian American for this group of interviewees? Many had taken classes on race, ethnicity, and gender in college. Several had not. All of them had informal opportunities, outside of classrooms, to learn and engage with knowledge and theories about Asian American histories, racialization, and community activism and resistance to intersectional forms of oppression. Just by living life and considering new ideas that came their way, they developed their understandings of the world around them and how they could enact social justice values. They learned that Asian American histories were interwoven with the experiences and stories of other people of color.

The people in this chapter were involved in expansive and often underresourced social justice work, as volunteers or through public interest careers. Twelve of them were US-born children of immigrants. Six of them had immigrated to the US as children or young adults. The youngest interviewee identified as third generation. His parents were children of immigrants. Unlike the policy opponents featured in the previous chapter, most (twelve) were women, and there was no dominant ethnic identity among these nineteen. They were Burmese, Cambodian, Chinese, Filipino, Indian, Korean, Taiwanese, Vietnamese, and mixed ethnic Asians.[4] They were a much more diverse group than the policy opponents I'd met.

Central to how these interview participants evolved in their identities and commitments were popular education experiences,[5] which drew strong connections between Asian American experiences and social systems that also marginalized other people of color. Some experienced community-based popular education programs outside of school or learned from their families about Asian American history—the everyday practices of popular education. Many encountered ethnic studies curricula or community-based learning opportunities in college. They all believed in the importance of affirmative action policies and race-conscious college admissions to the vitality of a diverse multiracial democratic society.

That said, if there is a well-established and long-standing Asian American social justice movement and community, and these are the people who represent the legacy of that movement, I wondered why the defense of affirmative action policies has been relatively lackluster. Even if the specifics of the policy and practice aren't inspiring, I have wondered why the ideals connected to them have not motivated much strategic action, when the opposition has continuously attacked them. I am not saying that affirmative action supporters have not done anything. However, compared to the activism among Asian American affirmative action opponents, policy supporters' engagements in this debate (e.g., signing onto letters of support and amicus briefs and occasional public demonstrations) have been less energized and impassioned.

To be clear, the people in this chapter did not share a unified view on social and political issues with each other, nor did their support for affirmative action show up in a cohesive way. Some were actively leading and contributing toward efforts to maintain the constitutionality of race-conscious admissions, recognizing how consequential these policy battles were to the future of racial justice advocacy more generally. All of them viewed the affirmative action debate as an existential one. However, some also saw affirmative action as just one tool and not a framework for their political investments and activities for social justice.

They did, however, share two things. One was a belief in the hopeful idea that "another world is possible."[6] The other was a commitment to engaging and investing in cross-ethnic and cross-racial solidarity for social justice.

### LEARNING OUTSIDE AND INSIDE OF SCHOOLS

Education and schooling are not the same. The institution of schooling is not the only place where vital education, teaching, and learning occur. Many times, some of the most important lessons occur outside of schools, colleges, and universities, as my friend Curtis Chin offers in his memoir *Everything I Learned, I Learned in a Chinese Restaurant.* The people I talked to for this chapter all shared that learning about Asian American historical, social, legal, economic, and political conditions—how we're positioned in complex systems of inequality *and* how we have taken collective action for racial justice—played a key role in informing their civic engagements, work in the world, and political perspectives and choices.

### "THE EDUCATION I NEEDED": FAMILY AND COMMUNITY-BASED EDUCATION

The youngest person I interviewed for this study was a high school student named Mason. Prior to our visit, I had only met him via social media. I was impressed and inspired by his impassioned blog posts and activism for affirmative action as a youth leader in an Asian American civil rights organization. He and his parents welcomed me into their home in a Southern California suburban community, which Mason described as a small, mostly White town that contrasted with the more racially and economically diverse surrounding communities in the region.

The predominantly White city where Mason and his family lived looked just like the beachside communities idealized in popular TV shows. As I drove toward Mason's house, I saw young people with sandy blond hair and sun-kissed skin carrying surfboards as they walked toward the beach. I noticed how close I was to Gardena and Torrance—two predominantly

Asian and historic Japanese American communities—and planned to get a bowl of ramen for lunch after I finished interviewing Mason.

After eighth grade, Mason told me, he opted not to attend the local high school in his city. He wanted to attend a more racially and ethnically diverse school in a neighboring community. No racial group represented a student majority at the high school he chose to attend. Some might be surprised that Mason, with the support of his parents, chose to opt out of a high school with higher test score averages. I wondered why his family would take on the inconveniences associated with this choice—four years of driving Mason through Los Angeles County traffic to and from school in a community where they had not purchased a home. Mason explained that he often felt alienated in his home community's schools, which were predominantly White, before high school.

Toward the end of my interview with Mason, his mom came into the living room. She was casually dressed in blue jeans and a V-necked black T-shirt. She could have been part of Gen X like me, but like so many East Asian women it was hard to tell (#AsiansDontRaisin). She had to leave to pick up her daughter and wanted to gift me with some children's books. I thanked her for the books, which included Sandra Cisneros's *The House on Mango Street* and Ken Mochizuki's *Baseball Saved Us*, about Japanese American children and the baseball league they started while incarcerated in an internment camp during World War II.

After she left, Mason told me that his mom and dad—US-born children of Chinese and Korean immigrants—had been ethnic studies students and activists in college. Perhaps as a result, he said, he was exposed to a diversity of stories, books, and art throughout his childhood. I smiled at the thought that I was getting a glimpse of my own family's future.

When he was twelve, Mason asked his father to take him to a rally in downtown Los Angeles to protest Arizona Senate Bill 1070, which included requirements for law enforcement to routinely ask people suspected of being undocumented immigrants to show their legal documents authorizing their presence in the US. Reflecting on this experience, he remembered feeling like, "Wow. I'm a participant in history. Some day in the future, people are going to talk about this bill and I'm going to have been there and participated in the rallies that they're going to talk about."

I realized that Mason's involvement in social justice activism and for affirmative action was something encouraged by his parents throughout his young life. In his family he learned early to question injustices and to consider how he could become a leader and contribute toward community-based efforts to transform society. Since Mason was very young his parents had shared stories of injustices, of hope and resistance to transform systems of inequality, and of solidarity. Not only did they talk with their children about the social and political complexities of the world, but they also encouraged them to participate in efforts for social justice. As a result, Mason was very interested in learning about his grandparents' experiences and getting involved in community campaigns for immigrant rights. His education started with his family.

For many in this chapter, K–12 schools would not be where they would learn about Asian American history or develop their political identities. Most would not encounter such learning opportunities until college or later. Still, Mason was not alone in his precollegiate learning experiences. Two other people I interviewed for this chapter—Ligaya and Tina—also began learning about social inequalities and community-based movements for justice during their high school years, through community-based youth organizations.

On a typically gloomy and chilly summer day in San Francisco in June 2016, I found a small table in the back corner of a crowded café. I made myself comfortable and took off my light blue puffy jacket, next to what seemed like a secondhand brown leather sofa sitting atop the intentionally distressed brownish-red painted cement floors. San Francisco bohemian chic, I thought to myself. The light blue walls and ceiling were painted with puffy clouds and a tree with leaves as a canopy from the neighbors above in the classic stucco three-story building. The din of conversation among café regulars was generally drowned out by the music on the speakers, occasionally punctuated by the steam squeals of the espresso machine and shouts of names. "Angela! Order for Angela!" Ligaya had recommended the neighborhood hot spot as a place that was convenient for her during her busy working mom schedule, shuttling her young children to and from school while juggling professional responsibilities.

I first met Ligaya in 2002 at the University of California Davis, where I had taken a job as the first student affairs officer in Asian American studies. Ligaya had been one of the student activists who held the university accountable to serving the diversity of students on campus and its public service mission. She and her peers represented one generation of many that sustained successful campaigns demanding more targeted institutional investments and supports for Asian American, Pacific Islander, Native American, and other students of color. My position at Davis was one of the wins from that intergenerational, decades-long movement. Like so many student activists fighting for new visions for the future, she would not directly benefit from the gains won. It didn't matter to her, though, because she recognized that generations of students before her had fought for institutional changes that allowed her to be one of the first to earn an Asian American studies bachelor's degree at Davis. She was one in a long line of seed planters and cultivators of change.

I reached out to Ligaya because she was on the board of directors of one of the Filipino American organizations that had signed onto amicus briefs and public statements supporting affirmative action. I was also excited to reconnect with her after many years of passively staying in touch with each other via Facebook. It had been at least seven or eight years since we had last seen each other in person. Since then, we had both become moms, and I was eager to learn about her experiences raising a young family, in addition to her perspectives on affirmative action—the principal reason for our meetup.

As with all the interviews, I started by asking Ligaya about her experiences growing up. "I was born in San Francisco. Raised in Union City for my younger childhood and then I moved" to a predominantly White suburb. As one of the first Asian Americans in the community, Ligaya and her sister found verbal and physical racial harassment jarringly commonplace. Unfortunately, she said, "It was a big part of our growing up."

To navigate the social terrain of her predominantly White high school, Ligaya explained that she and her fellow students of color generally had the choice between two strategic paths. You either assimilated and tried to be as White as possible, or you connected with other students of color "who were like 'fuck this.'" Her best friends were Vietnamese and Pakistani, and the multicultural club they formed with the few other students of color—Latinx and African Americans—in school was central to their social life.

To find a place to thrive in her predominantly White high school context, she intuitively chose to build community with fellow Asian Americans and other students of color.

In her junior year of high school, Ligaya got involved with a youth group program affiliated with a nonprofit organization—Filipinos for Affirmative Action (FAA). FAA and the Filipino Youth Coalition's annual "K(no)w History, K(no)w Self" conference provided an education about Filipino culture and Filipino American history that was missing in her schooling and at home. Her immigrant parents, she told me, had decided it would be best to encourage their children to assimilate into White middle-class norms. Moving away from their ethnic community into a suburb with "supposedly better schools" was a choice her parents made with the intention of increasing their girls' opportunities for upward mobility. However, their new community and school made Ligaya feel isolated and hungry for a different kind of education. Attending weekly youth group meetings helped her grow in her curiosity and formal educational pursuits. Ligaya would go on to major in Asian American studies in college, complete a master's in African studies, and pursue a career in public health and education.

Like Ligaya, Tina had also participated in a community-based youth organization during her high school years. Born in Oakland into a Cambodian refugee family whose scars and traumas from the American war in Southeast Asia remained present in their home, she grew up navigating underfunded schools and violence in the city. Tina found a nurturing place of healing, learning, and community empowerment as a young person at AYPAL.

Founded in 1998, AYPAL's mission is to "empower Oakland's low-income Asian & Pacific Islander immigrant and refugee families to be leaders for school reform and neighborhood change."[7] AYPAL's programs helped Tina better understand her family's resettlement experiences connected to the history of US war in Southeast Asia. Through tears, she told me about how AYPAL helped her process feelings of shame that had developed over years of racial microaggressions and socioeconomic marginalization that disparaged her family's economic and Southeast Asian refugee background. Learning about the multiple systems of oppression at play in her family's experiences made her feel "really sad and really angry." These emotions and the AYPAL community motivated her to continue her learning in college and pursue a career in environmental justice work.

To be clear, the kind of popular education Tina experienced didn't just leave her sad and angry. AYPAL encouraged Tina and other youth members to be curious and develop a critical analysis of social, political, and economic systems of inequalities. Empowered by what they were learning, they were motivated to collectively design, mobilize, and lead strategic efforts for improvements to social conditions in collaboration with other communities of color.[8] As she finished dabbing the tears from her eyes, Tina told me that she found "a lot of joy in doing work to uplift low-income immigrant and refugee communities." Her work was meaningful and personal to her. The community and collectivist nature of the work felt fortifying. She was in this work together with many other people. Her community-based educational journey helped her heal from intergenerational family traumas and start a personally meaningful career in contributing toward the betterment of systemic conditions that kept her community marginalized.

These kinds of outside-of-school learning that Mason, Ligaya, and Tina experienced through their families and community-based organizations represented key legacies of the Asian American studies movement in the 1960s and '70s. College student–led campaigns for Asian American studies, African American studies, Native American studies, and Latinx studies were fueled by desires to transform higher education curriculum, expand popular education, and create new possibilities for broader social justice change.[9] We can trace these interviewees' community learning engagements directly to the historical goals and visions of the Asian American studies movement, which was a part of the broader ethnic studies movement.[10]

### DEVELOPING PEOPLE-OF-COLOR SOLIDARITY POLITICS IN COLLEGE AND BEYOND

Many of the people in this chapter had critical learning experiences in college, whether through their classes or in cocurricular activities. Others' learning journeys were sparked after college. Cross-ethnic and cross-racial solidarity, and their centrality to forging a more just world, were key to what they learned. Solidarity as a value and a practice was fundamental to how they came to their understandings of what it meant to be Asian American.

### LEARNING TO "TRANSFORM THEIR COMMUNITIES AND THE WORLD" IN COLLEGE

According to many in this chapter, affirmative action and related diversity initiatives deserved credit for their LIFE-AFFIRMING learning experiences. To them, these initiatives led to institutional investments in the racially diverse campus environments, faculty, staff, and programs and classes that supported and encouraged their learning and growth. They benefited from the diversity resulting from RACE-CONSCIOUS admissions. However, only four—Vanessa, MIN-JI, Mya, and Arnold—expressly said they were direct beneficiaries of affirmative action in getting into college. MIN-JI, Mya, and Arnold all said at one point in their interviews that they were confident they would not have been admitted to their colleges had it not been for affirmative action. Vanessa, however, offered clear evidence that she was part of an affirmative action "cohort" at UC DAVIS.

Vanessa's father had immigrated from the Philippines to Stockton, California, in the 1920s. Her mother and older sibling joined him after World War II. Vanessa was born shortly after in 1948. The whole family—Vanessa, her parents, and three siblings—would work in the farms, growing sweet potatoes and asparagus, during busy harvest times. They lived in an unincorporated area of the city, near the fields, south of Main Street. Most White people lived north of Main Street. Most people of color lived in East Stockton, where public housing projects were built, and south of Main, where neighborhoods had few streetlights or sidewalks.

After graduating from the high school where most students of color in Stockton were enrolled, Vanessa attended the local community college. Just as she was about to transfer to San Jose State College, a recruiter from the newly established Educational Opportunity Program (EOP) at UC Davis offered her a scholarship if she applied to attend that university to complete her bachelor's degree. UC Davis and the surrounding community were "very White and there were a hundred kids that they recruited for that first major affirmative action cohort," she told me.

In this very early form of affirmative action in higher education, colleges and universities supported promising students like Vanessa in their application, enrollment, and completion of their collegiate goals. EOP students were provided with scholarships, regular peer support groups, tutoring, and counseling. What Vanessa told me reminded me of what my doctoral mentor, Don Nakanishi, shared about his experiences being recruited from the Boyle Heights neighborhood in Los Angeles to attend college, clear across the country, at Yale.

Vanessa and Don were part of the pathbreaking generation of student activists and leaders who transformed higher education and other social institutions. They were among the first cohorts of students of color to integrate colleges and universities in the 1960s and endured "pretty alienating" campus environments. Don once told me about how the grandson of FDR and his friends barged into his room on December 7 of his first year at Yale to read the "Day of Infamy" speech, which was originally delivered by President Franklin Roosevelt following Japan's bombing of Pearl Harbor. As FDR's descendant finished reading the speech, his classmates assaulted Don with water balloons. Don would go on to start and lead a foundational academic journal for the nascent field of Asian American studies in his junior year. *Amerasia Journal* remains a central academic journal in the field.

As a Davis student, Vanessa would work on a Ford Foundation–funded project in 1968 to develop readers, materials, and curriculum for Asian American studies courses. Mentored by the late professor Isao Fujimoto,[11] she and her classmates returned to their home communities of Stockton, Oakland, San Francisco, and Sacramento to document oral histories and ethnic community development. This project would offer key contributions to the groundbreaking *Roots: An Asian American Reader*, which provided one of the first texts for new Asian American studies classes to use in their learning communities.

Even though she never intended to become a student activist, Vanessa and her friends would join in the anti-war movement and protests. They would often carpool from Davis to Berkeley and San Francisco State University to join in the Third World Liberation Front and ethnic studies strikes. "Student activism is contagious!" she said, smiling as she remembered her college years. Vanessa would lead a long career leading, developing, and strengthening Filipino American communities in Northern California. She was also involved with Filipino organizations that developed "a lot of solidarity with Central American liberation struggles and Free South Africa efforts," because they saw how interconnected the goals of freedom movements were around the world. The leadership of her generation of student activists would transform higher education and create organizations and social institutions that would open new possibilities for the next generations of Asian Americans, including so many people in this chapter.

Mya could not pinpoint an EOP program as evidence that she was a direct beneficiary of affirmative action in her admission to college and law school. However, she was convinced that her test scores and grades alone, compared to her classmates in college and law school, would not have allowed her to stand out from other applicants. When she was twelve years old, Mya and her family immigrated from Burma to the US. After a few years in Indiana and Georgia, her family resettled in Northern California. At the time of our interview, Mya was a civil rights lawyer living in New York with her husband and two children. She shared that recognizing herself as a beneficiary of affirmative action in her college and law school education was how she began seeing herself as a person of color. It was when she began to understand how her experiences as a Southeast Asian American woman were connected to the conditions shaping the experiences of other people and communities of color.

Several others I interviewed talked with me about how they developed identities as both Asian Americans and people of color during their college years, through classes and other campus experiences. For example, Helen told me she didn't identify as a woman of color until she was in college. Before college, she knew she wasn't White, and she identified as Filipina and Asian American. It wasn't until another student invited her to the annual Students of Color Conference coordinated by the University of California Student Association that she started considering what it meant to identify as a person of color. From this foundation of her identity, developed through her civic engagements in college, she continues to work in solidarity with people across ethnic and racial identities to support "progressive folks of color and women to run for office." Helen was not invested in a project of racial representation, but rather in a political project rooted in her identity as a woman of color, premised on cross-racial feminist solidarity.

For many, like Olivia, college was a time for people to "transform themselves and to learn how to transform their communities and the world." Olivia was a second-generation Korean American woman who was a recent UCLA graduate. She was raised by her single mother, who owned and operated a small dry-cleaning business. Olivia worked there each day after school as a kid and continued to work with her mom every Saturday in the shop. In college she recalled learning through friends and campus events about social justice issues that challenged her to clarify her values for "institutional change" to address inequalities.

Olivia also took a class in Asian American studies her senior year that led her to make sense of her own family's history and the struggles she and her mom had experienced. She never really understood why her father had left their family in the 1990s, and her mother didn't want to share details of their divorce, because she "never wanted to say anything bad about him." Part of the course covered the 1992 Los Angeles uprising, which was triggered by the acquittal of four LAPD officers who were video-recorded while mercilessly beating Rodney King, an unarmed Black man, on the side of a road. Olivia was about four years old in 1992 and didn't remember much from that time, but she knew that was around the time her parents divorced. Doing research in the basement of the university library for her final project for the class, she found a government document listing names of people whose businesses were damaged. She froze when she came across the names of her paternal grandfather and now-estranged father. "They were listed under a government document of businesses that applied for insurance after the fires. I was in complete shock."

Until that moment, Olivia did not know that the looting and violence during the 1992 Los Angeles uprising played a role in her family's trauma. With frustration in her voice, she shared, "No one talks about anything bad in my family!" Her Asian American studies class triggered a process of healing for her, she told me. It also propelled her to pursue a public interest career. After college, she started working at the NAACP. She was eager to develop her career as someone who engages in community bridging and reconciliation projects.

Similarly, Asha found her college classes eye-opening and her professors supportive in her exploration of questions about racism and her family's economic status in the US and in India. As a student at the University of Illinois at Chicago, her professors helped her learn new ideas and become aware of her own views, and they supported her in struggling to define what she thought about racism, class, and patriarchy.

While many interviewees talked about their classes, many also spoke about pivotal moments of learning that took place outside of their coursework in college. Melissa, a second-generation Chinese Canadian who now resides in the US, told me about "a really violent racialized sexual assault" of an Asian American woman right next to her residence hall her first year in college. The incident's proximity to her residence hall propelled her development as an Asian American feminist. She remembered being frustrated that "there wasn't enough resources to talk about it as a racist *and* sexist incident." Feeling compelled to do something, she joined the Asian American Student Association on campus, and they organized campaign efforts to hold the university accountable. From this experience, Melissa began "learning about structural inequities, facing not just me as an Asian American or a woman of color, but also other people of color, and other women of color, and other forms of marginalized identities." It was her origin story as an Asian American feminist who became deeply committed to cross-racial women of color solidarity.

These experiences led Melissa to sign up for every Asian American studies class available to her and to take ownership of her educational experiences. She petitioned the college to acknowledge her completion of a self-designed academic minor in Asian American studies. It mirrored Arnold's experiences at his college campus, where he cobbled together independent study experiences to create an Asian American studies major for himself when such a major was typically unavailable to students. There were so many stories like these about Asian American studies turning on light bulbs for people in their educational journeys, motivating them to powerfully shape their educational pathways, to understand their experiences at the intersections of systemic oppression. While Melissa talked about the intersection of sexism and racism, Arnold, an openly gay second-generation Filipino American man, was very invested in advancing the rights of queer people of color.

Intersectionality was also an important framework for Anh in her understanding of the world. She and her family left Vietnam as refugees at the end of the war in 1975. They resettled in a predominantly Black and low-income community in Milwaukee after they were sponsored by a local Lutheran church. In this community, she said she knew she wasn't Black or White. "I was just me, whatever that was, floating along." She told me she didn't have a distinct Asian American identity until she got to college.

For Anh, being a person with a physical disability was initially the most salient identity for her. Starting college away from her family before the American Disabilities Act was particularly challenging.[12] "That started my whole railing against the system and I think it spilled over into race," she told me.

In her first few years in college, she didn't get involved in Asian American student organizations that were mostly social and cultural in orientation and didn't interest her. One night during her second year of college, someone slipped an invitation under her door to join an organization for women of color, with an explicit note explaining that people who didn't identify as women of color were not welcomed. "It was just what I needed," Anh remembered.

Most of the group identified as African American women, but there was also a critical mass of Asian American women to organize into smaller caucuses of East Asian, South Asian, and Southeast Asian women. One of the coleaders of the women of color group also announced that she was going to start a panethnic Asian American Student Association (AASA) to advocate for community interests and for an Asian American studies program. In the absence of an Asian American studies program, AASA students coordinated student-led seminars.[13] That's where Anh started "learning about an Asian American identity and words and tools to talk about racism, structural and internalized racism." Imperial wars and systems of ableism, patriarchy, and racism all collided to shape Anh's world and experiences. Campus student organizations and activist teach-ins allowed her to reclaim power to define who she was and what it meant to be Asian American for her, to affirm and not gaslight her experiences with racism, and to work to transform unjust systems.

The stories I heard in these interviews felt very similar to my own educational experiences. Taking a class on Asian American history in a classroom community during my junior year of college with about a dozen other Asian American college students who represented a diversity of backgrounds and perspectives was life-changing for me. It gave me a language I didn't know I needed to learn. I remember few college classes outside of Professor Liem's sunlit seminar room. Confession: I think it was the only college class for which I read every assigned text. I developed a new confidence. New possibilities came into view as I learned concepts to understand daily life experiences, and how Asian American experiences were connected to other communities of color and transformative efforts for equity.

These college experiences—both in and out of classes—helped us learn how to make sense of what it means to be Asian American in relationship to the experiences and histories of other people of color. They were opportunities to develop a sense of solidarity as a path for social justice, allowing us to claim identities as people of color. As Arnold explained, developing and practicing solidarity required an understanding of the notion that "until we're all safe, until we all have justice, until that happens, none of us do." This is what it means to claim an identity as an Asian American and a person of color.

**POST-COLLEGE ON-RAMPS TO LEARNING** As powerful as these college-based learning experiences were, most people never get the chance to benefit from such programs, for a variety of reasons. That said, several people talked about having learning opportunities to make meaning of race, racism, and what it means to be Asian American outside of college. They also advocated for more informal opportunities for anyone to learn about the complexities of race and racism.

Charles was on the board of directors of one of the pro–affirmative action Asian American organizations. He was also a partner at a major global corporate law firm. Toward the end of our interview, he said he had a confession to make. For a long time he had been a conversative who didn't agree with affirmative action. "I didn't see the point of it," he said. He had been on a long learning journey, "becoming more aware of social injustice and things that are happening now in underserved communities," turning him around in his views.

Charles's immigrant parents were like Ligaya's Filipino immigrant parents. They moved their family to a predominantly White suburb to take advantage of the well-resourced schools, and spoke only English with the children to help them assimilate into a White-dominated society. Unlike Ligaya, Charles had no opportunities to connect with youth groups in his area, and as a result he felt little affinity with Asian American communities and organizations in college and law school. His pathway of learning about race, racism, and Asian American identity began when he was a young associate at his law firm, where he was encouraged to join various bar associations to network and get ahead in his legal career.

Initially he was hesitant to join Asian American bar associations, but eventually he made some good friends in those spaces. One of those friends encouraged him to go to a national convention of the National Asian Pacific American Bar Association (NAPABA) in New York City. He didn't know anyone and said, "Why would I go to that?" The friend told him, "Just go. You'll get it."

What Charles got was a two-day community-based Asian American studies crash course. He found the space to be very welcoming. People took him to an off-Broadway production of *Carry the Tiger to the Mountain*. Put on by the Pan Asian Repertory Theater, the play told the story about the murder of Vincent Chin in Detroit and the subsequent Justice for Vincent Chin campaign.[14] Charles had never heard about the case and appreciated that people at NAPABA took him "under their wing." The two days were culminated by a formal gala, where he was shocked and exhilarated to see a thousand Asian Americans dressed to the nines. "I was floored," he said. "I'd never been in a room like that before. It was cool. I felt like I fit right in and I had never felt different from anybody else."

In addition to the racially immersive and personally transformative experience at NAPABA, Charles chose to attend panels with representatives from the US Department of Justice, on topics like anti-Asian hate crimes, xenophobia, and racial profiling. It was also his first introduction to Asian

American civil rights organizations like the Asian American Legal Defense and Education Fund and Asian Americans Advancing Justice. The way he was sharing with me about this experience felt like he was telling me how he was born again, with a new perspective that affirmed the wholeness of his life experiences.

In the two decades since connecting with the Asian American civil rights community, Charles shared that he had learned that being Asian American means showing up in solidarity for other Asian Americans. Given his own personal and family history of experiences with racial harassment, he was particularly sensitive to Islamophobia targeting South Asian Americans, and especially Sikhs. He felt that the Asian American affirmative action divide could be reconciled with more opportunities for the public to develop their racial literacy.[15]

Annabelle, a staff member at an Asian American community-based organization, agreed that there was "a real hunger" among people who didn't work in Asian American identity-based organizations for community dialogues to provide an "on-ramp" to learn and make sense of social inequalities around them. Unpacking the Asian American affirmative action divide, she shared her frustration over a lack of strategy to reconcile community conflicts. She observed some people in Asian American activist circles dismissing immigrant Asians as "just racist" rather than considering how to engage them in community dialogues and popular education, with the assumption that people can learn.

Annabelle was concerned that some Asian Americans who worked in civil rights organizations were too dismissive of Asian Americans who opposed affirmative action policies. Racial illiteracy and racist ideologies are not just problems found exclusively among Asian Americans. Thankfully, there are some notable creative popular political education efforts found across Asian American organizations, including those that serve immigrant communities, that cultivate cross-racial solidarity as a foundational pathway toward collective uplift and liberation.

For example, when I interviewed Min-Ji, a Korean American immigrant woman, in the community center for which she was the executive director, I noticed that part of the office had a sign for the local chapter of a Black youth activist organization. Toward the end of our interview, I asked Min-Ji how her Korean service organization and BYP100 came to share space. "We're the fiscal agent for BYP100," she said. "It's one way we do organizational solidarity."

Moving the organization to do this was not easy, though. Some of the immigrant elders didn't understand why their Korean community center would consider offering space and organizational resources to "somebody else's issue," Min-Ji noted. What moved the Korean immigrant constituency to welcome BYP100 was a community dialogue and presentation of photos during Min-Ji's organization's annual commemoration event memorializing the May 18 uprising in Gwangju, South Korea. Min-Ji explained to me that in May 1980 the US-backed South Korean military dictatorship sent in tanks and machine guns, slaughtering two thousand civilians who were peacefully protesting for democracy.

At the 2015 Gwangju commemoration event, photos of violent police repression of peaceful Black Lives Matter protestors in Ferguson and Baltimore were displayed next to photos from the Gwangju uprising. Min-Ji remarked, "People couldn't tell the difference between Gwangju and Ferguson and Baltimore. Then the Korean first-generation [immigrant elders] said, 'Oh my God. This is happening here, same way.'" The Korean American elders felt Gwangju viscerally. It was a poignant example of culturally relevant and affirming popular education that opened up space for community solidarity.

### BATTLING FOR THE HEART AND SOUL OF OUR COMMUNITY

"I feel like we're battling for the heart and soul of our community," Emily told me, as we sat in the windowless conference room with light beige chairs on deeper beige carpet at the civil rights legal organization where she worked. From Emily, a second-generation Taiwanese American woman, and others in this chapter, I heard rhetorical hand-wringing over what to do about the affirmative action divide within the Asian American community. Armed with their critical analyses of the social world, they worried over how outsiders, mostly White conservatives, were using racial stereotypes of Asian Americans to claim that the policy harmed Asian American students. Few were taking up an active fight for affirmative action commensurate with policy opponents' fervor or even their own understanding of this debate being an existential one.

Still, for the people in this chapter, the affirmative action debate was more than a niche policy disagreement over admissions at hyper-selective colleges and universities. There were broader implications for where Asian Americans would align in US racial politics. Would we fall on the side of expanding rights? Or would Asian Americans play a role, even a symbolic one, in narrowing education access?

In these existential Asian American community discourses, what "affirmative action" meant seemed to take on wide-ranging definitions. In the WeChat realm, affirmative action seemed restricted to selective college admissions. But for several people I interviewed in this chapter, it could encompass all anti-oppressive initiatives. For others, it was a narrow policy tool to advance equity.

For Emily and others, campaigns against affirmative action served to perpetuate inequalities, countering values and ideals of a multiracial democracy. Because Asian Americans were situated as a racial wedge in these political debates, Emily felt that Asian Americans "have a responsibility to counter that." I saw this sense of responsibility deepest during my interview with Dean, a Chinese American immigrant.

When I first met Dean, I thought of him as a unicorn: a well-known Chinese American immigrant social justice influencer with a large following on WeChat. His anti-racist and pro–affirmative action micro-blog posts regularly went viral, suggesting to me that the values Dean and I shared resonated with many more members of the Chinese diasporic community than I had thought. Meeting and talking with Dean was pivotal for challenging me to develop a deeper understanding of the Chinese American diasporic community.

Connecting with him helped me learn about networks of Chinese American immigrants who were invested in countering anti-Black ideologies and racism. They also understood that our fates were linked with the welfare of other communities of color. Dean regularly went on WeChat to counter those who would assert racist stereotypes and ideologies about other communities of color, asking readers, "Why come to the US if you're not OK with a multiracial shared society?"

Dean taught me a lot about how affirmative action discussions had shifted over a relatively short amount of time on WeChat. He wanted me to know that the original Chinese phrase for affirmative action had a very "beautiful underlying meaning" that made it difficult for opponents to say they were against the policy. Since 2013, around the time of the SCA-5 debate in California, he began noticing that people on WeChat stopped using the Chinese characters for affirmative action and started using "AA" instead. Concurrently, he explained, the discourse on WeChat shifted. Increasingly, WeChat discourses turned ugly and contentious over affirmative action.[16]

In many ways, Dean was like most of the policy opponents in the previous chapter. He was a successful professional in the tech industry, raising a family in a suburban community. What made Dean different was that he had not immigrated to the US for graduate school. More importantly, he routinely lived life in racially integrated spaces.

Dean immigrated from China in 1988, two years before the 1990 Immigration Act shifted the balance of immigration toward more heavily favoring highly educated and professional-class immigrants. When he first arrived in the US, he worked various part-time jobs to make ends meet. In his workplaces he regularly interacted with a diversity of people, including Filipinos, Latinx, and African Americans. One of his jobs was as an accounting assistant, where his supervisor was Black. During a call over a financial dispute, the client on the other end of the phone starting yelling at Dean and complaining that his English was not good. Dean handed the phone to his supervisor, who said to the client, "I can understand Dean's English very well. If you can't understand him, that's your problem." This was a defining experience for Dean that shaped his anti-racist values. He offered this story as an example of cross-racial solidarity and one of many experiences in integrated spaces that made him frustrated over racist ideologies that floated through WeChat.

When I asked Dean why he spent so much time engaging in political discussions, writing, and posting persuasive anti-racist essays in WeChat, he told me he was deeply concerned about the future of Chinese Americans and what he called our "brand name." He had studied Chinese American history and had learned that there was a positive relationship between the social and political advances made by other people of color and the uplift of Chinese Americans. He worried that if Chinese Americans "only think about our race, then other people won't respect us. They won't respect our children." On WeChat he was trying to challenge members of the Chinese diaspora to expand their views.

I have remained in touch with Dean over the years. He has taught me so much about Chinese diasporic communities and Chinese idioms. My favorite idiom is 鼠目寸光. It means "rat's eyes." He has used that expression on more than one occasion in our conversations to comment on how short-sighted Chinese and other Asian American affirmative action opponents are. Without solidarity and harmony, Dean has told me, we will all suffer.

Among the people I spoke with for this chapter, Jacob was one of the few who had put a lot on the line to fight for affirmative action. I have long held a lot of respect for Jacob, a second-generation Taiwanese American, and how he thought and strategized about advancing campaigns for equity. A few years after I had met him for this interview, he and others in California launched a failed ballot measure attempt in 2020 to repeal the affirmative action ban in the state.

Back in 2016 I met up with Jacob on a chilly June day in a San Francisco public park for our interview. The organization he led centered affirmative action advocacy in its mission. Since the organization was founded in 1969, it has advocated to expand employment opportunities, immigration, language access, and voting rights. Jacob told me that enacting affirmative action was about working to change an unacceptable status quo of inequities. Like him, Ethan, a fellow executive director of another Asian American community-based organization, defined affirmative action as "action to address injustices." Affirmative action, therefore, could mean everything for them.

In contrast, affirmative action was just a narrow tool to advocate for equity, according to Min-Ji. Her organization had signed onto amicus briefs supporting affirmative action. When I asked her what she was hoping to accomplish in advocating for the policy, she clarified that her organization's work was not centrally about affirmative action. "We're actively fighting against racism," she explained. "In that context, we're supporting it." Her organization supported affirmative action as an "inclusive practice" that was part of a larger umbrella of "working on racial justice."

Between those who understood affirmative action as a broader framework for racial justice and those who saw racial justice as the frame, with affirmative action serving as one tool for that work, I started understanding why there was little coordinated mass mobilization to clearly defend and advance affirmative action. Along these lines, Vanessa also gave me additional insights into the general lack of collective energy for affirmative action. I asked her why she thought so many Asian American civic organizations like hers did little more than issue statements and sign onto amicus briefs in support of the policy. She reasoned that this was an issue tied up in the legal courts. Therefore, the "leadership lane" for this matter was in the hands of Asian American legal nonprofit organizations. Historically, many of these organizations were founded to offer legal aid. They were not set up to lead and organize communities for political campaigns or to intervene in media and public discourses.

In the battle for the Asian American community's heart and soul, there isn't a shared conception of affirmative action. Perhaps as a result, there seem to be few clear strategic pathways and efforts to activate, energize, and reassert Asian American voices of support for affirmative action. There was, however, a shared commitment to working for racial equity. I worry that as a result of the Supreme Court's 2023 ruling ending race-conscious admissions in *SFFA v. Harvard/UNC*, work for racial equity in any form will become even more difficult than it already is.

### TOWARD AN ASIAN AMERICAN FUTURE BUILT ON COMMUNITY EDUCATION AND SOLIDARITY

Cross-racial and cross-ethnic solidarity was both a value and practice that are central to what it means to be Asian American, among the people I interviewed in this chapter. "I don't think of the Asian American agenda as separate from the agenda advanced by other people of color for racial justice," Jimmy, a second-generation Korean American man, told me in a classic Chicago mid-rise office building overlooking a working-class and gentrifying Uptown neighborhood. Jimmy and others in this chapter saw their own fates as linked with others and recognize the need to work toward what Heather McGhee called a "solidarity dividend."[17]

Unlike the people in the previous chapter, those I interviewed for this chapter did not see an agenda for the betterment of Asian American communities as separate from the welfare of other people of color. These people had benefited from the legacies of the ethnic studies movement, including the Asian American studies movement, inspired by the civil rights movement, both in and outside of schools.[18] If we understand the ethnic studies movement as the original diversity, equity, and inclusion (DEI) efforts in higher education, we can also recognize contemporary anti-DEI efforts and book bans as blowback against the powerfully transformative learning such programs offer. Informed by the ethnic studies tradition of education, both in and outside of schools, the people I interviewed in this chapter were all committed to questioning social injustices. They were all working in various, but not necessarily unified, ways to bring forward a more just world. These kinds of education and ethics are dangerous to those who hold the most power in our society. There is power in knowing history and ourselves, and recognizing that our collective communities are capable of transforming institutions, communities, and the power arrangements in the world.

When we moved back to Chicago in July 2020 and were looking for a new home in the city and figuring out how to navigate Chicago Public Schools (CPS), Té Té, I didn't want you to enroll in a predominantly White school or a school where you would be the only Asian American student. We chose a home in a racially and ethnically diverse neighborhood. Our neighbors were Latinx, Black, Filipino, Asian Indian, Korean, and White. The back alley of our block was the dividing line between two school zones. Homes on our side of the alley were assigned to Cicero Elementary School. Some of our neighbors conveyed their trepidations about Cicero with us and shared their strategies for enrolling their children into Haskins Elementary School—the school zoned for homes on the other side of our alley.

I wondered why some people actively avoided our neighborhood school. The great majority of students at Cicero identified as Latinx, 7 percent as White, and 2 percent identified as Asian. The school is also federally designated as a Title I school, meaning most of the attendees come from low-income families and the school receives some additional resources to serve the school community. In contrast, Haskins was not a Title I school, and almost half of its students were White. Slightly over 40 percent identified as Latinx. Six percent identified as Asian, and 5 percent were Black. Interestingly, both schools performed about the same along state tests, but test score averages aren't something I really buy into as a measure of school quality anyway, especially when testing has played a role in school inequalities.[19] The thing that caught my attention about Cicero, and what I have appreciated most, was that the average teacher in the school had at least a decade of teaching experience and there was very low staff turnover.

Your father and I followed through on our values and the agreement we came to during our discussion about neighborhood schools on the L many years earlier. We enrolled you at Cicero. We looked forward to connecting with other families in the neighborhood. Admittedly, though, I didn't anticipate the culturally sustaining and affirming education the school would deliver. I had heard enough aspersions cast on Cicero that I started buying into the idea that this neighborhood school wouldn't be that great, and we would need to substantially supplement your education.

I soon learned that I was wrong to have such low expectations of the school. My assumptions about the kind of education you would get at Cicero drastically shifted on a typical cold and dreary winter day when you were in the second grade. I couldn't remember where we were driving from, but as I turned our car into our neighborhood, I heard your voice from the back seat. "Mama, I got a question for you." I took a deep breath to get ready to answer what you had for me that day.

"Are we colonizers?" you asked.

I responded, "Hmmm. Why are you asking?" In our eighth year as mother and daughter, I had learned to ask you to help me understand what you were thinking and where your wonderings were coming from. It bought me some time to get ready.

You plainly responded, "We're learning about the colonization of Haiti and the Haitian Revolution at school. America colonized Haiti a hundred years ago. You say we're American, so doesn't that make us colonizers?"

I was shocked by what was coming out of your mouth.

You went on, "Also, since we're not Native Americans, are we colonizers?"

You were learning about the history of Jean Baptiste Pointe du Sable, the Haitian migrant celebrated as the founder of Chicago. I noted that you didn't indicate that you had learned about his wife, Kitihawa,[20] a Native Potawatomi woman, with whom he created the settlement along the river that would eventually be incorporated into the city of Chicago. When du Sable arrived in the area that we now know as Chicago, it was already home to vibrant tribal communities and nations of Potawatomi, Ojibwe, Odawa, Miami, and many other American Indians.

I was thrown by your question. Was I driving with my second grader seated in a booster seat in the back of our SUV, or someone much older? As I prepared to answer you, I wondered if some of the "anti-CRT parent choice" and "divisive concepts" book-banning activists had children who similarly asked them challenging questions. Did these parents feel a sense of inadequacy and general discomfort that motivated them to form campaigns seeking an end to teaching and learning about the ugly realities of settler colonialism and chattel slavery foundational to the US? According to PEN America, legislators in thirty-six states had introduced 137 educational gag order bills in 2022, with twelve laws passed in 2021 and seven in 2022.[21] These gag orders would censor and prevent K–12 and postsecondary educators from addressing subjects like race and racism, gender, and LGBTQ+ identities.

I was surprised but not offended by your question. In fact, I was so pleased you were asking such questions. I made a mental note to email Mrs. Smith with kudos and encouragement to incorporate stories and learning about Kitihawa and the American Indians of Chicago.

Your question created an opportunity for conversation about our family history. I reminded you that your maternal grandparents were born in southern China and left as young children shortly after World War II, when many families became displaced migrants because of the turmoil of the Communist Revolution and postwar famine. They grew up in Hong Kong, which was a British colony until 1997. With their British Dependent Territories Citizen passports, my parents immigrated to the US in the 1970s, continuing our family's diasporic migration journey. I was born in

New England in the US Empire to colonial subjects of the British Empire during the reign of an English queen.

Our family elders were colonized people and not colonizers. They migrated across the globe and settled in the US. We are settlers in Chicago—on the native lands of the Ojibwe, Odawa, and Potawatomi peoples, who continue to make their homes here. As we got out of the car, I shared this with you, using vocabulary I thought you could understand. I explained that colonization was partly why your grandparents immigrated. I told you that we are settlers, not necessarily colonizers, but we can definitely act like colonizers. We have to watch out for that and try not to behave in colonizer ways. I felt myself uncomfortably and uncertainly pushing back against the label "colonizer."

"What's the difference between settlers and colonizers?" you asked as we walked from the garage into our home. And I thought to myself, "I hope you never stop asking questions like these, but I wasn't prepared for today's defense!" Taking our shoes off in the entryway littered with shoes, boots, and house slippers, I took another deep breath and did my best to answer your question the best I knew how.

I told you that we should keep thinking and learning together about whether there are differences and similarities between colonizers and settlers. I think the difference might be in our power. Colonization is about extraction—going to a place to purposely take things away from the people, and not sharing. Our family didn't come here looking to take things away from American Indians. They came here trying to find and make a home someplace in the world, and they settled in lands where we are not Native.

I told you that we should remember that we did benefit from something unfair to American Indians—the colonization that created this country—even if we didn't mean to take things away from American Indian nations and tribal communities; like this land our house is on, which was taken away from American Indians. Settlers can and do participate in colonization. We can be both settlers and colonizers, I think. As we continued our conversation, I felt uncertainty and discomfort creep up. Learning about settler colonialism and my own complicity remains one of the deep learning edges for me, after decades of receiving and accepting settler-colonial teachings.[22]

You took some time to consider what I said. After getting a drink and snack, you said, "Well, that's not fair to take things away from people."

I asked, "Because we know we benefited from something that was and is unfair to American Indians, what should we do about it?"

Matter-of-factly, you said, "We should give back their lands."

The kind of critical thinking, inquiry, and values expressions you are practicing and developing is astounding to me sometimes. I am grateful to your teachers at Cicero for being my partners in your education. I felt warm knowing there was a connection between what you were learning in school to the ethnic studies educational tradition I experienced as a college student. I cannot imagine how much harder it would be to walk with you in your learning journey without the leadership of professional and caring teachers in our Chicago public school where race and ethnic studies content is not banned by state law.

With or without schools and teachers engaged with this kind of learning, and whether governments ban learning and teaching about race and racism, I know you, like so many other children, will still naturally have all kinds of wonderings and questions about the world. No matter what governments do, it is human to want to make sense of things that just don't make sense, like racism, poverty, and patriarchy. And when you know history, you know yourself better, and you know what you're capable of in relationship with others. You can collectively imagine and enact new possibilities in uplifting people with whom we share community. Know history, and learn how to build a future with solidarity as the foundation.

# ASIAN AMERICAN IDENTITY IS A SOLIDARITY ETHIC AND PRACTICE

My Dear Daughter,

When you were seven and your friend Jaya had just turned eight, he came over to our house for a spaghetti dinner. As Jaya asked for seconds, I noticed you picking at your still nearly full plate of noodles. And then I did something that I swore as a kid I would never do as a parent. I remarked to Jaya, "Wow! You are such a good eater! I wish Té Té was more like you!"

Jaya smiled briefly, looked at you, and the smile disappeared. You glanced at Jaya's empty plate and then up at his face, with red sauce around his lips, framed by his brown curly hair. With a frown, you quietly looked down at your lap. My heart fell and I immediately regretted my words.

Jaya turned to me and said, "That's not fair. There's nothing wrong with how Té Té eats. Sometimes, I'm not a good eater." He could have accepted my praise, but Jaya refused it when he saw that it came at your expense and realized that my characterization of him was too simple.

Jaya's words seemed to empower you to look up at me and say, "Mama, that hurt my feelings. You made me feel like you don't love me, and you wished Jaya was your child."

Together, the two of you told me that I had disguised criticism of Té Té within an insincere compliment of Jaya. You collectively rejected my double-edged words that could have seeded a resentment between you and splintered your friendship. I offered a sincere apology to you over dinner that night and promised to do better in the future.

You and Jaya are two third-generation Asian American children—one mixed-ethnic Chinese and Thai and one Black, Jewish, and Indian mixed-race. In that dinner-table exchange, you embodied what it meant to be Asian American through your instincts to act in solidarity with each other. Motivated by care and love for each other, you intuitively rejected my words aimed at dividing you and Jaya. That moment was one of my low points as a parent, especially when I realized that I was engaging in a form of wedge politics that so often gets enacted between Asian Americans and other people of color within power-laden social contexts.

"Asian American is not a color," you told me when you were just three years old. You weren't wrong. With that simple and powerfully observant quip, you propelled me into wondering how I could best support you as you began pondering our social place in a racialized world and questioning what it means to be Asian American. Explaining the complex and absurd realities of the world around us without overly complicated scholarly words doesn't come very easily to me. I wrote you this book to share my hopes for the future and continue engaging in the conversation you started when you were a toddler. All along, you already understood the practice of political solidarity that I believe is central to what it means to be Asian American.

I want you to know that what it means to be Asian American in this world has always been contested and is evolving within a racial hierarchy that keeps Whiteness at the top and Black people at "the bottom of the well," all in relationship to transnational empire and settler colonialism.[1] Asian Americans participated in the collective creation of affirmative action policies and programs, recognizing that our future was interlinked with those of other systemically marginalized peoples.[2]

To be clear, though, Asian American leadership in the movement for affirmative action and more broadly for civil rights was not a simple forgone conclusion. There were always tensions and conflicts within our communities and disagreements about how to uplift Asian American communities in an unequal society. Those of us who have been governmentally categorized as Asian or Asian American (or "Oriental" before these labels) bring a vast array of cultural and community groundings, migration histories, economic class statuses, perspectives, ideas, and understandings of who we are in relationship to the world around us. All of this challenges the idea that we can ever have a shared identity.

Asian American is not a color, but it is an identity that centers community care and uplift across an array of diasporic communities. Asian Americans across ethnic communities have historically survived and thrived through collective support and struggle against oppressive systems. Being Asian American doesn't mean that we are always in lockstep with each other.

One thing I learned at a young age in my loud immigrant Chinese American family and community was that it was part of our cultural ways to share impassioned disagreements with each other, especially about politics. My civics education started from the many lively debates during family and community get-togethers that had as their soundtracks Cantopop, off-key karaoke songs, the clicking and banging of mah-jongg tiles, and political points made in between laughter, food, and joy. Civic cultural community discourses and community connections can fill hearts and bellies and nurture joy and dreaming, like it did for me within my social context of struggle.

What I have witnessed, however, in debates between some contemporary Asian Americans over race-conscious admissions policies has not often included real community connection, joy, or care. Melissa, one of the people I interviewed, put it best when she said that it's one thing to engage in a practice of disagreement and debate that centers love: "I love you; therefore, I challenge you." It's another thing when I engage in debate with this disposition, and it's heartbreaking to encounter fellow Asian Americans in debates who disagree in toxic, personal, and violent ways.[3]

In my idea of an aspirational identity, Asian American does not include the toxicity of self-interested ethnic chauvinism, which has resulted in a complicity with White supremacy undergirded by anti-Black ideologies. Asian American identity is rooted in ethics of cross-ethnic and cross-racial solidarity and movement building toward a better world for all. The young people who first created the term "Asian American" came together across their ethnic identities—Filipino, Chinese, Japanese, and so on—to look out for each other and lift each other up, which sometimes requires sacrifices for long-term collective benefit.

The imperfect and challenging practice of political solidarity for a shared desire for justice is central to what it means to be Asian American. It is a practice that resists invitations of power seeking to sow division with disingenuous compliments that flatten Asian Americans into a "model minority" stereotype of self-sufficient high achievement to propagate White dominance and the oppression of Black, Indigenous, and other people of color, including Asian Americans. This is why the wonky legal battle over race-conscious college admissions in the federal court system has been so personal for me. I simply cannot tolerate the idea in the SFFA lawsuits against race-conscious admissions that a White man sold deceitful praise of Asian Americans, contrasting a stereotype of us against stereotypes of other people of color to strike down race-conscious admissions. Ed Blum's win in the SFFA cases will ultimately hurt all of us.

I have never believed that affirmative action was the silver bullet for curing systemic intersectional racism. However, this policy has been an important touchstone of larger efforts seeking to advance equitable op-portunity in a society that was historically built on the dispossession of Indigenous land and life, anti-Black chattel slavery and apartheid, transna-tional empire, and labor exploitation.[4] Now that the Supreme Court has struck down race-conscious admissions practices, will people understand that most Asian Americans were unwillingly pulled into Ed Blum's lifelong campaign against policies for a multiracial democracy?

### HALLOWEEN 2022 AT THE SUPREME COURT

On Halloween in 2022, you and I traveled to Washington, DC, to the US Supreme Court steps for the day of oral arguments in the SFFA cases. For months you had asked me when we would take a mommy-daughter trip. When I found out when oral arguments would take place, I asked you if you wanted to join me on a trip to DC.[5]

On Halloween morning we woke up early and got ourselves ready for the day. When we arrived at the court, there were already several hundred people—a beautiful tapestry of people of all colors and genders. You were probably the youngest person in the gathering. It was an intergenerational crowd, but most of the group looked to be in their twenties. Busloads of students from Harvard, Morgan State University, the University of Maryland at College Park, and Yale were present. There was also a strong contingent of students from Howard University. It was simply beautiful.

You asked me, "How many people are here for diversity?"

Hundreds, I told you.

It felt amazing and so hopeful to be together with so many people rejecting division and embracing solidarity. Among the folks older than thirty, I recognized so many people I had worked with for more than a decade through email, phone calls, and, eventually, Zoom conferences. The community connections, relationships, and coalitions built could never be overturned or banned.

Even during a torrential downpour, we all stayed on the court steps. Listening to oral arguments, many of my lawyer friends were visibly frustrated by the conservative justices' questions and commentary. You asked several times, "Is the sky crying because our arguments aren't working?" For the first time, I allowed myself to think about what it would be like if we lost, and an unshakable sadness came over me.

At the airport on our way home to Chicago, you must have seen the worry that had crept into my face after the highs of being in community with so much energy and hope. You asked, "What happens if we lose?" I did everything I could to hold back my tears in that moment, especially since I had just seen someone with a large following on Twitter call out Asian Americans for bringing the SFFA lawsuits to the federal courts. They were angry that Asian Americans had betrayed the cross-racial coalition for racial progress. It didn't matter that it wasn't Asian Americans filing the lawsuits, or that opinion polls showed that the majority of Asian Americans supported affirmative action. Ed Blum had made everyone think it was Asian Americans bringing forward the Harvard case.

## JUNE 2023

June 2023 was the tenth anniversary of my mother's death. As we got closer to the inevitable ruling from the court on the SFFA cases that month, I was haunted by memories of the sound of my mom's death rattle. I swore I could hear it as I sat on a quiet train or suddenly when I was meditating.

In June 2013 no one had prepared me for the death rattle. The sound is caused by the relaxing of the muscles around air passages. As the end nears, the death rattle sounds a lot like the gurgling sound when you finish drinking something through a straw. I remember feeling frightened by the shocking sound.

One week before my mom's tenth death anniversary and a few weeks before the Supreme Court ruling was announced, I recorded an interview with higher education reporter Lisa Philip at WBEZ, the Chicago NPR affiliate.[6] It was by no means my first media interview about the admissions cases. After dozens of media appearances over the years, I had become relatively comfortable in these interviews. But as I set up my computer for this Zoom interview in a quiet corner, I thought I heard the death rattle again. Shaking it off, I hopped on Zoom for the recorded conversation.

Toward the end of the interview, Lisa asked me a question about the implications if the Supreme Court struck down race-conscious admissions, and I caught myself getting choked up. I was surprised and unprepared for the emotions of grieving and fear that were taking over my body. I finished the recorded conversation through tears streaming down my face and several breaks so I could collect myself enough to get my words out.[7]

It felt like an ending was near and inevitable. I don't like the feeling that our Asian American faces will be framed as the enemy of racial progress, especially when Asian Americans continue to confront racism. I have lived my entire life in a world where affirmative action was an available policy tool for educational opportunity. It's hard and emotional to confront what is to come in light of the court's ruling.

Although the Supreme Court ruled against race-conscious admissions in the SFFA cases against Harvard and the University of North Carolina, the justices' opinions cannot change ethics and practices of solidarity. When I reflect on my professional educational career, which started in 2002 shortly after California banned affirmative action, I am reminded that community-based movements for collective racial justice and uplift can always win. Bans be damned!

## POST-AFFIRMATIVE ACTION CALIFORNIA

In 1996 voters in California passed Proposition 209, which banned the state from practicing affirmative action in public employment, contracting, and education. This ban did not mean the end of racism. Although it meant there was one less policy tool to promote equitable opportunity, affirmative action bans cannot stop the creative energy, dreams, and leadership for change among communities of people with visions for justice and the wherewithal to make things happen.[8]

As a young twenty-something college student affairs professional in the late 1990s and early 2000s, I followed an interesting Asian American student campaign at UC Davis through a new tool at the time called email listservs. Through these new national listservs that connected Asian American student affairs professionals, I learned that Asian American students, faculty, staff, and community members at Davis had organized mass rallies and teach-ins to protest a string of violent anti-Asian incidents on campus and the surrounding Sacramento area. The fact that Asian Americans in California—a place I had thought of as an Asian American mecca—were struggling with similar anti-Asian racism found east of California captured my attention.

Revisiting the February 9, 2001, issue of the student newspaper the *California Aggie*, I remember feeling excited by how the campaign, advocacy efforts, and demands for institutional changes were fueled and sustained by cross-racial solidarity.[9] The demands included increased investments in campus supports for survivors of racial violence, the creation of a permanent Cross-Cultural Center (CCC) building, a new staff line in the Academic Advising and Support department to focus specifically on supporting emergent bilingual students, new staff lines in Counseling and Psychological Services with expertise in Asian American and Pacific Islander mental health, and Student Affairs Officer positions in the Native American studies and Asian American studies programs. Several students and faculty who didn't identify as Asian American spoke on the record to support the demands and efforts. Students from UC Berkeley traveled the seventy miles to join in the rallies. They blocked entrances to Mrak, the university administration building.

This campaign would lead to several transformative wins for racial equity, which were decades in the making, at UC Davis. I was the first person hired in the Asian American studies student affairs officer position in 2002.[10] Over three years, this job and the Davis community transformed my life and career. I learned so much about the ups and downs of negotiating cross-ethnic and cross-racial relations and solidarity. I never really got to pursue Asian American studies in college or during my master's program, but living and working at Davis gave me a deeply enriching civic education that invited me into relationships that made it possible to dream boldly and participate in collective solidarity efforts to change the world.

States and courts can ban affirmative action and race-conscious admissions, but they cannot ban community desires and movement building for justice. In my professional capacity I supported student efforts and advocated to make the campus climate more culturally affirming to all students. My work was informed by the detailed demographic data available from the University of California. The post–affirmative action environment made these data especially valuable, and when I was a doctoral student at UCLA, Asian American students in 2007 led a successful campaign to expand the demographic data collected throughout the system.[11] My time as a professional and student at the University of California taught me that the fight for a more just society does not end at the courts or in policymaking systems.

### "PEACE BE WITH EVERYONE"

Té Té,

There are people who seek to seize power through strategies of racial division.[12] There are also many Asian American stories and models of solidarity, mutual aid, and community care. For example, performance artist Kristina Wong founded the Auntie Sewing Squad, a national network of volunteers that sewed masks during the COVID-19 pandemic for marginalized communities to make up for a national shortage of masks.[13] I mentioned the Vigilant Love grassroots organization in chapter 3. The Vietnamese American Youth Leaders Association (VAYLA) is another example. Vietnamese American youth founded the organization in New

Orleans following Hurricane Katrina to build an environmental justice movement in their community. Since its founding, it continues to support the development of Asian American and Pacific Islander "leadership to address social inequities facing our community while anchored in an anti-racist, Queer, Feminist lens."[14] When I was a visiting researcher at VAYLA in 2010–12, I was in awe over how the organization—the only youth organization on the east side of the city—welcomed Black and Latinx young people as leaders as well, while still rooted in the dynamic Vietnamese American community.[15]

More recently, in Philadelphia people across ethnic and racial identities took over city streets on June 10, 2023, to protest a proposed new 76ers basketball arena that would displace the Chinatown community. News videos and photos featured young people and elders, interfaith clergy, and Latinx, African American, and White protesters rallying alongside Asian Americans.[16] Twenty community-based organizations in the city coordinated the collective action and campaign to save Chinatown. This kind of rapid mass mobilization requires established relationships between groups.

To be sure, cross-ethnic and cross-racial solidarity work isn't easy. It requires deep investments and efforts to navigate through conflicts. That said, I want to celebrate examples of solidarity work. These stories often get buried by stories of division, like the ones amplified by Ed Blum and SFFA's false claims in the Harvard case that race-conscious admissions hurt Asian Americans in favor of Black and Latinx students. We have so much to learn from contemporary and historical solidarity movements for justice that reject the false notion that Asian American interests are mutually exclusive from those of other people of color. We win together!

We can also practice cross-ethnic and cross-racial solidarity daily, as individuals. Your friend Jaya demonstrated just one example. Another example is Ruhel Islam and his daughter Hafsa's reaction when their restaurant, Gandhi Mahal, burned down in Minneapolis during the protests following the police murder of George Floyd in 2020. Hafsa posted in a viral Facebook post that her father told someone on the phone, "Let my building burn. Justice needs to be served. Put those officers in jail." Hafsa continued in the post that, "Gandhi Mahal may have felt the flames last night, but our fiery drive to help protect and stand with our community will never die! Peace be with everyone."[17] Practicing solidarity challenges self-interest instincts. It can lead to changes in social conditions that end violence and trauma.

Asian American is not a color and has always been an idea that emerged from an Asian diasporic community praxis of learning and action for cross-ethnic and cross-racial solidarity. We learn about Asian American identity through trial and error, building, and working in relationship with others toward a more just world.

There are many Asian American histories, legacies, and contemporary stories and models of advocacy, solidarity, and movement building to learn and explore.[18] Asian Americans across the affirmative action divide have offered various models and possibilities. As you reflect on our stories, you can decide to follow established pathways, break and transform them, or envision something completely different.

What stories and new possibilities will we create together? I hope that we can generate new approaches for a more just and humanizing future, in community with others. This is how we build new Asian American futures.

# ACKNOWLEDGMENTS

This project was the product of years of conversations and support from so many.

I must start by thanking my late doctoral advisor Don Nakanishi for sending weekly emails pointing out news stories raising questions about how Asian Americans fit within racial equity discourses in education. Don was a pathbreaker and a model of cross-racial solidarity and transformative leadership who opened possibilities for generations after him. Thank you, Paul Ong, for pointing out the "Asian American affirmative action divide" as a problem for study, and Peter Kiang for challenging me to actually talk with Asian Americans across this divide.

Thank you to Jeffrey Alton and the University of Illinois at Chicago's Asian American Student Center for inviting me to workshop early ideas for this book in 2016, and to Z Nicolazzo for being in the audience and offering so much encouragement. Thank you to Jennifer Chau, Cat Fung, Vincent Pan, and Alex Tom for helping me identify interview leads. Taiyo Na, thank you for introducing me to Chris Iijima's widow, Jane, who graciously gave me permission to include lyrics from "Asian Song" in this book.

I owe deep gratitude to the colleagues I got to work with at Loyola University Chicago, where I received funding to conduct the interviews for this book. Bridget Turner Kelly, Mark Engberg, John Dugan, and Sabina Neugebauer—I'm so glad we were brought together at the Water Tower. I treasure your friendship and mentorship. At Colorado State University, I'm grateful to Susana Muñoz, D-L Stewart, Kari Dockendorff, Dave McKelfresh, Vincent Basile, Ricki Ginsberg, Jess Jackson, Jessica Gonzalez,

Danny Birmingham, Louise Jennings, and Gene Gloeckner for welcoming me and my family to the mountains and for the intellectual community.

I am grateful to all the students I've worked with and learned with, at both Loyola and CSU. Thank you, Megan Segoshi, for joining me on the wild ride of interviews for this book and trusting me to be your doctoral advisor to boot! Dian Squire, Ester Sihite, Naseeb Bhangal, Ajani Byrd, Lester Manzano, Sara Furr, Kristen Surla, Lilianne Tang, Caressa Nguyen, Devita Bishundat, Joliana Yee, Cori Kodama, Peter Limthongviratn, Mavis Meng, Josie Carmona, Kerry Wenzler, Douglas Lee, Eileen Galvez, Bri Sérráno, Nikki Chun, Joanne Song Engler, Jess Hurtado, Ali Raza, Daisy Torres-Baez, and Elias Quiñonez—thank you for the many hours of intellectual conversations and joy!

Thank you to the community of friends, colleagues, and mentors that have supported me at the Spencer Foundation. Emily Krone Phillips, Maricelle Garcia, Cindy Soto, Jasmine Knetl, Doris Fisher, Tafadzwa Tivaringe, Jenny Zhang, Kevin Close, Krystal Villanosa, Kenly Brown, Naomi Mae, Rhoda Freelon, Megan Bang, Na'ilah Nasir, and of course my work spouse Leah Bricker, and the whole Spencer team—I'm so thankful to be part of this dream team!

Thank you, Akil Bello, Katherine Cho, Derek Houston, Douglas Lee, Maxwell Leung, Amanda Tachine, Brit Williams, Corey Winchester, and most of all Aujean Lee for reading drafts of the manuscript. Your feedback and encouragement were invaluable!

To my Bruin Book Club buddies—Anthony Ocampo, Janelle Wong, and Ellen Wu—how did I get so lucky to meet with you every month to share writing and support each other? You've been with me through at least two different book proposal drafts and multiple drafts of chapters. Thanks for believing in me.

Thank you, Badia Ahad-Legardy, for teaching me how to write a book proposal and for your friendship. I would never have figured out how to get tenure without you! Jeff Chang and Leigh Patel, thank you for giving me the courage to submit my book proposal to Beacon Press.

To the team at Beacon, you really know how to make an author feel special! You have been a dream to work with. Thank you, Rachael Marks, for believing in my idea from the moment we met in that quiet AERA exhibit hall in 2021!

Thank you to my wonderful network of friends and mentors, both in and outside of the academy, who have supported me personally and intellectually through many years—Taz Ahmed, Xiaojing Wang, Sherry Deckman, Sheeba Jacob, Joanna Lee, Phil Yu, Kai Ma, Marsha Kwong, Nitasha Sharma, Brittany Hsiang and Mike Chen, Julie Park, Yen Ling Shek, Dina Maramba, Robert Teranishi, Dominique Baker, Liliana Garces, Mike Hoa Nguyen, Tim Yu, Terry Hong, Nolan Cabrera, Liza Talusan, Natasha Warikoo, Les Talusan, Cheryl Matias, Wayne Au, Delia Cheung Hom, Dawn Lee, Anurima Bhargava, Connie Wun, Rosaline Chan, Monica Thammarath, Oliver Wang, Jeff Yang, Jenn Fang, Olivia Lee, Sarah Park Dahlen, Margaret Chin, Jeannie Park, Jane Bock, Steven Chen, Betina Hsieh, Jung Kim, Noreen Naseem Rodriguez, Hina Mahmood, Sonia Mathew, Tuyet Ngo, the McPaks, Rema Reynolds (and Cadence), Rosie Perez, Kim Griffin, Cindy Mosqueda, Chrystal George Mwangi, Leslie Gonzales, Carson Byrd, Allyson Tom, Jude Paul Dizon, and Marie Bigham. Also shout out to the legendary Toledo Lounge Collective!

To my family—爸爸, Chester, Felix, and Mommy in heaven—thank you for everything.

Finally, words cannot convey my love and gratitude to my ride or die, Todd. None of this would be possible without you, Nerdlinger. And of course, Té Té. I struggled to find my voice and direction for this book before you made me a mom. Baby girl, I'm finally done with your book! Let's go play!

# INTERVIEW PARTICIPANTS

| PSEUDONYM | POLICY POSITION | IDENTITIES | LOCATION |
|---|---|---|---|
| Albert | Opponent | 4th-generation Chinese American gay man | Southern California |
| Anh | Supporter | 1.5-generation Vietnamese American disabled refugee woman | Chicago |
| Annabelle | Supporter | 2nd-generation Korean American woman | Chicago |
| Arnold | Supporter | 2nd-generation Filipino American gay man | Northern California |
| Asha | Supporter | 1st-generation Indian American woman | Chicago |
| Bingwen | Opponent | 1st-generation Chinese American man | Southern California |
| Charles | Supporter | 2nd-generation Chinese and Filipino American man | Chicago |
| Dean | Supporter | 1st-generation Chinese American man | Southern California |
| Emily | Supporter | 2nd-generation Taiwanese American woman | Southern California |
| Eric | Opponent | 2nd-generation Chinese American man | Northern California |
| Ethan | Supporter | 2nd-generation Chinese and Vietnamese American man | Northern California |
| Evan | Opponent | 1.5-generation Chinese American man | Southeast US |
| George | Opponent | 1st-generation Chinese American man | Southern California |

| PSEUDONYM | POLICY POSITION | IDENTITIES | LOCATION |
|---|---|---|---|
| Grace | Opponent | 1st-generation Chinese American woman | Chicago |
| Helen | Supporter | 1.5-generation Filipina American woman | Northern California |
| Jacob | Supporter | 2nd-generation Taiwanese American man | Northern California |
| Jake | Opponent | 2nd-generation Chinese American man | Southern California |
| Jian | Opponent | 1st-generation Chinese American man | Northern California |
| Jimmy | Supporter | 2nd-generation Korean American man | Chicago |
| Jun | Opponent | 1st-generation Chinese American man | Northeast US |
| Ligaya | Supporter | 2nd-generation Filipina American woman | Northern California |
| Mason | Supporter | 3rd-generation Chinese and Korean American man | Southern California |
| Melissa | Supporter | 2nd-generation Chinese Canadian woman | Northeast US |
| Min-Ji | Supporter | 1.5-generation Korean American woman | Chicago |
| Mya | Supporter | 1.5-generation Burmese American woman | Northeast US |
| Olivia | Supporter | 2nd-generation Korean American woman | Southern California |
| Richard | Opponent | 4th-generation Chinese American man | Pacific Northwest |
| Ruth | Opponent | 2nd-generation Chinese American woman | Northern California |
| Sheng | Opponent | 1st-generation Chinese American man | Northeast US |
| Stanley | Opponent | 1st-generation Chinese American man | Northeast US |
| Thomas | Opponent | 1st-generation Chinese American man | Southern California |

| PSEUDONYM | POLICY POSITION | IDENTITIES | LOCATION |
|---|---|---|---|
| Tina | Supporter | 2nd-generation Cambodian American woman | Northern California |
| Vanessa | Supporter | 2nd-generation Filipina American woman | Northern California |
| Wei | Opponent | 1st-generation Chinese American man | Southern California |
| William | Opponent | 1st-generation Chinese American man | Southern California |
| Wilson | Opponent | 1st-generation Chinese American man | Northern California |

# NOTES

## INTRODUCTION: "BUT ASIAN AMERICAN ISN'T A COLOR"

1. Jerry Flores, "Why Does the Migrant 'Caravan' Exist? And How Did It Come to Be?," *The Conversation*, October 30, 2018, https://theconversation.com/why-does-the-migrant-caravan-exist-and-how-did-it-come-to-be-105781.

2. I capitalize "Black" to acknowledge Black people, history, identity, and cultures. I choose, in this book, to capitalize "White" to draw attention to the racial "specificity and significance of Whiteness," persuaded by Eve Ewing's essay. However, I do not edit the letter casing within quotations. Eve Ewing, "I'm a Black Scholar Who Studies Race. Here's Why I Capitalize 'White,'" *Medium,* July 2, 2020, https://zora.medium.com/im-a-black-scholar-who-studies-race-here-s-why-i-capitalize-white-f94883aa2dd3.

3. Robin D. G. Kelley, *Freedom Dreams: The Black Radical Imagination* (Boston: Beacon Press, 2003). Kelley defined freedom dreams as hopeful visions for new possibilities that are fundamentally different from current realities.

4. Like so many professors, I moved a lot pursuing professional opportunities. In 2017 we moved from Chicago to Colorado for my career. We moved back to Chicago for another job, but also to go back to a place that feels most like home.

5. The "City of Big Shoulders" comes from Carl Sandburg's poem "Chicago."

6. "Community cultural wealth" is a term first defined by Tara J. Yosso, "Whose Culture Has Capital? A Critical Race Theory Discussion of Community Cultural Wealth," *Race Ethnicity and Education* 8, no. 1 (2005), doi:10.1080/1361332052000341006. On anti-Asian immigration laws, racial covenants, segregation, and ethnic enclave economies, see works by Bill Ong Hing, Angelo Ancheta, Wendy Cheng, Nitasha Sharma, Michael Liu, Pyong Gap Min, Min Zhou, Scott Kurashige, and Dawn Mabalon, among others.

7. Johanna Ho, *Eyes That Kiss in the Corners* (New York: HarperCollins, 2021).

8. I grew up calling my immigrant parents' friends my aunties and uncles—our chosen diasporic family. In our family Té Té calls my friends with doctorates "Dr." So in this case, we call my friend Sarah "Dr. Sarah."

9. Jessica Colarossi, "If Babies and Toddlers Can Detect Race, Why Do So Many Parents Avoid Talking About It?" *The Brink,* November 9, 2020, https://www.bu.edu/articles/2020/if-babies-and-toddlers-can-detect-race-why-do-so-many-parents-avoid-talking-about-it.

10. In September 2022 the Texas State Board of Education unfortunately chose to delay their deliberation, review, and vote to 2025, postponing controversy and debate over updating state social studies standards to include Asian American history and Native American history. As I've expressed to my collaborator on the initial framework draft for Asian American history—Dr. Noreen Naseem Rodriguez—I'm still surprised the effort made it as far as it did and did not get defeated outright.

11. Although Florida governor Ron DeSantis signed legislation in 2023 to include Asian American history in public schools, the state simultaneously and paradoxically restricted diversity, equity, and inclusion in education. Additionally, state officials barred the teaching of an Advanced Placement African American studies course in Florida. These are cynical moves to position Asian Americans as a racial wedge that disrupts collective racial justice advances. Kimmy Yam, "DeSantis Criticized for Mandating Asian American History while Banning Courses on 'Systemic Racism,'" NBC Asian America, May 17, 2023, https://www.nbcnews.com/news/asian-america/desantis-criticized-mandating -asian-american-history-banning-courses-s-rcna84972.

12. Khushbu Shah and Juweek Adolphe, "400 Years Since Slavery: A Timeline of American History," *The Guardian*, August 16, 2019, https://www.the guardian.com/news/2019/aug/15/400-years-since-slavery-timeline.

13. I am forever grateful to have benefited from Professor Ramsay Liem's teaching and guidance. He, along with generations of students, advocated for Asian American studies classes on campus. By the time I was a junior at Boston College, there were two Asian American studies classes, and I enrolled in Professor Liem's class on Asian American history and identity.

14. In a 1965 commencement address at Oberlin College titled "Remaining Awake Through a Great Revolution," Dr. Martin Luther King Jr. implored the audience to stay faithful and committed to the hard work and struggle for peace and justice. He encouraged people to maintain hope, explaining that "the arc of the moral universe is long, but it bends toward justice."

15. To be clear, affirmative action is not the same as race-conscious admissions. However, because most people conflate these concepts and practices, at times I use the term "affirmative action" and "race-conscious admissions" interchangeably. Liliana Garces and I wrote a fairly extensive footnote distinguishing between the two in a 2018 research report. Liliana M. Garces and OiYan Poon, *Asian Americans and Race-Conscious Admissions: Understanding the Conservative Opposition's Strategy of Misinformation, Intimidation and Racial Division* (Los Angeles: UCLA Civil Rights Project/Proyecto Derechos Civiles, 2018), https://bit.ly/3dNLiI7.

16. Pulitzer Prize–winning author and professor Viet Thanh Nguyen coined the phrase "narrative plenitude." It is the opposite of "an economy of narrative scarcity, in which we feel deprived and must fight to tell our own stories and fight against the stories that distort or erase us." Viet Thanh Nguyen, "Asian Americans Need More Movies, Even Mediocre Ones," *New York Times*, August 21, 2018, https://www.nytimes.com/2018/08/21/opinion/crazy-rich-asians-movie.html.

17. American studies professor Lisa Lowe explained that there are no singular Asian American identities and cultures, and that we should recognize and

be open to a diversity of cultural politics among those who identify as Asian American. Lisa Lowe, "Heterogeneity, Hybridity, Multiplicity: Marking Asian American Differences," *Diaspora: A Journal of Transnational Studies* 1, no. 1 (1991): 24–44, doi:10.1353/dsp.1991.0014.

18. Y. Joel Wong, Kelly Koo, Kimberly K. Tran, Yu-Chen Chiu, and Yvonne Mok, "Asian American College Students' Suicide Ideation: A Mixed-Methods Study," *Journal of Counseling Psychology* 58, no. 2 (2011): 197; Michelle Samura, "Remaking Selves, Repositioning Selves, or Remaking Space: An Examination of Asian American College Students' Processes of 'Belonging,'" *Journal of College Student Development* 57. no. 2 (2016): 135–50, Project MUSE, https://doi.org/10.1353/csd.2016.0016.

19. In the *SFFA v. Harvard/UNC* Supreme Court decision, in June 2023, Justice Roberts's ruling opinion never mentioned "affirmative action." The case focused on whether colleges and universities could consider race as one of many factors in the selection of students to admit. In the opinion, the court recognized the importance of racial diversity as a public interest, even allowing the military academies to continue practicing race-conscious admissions. However, other colleges and universities would need to discontinue this practice, which is technically not the same as affirmative action, even though in this book and broad public discussions, we colloquially use the term "affirmative action" to include race-conscious admissions.

20. For more details on the research methods and design for this study, see OiYan A. Poon, Megan S. Segoshi, Lilianne Tang, Kristen L. Surla, Caressa Nguyen, and Dian D. Squire, "Asian Americans, Affirmative Action, and the Political Economy of Racism: A Multidimensional Model of Raceclass Frames," *Harvard Educational Review* 89, no. 2 (2019), doi:10.17763/1943-5045-89.2.201.

21. Even after the Supreme Court ruling in *SFFA v. Harvard/UNC*, debates continue among Asian Americans over whether race-conscious admissions policies are good or bad.

22. Although I occasionally use the term "selective" to describe colleges and universities that have low admission rates each year, I also use the terms "rejective admissions" and "rejective institutions," which are terms credited to Akil Bello. These terms more accurately describe institutions that reject more students than they invite to enroll. For example, Harvard, Yale, Princeton, and Stanford reject more than 95 percent of the qualified applicants they review each year. The majority of the more than 1,500 four-year baccalaureate-granting institutions in the US admit more than half of their qualified applicants annually.

23. See, for example, the debates over enrollment policies at selective public high schools such as Stuyvesant in New York and Thomas Jefferson High School in Fairfax County, Virginia.

24. Michele S. Moses, *Living with Moral Disagreement: The Enduring Controversy About Affirmative Action* (Chicago: University of Chicago Press, 2016).

25. Angelo Ancheta, *Race, Rights, and the Asian American Experience* (New Brunswick, NJ: Rutgers University Press, 2006); Robert S. Chang, *Disoriented: Asian Americans, Law, and the Nation-State* (New York: New York University Press, 1999).

26. I want to note that the idea of Asian Americans as settlers in North America is a contested notion. As Wayne Au (2022) explained, drawing from Iyko Day's work, it may be more accurate to recognize Asian Americans as alien labor in North America. Doing so allows us to acknowledge the differences between White settler colonialism and Asian American transnational diaspora. Wayne Au, "Asian American Racialization, Racial Capitalism, and the Threat of the Model Minority," *Review of Education, Pedagogy, and Cultural Studies* 44, no. 3 (2022), doi:10.1080/10714413.2022.2084326.

27. See, for example, Yen Espiritu, *Asian American Panethnicity: Bridging Institutions and Identities* (Philadelphia: Temple University Press, 1993); Dina Okamoto, *Redefining Race: Asian American Panethnicity and Shifting Ethnic Boundaries* (New York: Russell Sage Foundation, 2014).

28. Demeturie Toso-Lafaele Gogue, OiYan A. Poon, Dina C. Maramba, and Vijay Kanagala, "Inclusions and Exclusions: Racial Categorizations and Panethnicities in Higher Education," *International Journal of Qualitative Studies in Education* 35, no. 1 (2022), doi:10.1080/09518398.2021.1982045.

## CHAPTER I: THE ANCESTORS AND THEIR CONTRASTING DREAMS

1. "I am my ancestors' wildest dreams" is a saying representing a deeply meaningful idea within the African American community and cultural tradition. It represents legacies of survivance in response to anti-Blackness and systemic anti-Black violence. In this chapter I offer my reflection on Asian American history, my family's past, and the legacies of Asian American ancestors. Acknowledging that Asian American experiences and histories are fundamentally structured differently from those of African Americans, I adapted the original idiom to characterize Asian American dreams as contrasting or, at times, in conflict with each other.

2. Chris Helms, "Forest Hills Cemetery Cancels Lantern Festival," *Jamaica Plain News*, June 5, 2014, www.jamaicaplainnews.com/2014/06/05/forest-hills-cemetery-cancels-lantern-festival/2098. The last festival was held in 2013.

3. Felix Poon, host, "Ginkgo Love," *Outside/In* (podcast), July 2, 2020, http://outsideinradio.org/shows/ginkgolove.

4. Nicole Alia Salis Reyes, "'What Am I Doing to Be a Good Ancestor?': An Indigenized Phenomenology of Giving Back Among Native College Graduates," *American Education Research Journal* 56, no. 3 (2019), doi:10.3102/00028 31218807180.

5. Thomas M. Phillip, Megan Bang, and Kara Jackson, "Articulating the 'How,' the 'For What,' the 'For Whom,' and the 'With Whom' in Concert: A Call to Broaden the Benchmarks of Our Scholarship," *Cognition and Instruction* 36, no. 2 (2018), doi:10.1080/07370008.2018.1413530; Eve Tuck, "Suspending Damage: A Letter to Communities," *Harvard Educational Review* 79, no. 3 (2009), doi: 10.17763/haer.79.3.n0016675661t3n15. I especially want to credit Dr. Megan Bang for encouraging me to expand my thinking.

6. Angelo Ancheta, *Race, Rights, and the Asian American Experience* (New Brunswick, NJ: Rutgers University Press, 2006); Robert S. Chang, *Disoriented: Asian Americans, Law, and the Nation-State* (New York: New York University Press, 1999).

7. Sally Chen, Douglas Lee, OiYan Poon, and Janelle Wong, "Sounding the Alarm and Reclaiming an Asian American Politics for Racial Equity," in *Asian*

*American Contemporary Activism: Movement Moments and New Visions for the 21st Century*, ed. Diane Wong and Mark Tseng-Putterman (New York: New York University Press, in press).

8. Ian Haney López, *White by Law: The Legal Construction of Race* (New York: New York University Press, 2006).

9. Haney López, *White by Law*, 31.

10. Mia Tuan, *Forever Foreigners or Honorary Whites? The Asian Ethnic Experience Today* (New Brunswick, NJ: Rutgers University Press, 1999).

11. Madeline Hsu, *The Good Immigrant: How the Yellow Peril Became the Model Minority* (Princeton, NJ: Princeton University Press, 2015); Erika Lee, *The Making of Asian America: A History* (New York: Simon & Schuster, 2015); Ellen Wu, *The Color of Success: Asian Americans and the Origins of the Model Minority* (Princeton, NJ: Princeton University Press, 2014). Each offer important historical works on Asian Americans, immigration, race, and racism.

12. Haney López, *White by Law*, 56.

13. Although Evelyn Brooks Higginbotham first coined the phrase "respectability politics" or "politics of respectability" in 1993, W. E. B. Du Bois also explored this notion in his essay "Of Mr. Booker T. Washington and Others" in *Souls of Black Folk*. Du Bois critiqued Washington and other leaders of his day for calling on African Americans to behave in accordance with White dominant norms in hopes of being socially accepted by the White powers that be.

14. Haney López, *White by Law*.

15. Haney López, *White by Law*.

16. Haney López, *White by Law*, 64.

17. Adrienne Berard, *Water Tossing Boulders: How a Family of Chinese Immigrants Led the First Fight to Desegregate Schools in the Jim Crow South* (Boston: Beacon Press, 2017), 62.

18. Berard, *Water Tossing Boulders*, 86.

19. Haney López, *White by Law*.

20. Imani Perry, "Lessons from Black and Chinese Relations in the Deep South," *The Atlantic*, June 10, 2022, https://newsletters.theatlantic.com/unsettled -territory/62a33ef133833200211f154b/mississippi-triangle-documentary -racism-in-the-jim-crow-south.

21. Perry, "Lessons from Black and Chinese Relations in the Deep South."

22. Notably, *jus soli* and *jus sanguinis* ideas of belonging and citizenship are connected to the Nazi ideologies represented by White nationalists' chants of "blood and soil" at the August 2017 "Unite the Right" rally in Charlottesville. Franklin Tanner Capps and SueJeanne Koh, "Blood Power: US v. Wong Kim Ark and the Theo-logic of Belonging," *Political Theology* 23, no. 5 (2022), doi:10 .1080/1462317X.2022.2090817.

23. However, the Trump era has emboldened those who subscribe to citizenship by *jus sanguinis* (citizenship by blood) to reinvigorate a project to make US citizenship an inherited privilege and not granted by birthplace. Jonathan M. Katz, "Birth of a Birthright," *Politico*, October 31, 2018, https://www.politico .com/magazine/story/2018/10/31/birthright-citizenship-wong-kim-ark-222098. This would notably whiten the population of US citizens. US citizenship has always been a contested racial question, with the debate more prominent in

some time periods than others. What has never been up for debate has been the White right to citizenship. This is probably what underlies all the birtherism we've seen targeting President Barack Obama, whose father was born in Kenya, and Vice President Kamala Harris, whose mother was born in India and whose father was from Jamaica. Alex Kaplan, "This Is How a Birther Smear About Oakland-Born Kamala Harris Spread Online," Media Matters for America, January 22, 2019, https://www.mediamatters.org/4chan/how-birther-smear -about-oakland-born-kamala-harris-spread-online.

24. Lau v. Nichols, 414 U.S. 563 (1974).

25. Ling-Chi Wang, "History of a Struggle for Equal and Quality Education," in *The Asian American Educational Experience: A Source Book for Teachers and Students*, ed. Don T. Nakanishi and Tina Yamano Nishida (London: Routledge, 1995), 58–94.

26. *Lau v. Nichols*.

27. Edward Steinman as cited by Haivan Hoang, *Writing Against Racial Injury: The Politics of Asian American Student Rhetoric* (Pittsburgh: University of Pittsburgh Press, 2015), 36.

28. Rachel F. Moran, "The Story of Lau v. Nichols: Breaking the Silence in Chinatown," *Education Law Stories*, ed. Michael A. Olivas and Ronna Greff Schneider (New York: Foundation Press, 2008), 111–58.

29. Victor Low, *The Unimpressible Race: A Century of Educational Struggle by the Chinese in San Francisco* (San Francisco: East/West Publishing, 1981).

30. Erika Lee, *The Making of Asian America: A History* (New York: Simon & Schuster, 2015); Hsu, *The Good Immigrant*; Wu, *The Color of Success*.

31. Kat Chow, "'Model Minority' Myth Again Used as a Racial Wedge Between Asians and Blacks," *Code Switch*, NPR, April 19, 2017, https://www .npr.org/sections/codeswitch/2017/04/19/524571669/model-minority-myth -again-used-as-a-racial-wedge-between-asians-and-blacks.

32. There is a lot written about the model minority myth, including Claire Jean Kim, *Asian Americans in an Anti-Black World* (Cambridge: Cambridge University Press, 2023); Stacey J. Lee, *Unraveling the "Model Minority" Stereotype: Listening to Asian American Youth*, 2nd ed. (New York: Teachers College Press, 2009); OiYan A. Poon, Dian Squire, Corinne Kodama, Ajani Byrd, Jason Chan, Lester Manzano, Sara Furr, and Devita Bishundat, "A Critical Review of the Model Minority Myth in Selected Literature on Asian Americans and Pacific Islanders in Higher Education," *Review of Education Research* 86, no. 2 (2016), doi:10.3102/0034654315612205; Wayne Au, "Asian American Racialization, Racial Capitalism, and the Threat of the Model Minority," *Review of Education, Pedagogy, and Cultural Studies* 44, no. 3 (2022), doi:10.3102 /0034654315612205; Iyko Day, *Alien Capital: Asian Racialization and the Logic of Settler Colonial Capitalism* (Durham, NC: Duke University Press, 2016).

33. Julie Hirschfeld Davis, "President Wants to Use Executive Order to End Birthright Citizenship," *New York Times*, October 18, 2018, https://www .nytimes.com/2018/10/30/us/politics/trump-birthright-citizenship.html.

34. Greer Mellon and Bonnie Siegler, "New Experimental Evidence on Anti-Asian Bias in White Parents' School Preferences," *Sociology of Education*, June 13, 2023, doi:10.1177/00380407231173933.

35. Amy Howe, "Coalition for TJ v. Fairfax County School Board," *SCOTUS Blog*, April 25, 2022, https://www.scotusblog.com/case-files/cases/coalition-for-tj-v-fairfax-county-school-board.

36. Association for Education Fairness v. Montgomery County Board of Education, District of Maryland, Casetext (2022); Legal Defense Fund, "Motion to Dismiss Association for Education Fairness v. Montgomery County Board of Education Granted by Federal District Court," press release, July 29, 2022, available on the Legal Defense Fund website, https://www.naacpldf.org/press-release/motion-to-dismiss-association-for-education-fairness-v-montgomery-county-board-of-education-granted-by-federal-district-court.

37. I want to credit my friend and political scientist Dr. Janelle Wong for sharing this observation with me.

38. Sociologist Charles Tilly defined this idea in his book *Durable Inequality* (Berkeley: University of California Press, 1998). His research focused on White, middle-class parents. Therefore, the concept may not be exactly fitting to describe what some Asian American parents are collectively doing through litigation. However, it doesn't feel terribly inaccurate, either.

39. John L. Rury and Aaron Tyler Rife, "Race, Schools and Opportunity Hoarding: Evidence from a Post-War American Metropolis," *Journal of the History of Education Society* 47, no. 1 (2018), doi:10.1080/0046760X.2017.1353142; Paul Hanselman and Jeremy E. Fiel, "School Opportunity Hoarding? Racial Segregation and Access to High Growth Schools," *Social Forces* 95, no. 3 (2017), doi:10.1093/sf/sow088; John B. Diamond and Amanda E. Lewis, "Opportunity Hoarding and the Maintenance of 'White' Educational Space," *American Behavioral Scientist* 66, no. 11 (2022), doi:10.1177/00027642211066048.

40. Pawan Dhingra, *Hyper Education: Why Good Schools, Good Grades, and Good Behavior Are Not Enough* (New York: New York University Press, 2020); Annette Lareau, *Unequal Childhoods: Class, Race, and Family Life* (Berkeley: University of California Press, 2011).

41. Dhingra, *Hyper Education*, 45.

42. Most non-Californians think of Southern California as perpetually sunny, but June is typically the month when marine clouds are most prevalent, hence the term "June Gloom."

43. "On the Asian Stereotype of Asian Parents Wanting Their Kids to Be Doctors," Netflix Is a Joke, YouTube, May 10, 2021, https://www.youtube.com/watch?v=DGMYP9Lgf94.

44. Daniel Kwan and Daniel Scheinert, *Everything Everywhere All At Once*, IAC Films, 2022. This idea is inspired by the scene where Alpha Waymond is explaining the multiverse of realities to Evelyn: "Every rejection, every disappointment has led you here to this moment. Don't let anything distract you from it."

## CHAPTER 2: COMMONALITIES ACROSS THE AFFIRMATIVE ACTION DIVIDE

1. Peggy Orenstein, *Cinderella Ate My Daughter: Dispatches from the Front Lines of the New Girlie-Girl Culture* (New York: HarperCollins, 2011).

2. Yao Ming, Wat Misaka, and Rex Walters, among others.

3. Even as a Celtics fan, I couldn't help but get swept up in the excitement of seeing the flashy play of a fellow Asian American. I even posted on Facebook

suggesting what Ben & Jerry's ice cream flavor should be named in Lin's honor, and why.

4. Mark Viera, "For Lin, Erasing a History of Being Overlooked," *New York Times*, February 12, 2012, https://www.nytimes.com/2012/02/13/sports/basketball/for-knicks-lin-erasing-a-history-of-being-overlooked.html.

5. Chuck Culpepper, "An All-Around Talent, Obscured by His Pedigree," *New York Times*, September 14, 2010, https://www.nytimes.com/2010/09/15/sports/basketball/15nba.html.

6. "Linsanity: Jeremy Lin's Rise to Stardom," *60 Minutes*, CBS News, April 8, 2013, https://www.cbsnews.com/news/linsanity-jeremy-lins-rise-to-stardom.

7. Robert T. Teranishi, "The Attitudes of Asian Americans Toward Affirmative Action," National Commission on AAPI Research in Education (CARE), 2012, http://care.gseis.ucla.edu/wp-content/uploads/2015/08/CARE-affirmative_action_polling-1v2.pdf. In 1996 California voters passed Proposition 209, which banned all considerations of race in employment, public contracting, and education. The majority of all voters of color, including Asian Americans, voted to reject the ballot measure.

8. It was defeated by an activist movement led primarily by Chinese Americans.

9. Clare Jean Kim, "Are Asians the New Blacks? Affirmative Action, Anti-Blackness, and the 'Sociometry' of Race," *Du Bois Review* 15, no. 2 (2018), doi:10.1017/S1742058X18000243.

10. William C. Kidder and Jay Rosner, "How the SAT Creates Built-In Headwinds: An Educational and Legal Analysis of Disparate Impact," in *The Scandal of Standardized Tests: Why We Need to Drop the SAT and ACT*, ed. Joseph A. Soares (New York: Teachers College Press, 2020), 48–75.

11. Julie J. Park and Amanda E. Assalone, "Over 40%: Asian Americans and the Road(s) to Community Colleges," *Community College Review* 47, no. 3 (2019), doi:10.1177/0091552119852161; Robert T. Teranishi, Miguel Ceja, Anthony Lising Antonio, Walter Recharde Allen, and Patricia M. McDonough, "The College-Choice Process for Asian Pacific Americans: Ethnicity and Socioeconomic Class in Context," *Review of Higher Education* 27, no. 4 (2004), doi:10.1353/rhe.2004.0025.

12. Kristen Surla and OiYan A. Poon, "Visualizing Social Influences on Filipino American and Southeast Asian American College Choice," *Journal of Southeast Asian American Education and Advancement* 10, no. 2 (2014), doi:10.7771/2153-8999.1132; Robert T. Teranishi, *Asians in the Ivory Tower: Dilemmas of Racial Inequality in American Higher Education* (New York: Teachers College Press, 2010).

13. This is what a friendly acquaintance, who identifies as an affirmative action supporter, texted me in spring 2019.

14. Gabriel Chin, Sumi Cho, Jerry Kang, and Frank Wu, "Beyond Self-Interest: Asian Pacific Americans Toward a Community of Justice: A Policy Analysis of Affirmative Action," *UCLA Asian Pacific American Law Journal* 4 (1996): 129–62.

15. OiYan A. Poon and Ester Sihite, "Racial Anxieties: Asian Americans, Selective College Admissions, and Questions of Racial Equity in Affirmative

Action Policies," in *Contemporary Asian America: A Multidisciplinary Reader*, ed. Min Zhou and Anthony C. Ocampo (New York: New York University Press, 2016); Julie J. Park, *Race on Campus: Debunking Myths with Data* (Cambridge, MA: Harvard Education Press, 2018); Daniel Kahneman, *Thinking, Fast and Slow* (New York: Farrar, Straus & Giroux, 2011).

16. Law and higher education professor Liliana Garces and I traced the history of these federal cases and rulings, if readers would like to get into some of the weeds of how the law evolved through 2016. Liliana M. Garces and OiYan Poon, *Asian Americans and Race-Conscious Admissions: Understanding the Conservative Opposition's Strategy of Misinformation, Intimidation and Racial Division* (Los Angeles: UCLA Civil Rights Project/Proyecto Derechos Civiles, 2018), https://bit.ly/3dNLiI7.

17. See, for example, Michael J. Dumas, "Against the Dark: Antiblackness in Education Policy and Discourse," *Theory into Practice* 55, no. 1 (2016), doi:10.1080/00405841.2016.1116852; Eve L. Ewing, *Ghosts in the Schoolyard: Racism and School Closings on Chicago's South Side* (Chicago: University of Chicago Press, 2018); Connie Wun, "Angered: Black and Non-Black Girls of Color at the Intersections of Violence and School Discipline in the United States," *Race Ethnicity and Education* 21, no. 4 (2018), doi:10.1080/13613324.2016.1248829.

18. Regents of the University of California v. Bakke, 438 U.S. 265 (1978), 307.

19. Aamer Rahman, "Aamer Rahman (Fear of a Brown Planet)—Reverse Racism," YouTube, November 28, 2013, https://youtu.be/dw_mRaIHb-M.

20. Devon W. Carbado, "Footnote 43: Recovering Justice Powell's Anti-Preference Framing of Affirmative Action," *UC Davis Law Review* 53, no. 1117 (2019), https://lawreview.law.ucdavis.edu/issues/53/2/essays/files/53-2_Carbado.pdf.

21. Nolan L. Cabrera, "White Immunity: Working Through Some of the Pedagogical Pitfalls of 'Privilege,'" *Journal Committed to Social Change on Race and Ethnicity* 3, no. 1 (2017), https://www.jstor.org/stable/48644492.

22. "Essential Blue Eyed," transcript, California Newsreel, http://newsreel.org/transcripts/essenblue.htm, accessed February 10, 2023.

23. *Regents of the University of California v. Bakke*, 317.

24. Dana Y. Takagi, *The Retreat from Race: Asian-American Admissions and Racial Politics* (New Brunswick, NJ: Rutgers University Press, 1992), xii.

25. German Lopez, "Why You Should Stop Saying 'All Lives Matter,' Explained in 9 Different Ways," *Vox*, July 11, 2016, https://www.vox.com/2016/7/11/12136140/black-all-lives-matter.

26. Kimberly Reyes, "Affirmative Action Shouldn't Be About Diversity," *The Atlantic*, December 27, 2018, https://www.theatlantic.com/ideas/archive/2018/12/affirmative-action-about-reparations-not-diversity/578005.

27. Gratz v. Bollinger, 539 U.S. 244 (2003), 22–23.

28. Grutter v. Bollinger, 539 U.S. 306 (2003), 22.

29. Garces and Poon, *Asian Americans and Race-Conscious Admissions*, 11.

30. Otoniel Jimenez Morfin, Victor Pérez, Laurence Parker, Marvin Lynn, and John Arrona, "Hiding the Politically Obvious: A Critical Race Theory

Preview of Diversity as Racial Neutrality in Higher Education," *Educational Policy* 20 (2006): 1, doi:10.1177/0895904805285785.

31. Stephanie Mencimer, "Here's the Next Sleeper Challenge to Affirmative Action," *Mother Jones*, July 19, 2016, https://www.motherjones.com/politics /2016/07/abigail-fisher-going-stay-mad.

32. Stephanie Mencimer, "Meet the Brains Behind the Effort to Get the Supreme Court to Rethink Civil Rights," *Mother Jones*, March/April 2016, https:// www.motherjones.com/politics/2016/04/edward-blum-supreme-court-affirmative -action-civil-rights; Sarah Hinger, "Meet Edward Blum, the Man Who Wants to Kill Affirmative Action in Higher Education," ACLU, October 18, 2018, https:// www.aclu.org/blog/racial-justice/affirmative-action/meet-edward-blum-man-who -wants-kill-affirmative-action-higher.

33. Liliana M. Garces and Uma Jayakumar, "Dynamic Diversity: Toward a Contextual Understanding of Critical Mass," *Educational Researcher* 43, no. 3 (2014), doi:10.3102/0013189X14529.

34. OiYan Poon, "Edward Blum: 'I Needed Asian Plaintiffs,'" YouTube, July 30, 2018, https://www.youtube.com/watch?v=DiBvo-05JRg.

35. *SFFA v. Harvard*, No. 19-2005 (1st Cir. 2020), 119.

36. Some would point out that Calvin Yang, a Chinese Canadian and sophomore at UC Berkeley, spoke alongside Ed Blum praising the Supreme Court ruling in June 2023. I would point out that when Blum filed the SFFA lawsuits in 2014, Calvin was barely a high school student in Canada who had yet to apply to college. To be sure, there were probably Asian American members of SFFA. I'm not sure they were members in 2014. Moreover, it remains factual that not one Asian American served as a plaintiff or testified on the side of SFFA in these cases.

37. In a very special mommy-and-daughter trip, Té Té and I traveled to Washington, DC, that Halloween to be with friends and colleagues in the fight for racial equity and justice during the oral arguments. "Chicago Professor Among Pro–Affirmative Action Demonstrators at Supreme Court," ABC 7 Eyewitness News, https://abc7chicago.com/supreme-court-justices-oral-arguments -today-affirmative-action-unc/12402805/.

38. Students for Fair Admissions, Inc. v. President and Fellows of Harvard College, 600 U.S. ___ (2023). (Majority opinion, Note 4).

39. Students for Fair Admissions, Inc. v. President and Fellows of Harvard College, 600 U.S. ___ (2023). (Justice Jackson dissenting, 29).

40. SFFA, Inc. v. Harvard, 600 U.S. ___ (2003). (Majority opinion, 39).

41. Daniel Hirschman and Ellen Berrey, "The Partial Deinstitutionalization of Affirmative Action in U.S. Higher Education, 1988 to 2014," *Sociological Science* 4 (August 28, 2017): 449–68, doi 10.15195/v4.a18.

42. Liliana Garces and colleagues encourage higher education leaders not to fall into patterns of repressive legalism. Frank Fernandez and Liliana M. Garces, "The Influence of Repressive Legalism on Admissions," in *Rethinking College Admissions: Research-Based Practice and Policy*, ed. OiYan A. Poon and Michael N. Bastedo (Cambridge, MA: Harvard Education Press, 2022), 3–18.

43. Margaret M. Chin, OiYan Poon, Janelle Wong, and Jerry Park, "Here Are TEN Reasons NOT to Fall for the 'Asian American Penalty' Trap in Admis-

sions!" *Medium*, February 23, 2019, https://medium.com/@dddefenddiversitydd
/anti-asian-american-bias-exists-but-here-are-ten-reasons-not-to-fall-for-the
-asian-american-71ef01195189.

44. See Julie Park's excellent 2018 book, *Race on Campus*, for all the ways
the notion of mismatch is a myth.

45. Park, *Race on Campus*.

46. After our interview, I explained to Tina that race-conscious admissions
policy and practices did not place a limit, or quota, on Asian American college
admissions, and that they did not create an inflexible preference for non-Asian
minority students.

47. Lyndon B. Johnson, "To Fulfill These Rights," transcript of speech delivered at Howard University, June 4, 1965, available at https://teachingamerican
history.org/document/commencement-address-at-howard-university-to-fulfill
-these-rights.

48. For example, Eric shared with me that he believed that "until we can
improve our K–12 system in which all students can ensure they get an equal access
to education and resources it would be difficult to [assume a level field of competi-
tion] because simply put already at the start . . . every student's educational opportunity is already pretty much almost determined by where their parents live. If you
don't live in a good [school] district it would be much harder for you to actually do
better than someone in a better district. Obviously hard work plays into that too as
well. I'm not saying that students born in poor districts can't achieve as much but
they definitely have a larger burden to take on. They definitely have more to take
on than students in a better district. That makes it ultimately harder for them to do
better. When we see that they achieve, it becomes a monumental success."

49. Michael N. Bastedo, Nicholas A. Bowman, Kristen M. Glasener, and
Jandi L. Kelly, "What Are We Talking About When We Talk About Holistic
Review? Selective College Admissions and Its Effects on Low-SES Students,"
*Journal of Higher Education* 89, no. 5 (2018): 785.

50. Kang uses "first-generation" to mean US-born child of immigrants.
Throughout this book, I generally use the term "second-generation" when
referring to US-born children of immigrants and "first-generation" in reference
to the immigrant generation, in alignment with social science research in Asian
American studies.

51. Jay Caspian Kang, "Where Does Affirmative Action Leave Asian-
Americans?" *New York Times Magazine*, August 28, 2019, https://www.nytimes
.com/2019/08/28/magazine/where-does-affirmative-action-leave-asian-americans
.html.

52. Thomas J. Espenshade and Chang Y. Chung, "The Opportunity Cost of
Admission Preferences at Elite Universities," *Social Science Quarterly* 86, no. 2
(2005): 303–4.

53. Cass Cliatt, "Thomas Espenshade: Perspective On: Affirmative Action
and the Racial Achievement Gap," Princeton University, January 14, 2010,
https://www.princeton.edu/news/2010/01/14/perspective-affirmative-action
-and-racial-achievement-gap.

54. Bastedo et al., "What Are We Talking About When We Talk About Holistic Review?"

55. In his speech, Atkinson shared that he "recommended that all campuses move away from admission processes that use narrowly defined quantitative formulas and instead adopt procedures that look at applicants in a comprehensive way. While this recommendation is intended to provide a fairer basis on which to make admission decisions, it would also help ensure that standardized tests do not have an undue influence but rather are used to illuminate the student's total record." Richard C. Atkinson, *The Pursuit of Knowledge: Speeches and Papers of Richard C. Atkinson*, ed. Patricia A. Pelfrey (Berkeley: University of California Press, 2007), 138.

56. Although research and punditry have often noted the declines in African American and Latinx students at the UC, as a student affairs professional at UC Davis (2002–5) I also witnessed drastic declines in Southeast Asian American and Pacific Islander student admission rates and enrollment numbers, which were rarely if ever discussed.

57. Fisher v. University of Texas, 579 U.S. 365 (2016), 17.

58. William C. Kidder and Jay Rosner, "How the SAT Creates Built-In Headwinds: An Educational and Legal Analysis of Disparate Impact," in *The Scandal of Standardized Tests: Why We Need to Drop the SAT and ACT*, ed. Joseph A. Soares (New York: Teachers College Press, 2020), 48–75.

59. I interviewed fifty admissions professionals at colleges and universities practicing race-conscious admissions with admit rates of less than 40 percent. The guiding question for this study was "How does race-conscious holistic admissions work?"

60. In this section of the chapter, I provide insights on how race-conscious admissions worked based on a study published in 2023. OiYan Poon, Douglas H. Lee, Eileen Galvez, Joanne Song Engler, Bri Sérráno, Ali Raza, Jessica M. Hurtado, and Nikki Kahealani Chun, "A Möbius Model of Racialized Organizations: Durability of Racial Inequalities in Admissions," *Journal of Higher Education*, April 25, 2023, doi:10.1080/00221546.2023.2203630.

61. Some media reports suggest that some Asian American college applicants choose not to identify their racial or ethnic background as a strategy to improve their chances of selective college admission. Jesse Washington, "Some Asians' College Strategy: Don't Check 'Asian,'" Associated Press, December 3, 2011, http://archive.boston.com/news/nation/articles/2011/12/03/some_asians _college_strategy_dont_check_asian.

62. *Fisher v. University of Texas*, 19.

63. Poon et al., "Möbius Model of Racialized Organizations."

64. Anthony Carnevale and Michael C. Quinn, *Selective Bias: Asian Americans, Test Scores, and Holistic Admissions* (Washington, DC: Georgetown University, 2021), https://cew.georgetown.edu/cew-reports/selectivebias.

65. Joshua Grossman, Sabina Tomkins, Lindsay C. Page, and Sharad Goel, "The Disparate Impacts of College Admissions Policies on Asian American Applicants," National Bureau of Economic Research, Working Paper 31527 (2023), doi:10.3386/w31527.

66. Kimmy Yam, "Most Asian Americans Favor Affirmative Action, New Pew Study Shows," NBC News, June 9, 2023, https://www.nbcnews.com/news/asian -america/asian-americans-favor-affirmative-action-pew-study-shows-rcna88614.

## CHAPTER 3: COMMUNITY DIVIDES

1. Brandon Johnson, "On the Issues," Brandon for Chicago, Friends of Brandon Johnson, https://www.brandonforchicago.com/on-the-issues, accessed May 20, 2023.

2. Sarah Schulte, "Chicago Mayoral Election: How Johnson, Vallas Differ on Dealing with Crime, Policing," ABC7, March 31, 2023, https://abc7chicago.com/chicago-mayoral-election-2023-crime-police-department-paul-vallas/13059762.

3. Julie J. Park and Amy Liu, "Interest Convergence or Divergence? A Critical Race Analysis of Asian Americans, Meritocracy, and Critical Mass in the Affirmative Action Debate," *Journal of Higher Education* 85, no. 1 (October 31, 2016): 36–64, doi:10.1080/00221546.2014.11777318.

4. It is important to remember that "Asian American" is a panethnic identity that also includes South Asian Americans. In other historical moments, anti-Asian racism has targeted South Asian Americans, such as the spike in racist violence following 9/11 and the 2012 mass shooting targeting a Sikh temple in Oak Creek, Wisconsin. In this chapter introduction I am referring specifically to anti-Asian racism targeting people who might appear Chinese.

5. Russell Jeung, Aggie J. Yellow Horse, and Charlene Cayanan, *Stop AAPI Hate National Report* (San Francisco: Stop AAPI Hate, 2021), https://stopaapihate.org/wp-content/uploads/2021/05/Stop-AAPI-Hate-Report-National-210506.pdf.

6. Neil G. Ruiz, Khadijah Edwards, and Mark Hugo Lopez, "One-Third of Asian Americans Fear Threats, Physical Attacks and Most Say Violence Against Them Is Rising," Pew Research Center, April 21, 2021, https://www.pewresearch.org/fact-tank/2021/04/21/one-third-of-asian-americans-fear-threats-physical-attacks-and-most-say-violence-against-them-is-rising.

7. SAALT, "Post 9-11 Backlash," https://saalt.org/policy-change/post-9-11-backlash.

8. Naseeb Bhangal and OiYan Poon, "Are Asian Americans White? Or People of Color?" *Yes!*, January 15, 2020, https://www.yesmagazine.org/social-justice/2020/01/15/asian-americans-people-of-color.

9. Cathy Park Hong, *Minor Feelings: An Asian American Racial Reckoning* (New York: One World, 2020), 56.

10. In my own life, I remember texting with Asian American friends about our fears and getting through them with humor where we could find it. For example, in late March 2020 my friend Joanna Lee texted me, "My garage door won't open so it's like a sign telling me to stay home with my mild cough cuz of Coronavirus racism." In response, I texted, "Stay home!!! The racism outside is bad." She quipped back at me, "Racism Forecast: Moderate to severe anti-Asian racism today." And we both texted a mess of laughing and crying emojis. I am reminded by my friend and colleague, Dr. Badia Ahad-Legardy (author of *Afro-Nostalgia: Feeling Good in Contemporary Black Culture*) that our lives are more than trauma, and that getting through trauma requires a practice of joy and love.

11. I say seemingly because there are conflicting reports about whether there has been an actual increase in violent assaults or really a consciousness of these incidents. Kimmy Yam, "One-Third of Asian Americans Fear Someone Might

Threaten or Physically Attack Them, Survey Finds," NBC News, April 22, 2021, https://www.nbcnews.com/news/asian-america/one-third-asian-americans-fear -someone-might-threaten-or-physically-n1265016.

12. VietRISE, "Vietnamese and Asian American Organizations Across the Country Denounce Upcoming March 15 Deportation Flight to Viet Nam, Say Deporting Refugees Is Anti-Asian Violence," press release, March 12, 2021, https://vietrise.org/vietnamese-and-asian-american-organizations-across-the -country-denounce-upcoming-march-15-deportation-flight-to-viet-nam-say -deporting-refugees-is-anti-asian-violence.

13. "Indianapolis FedEx Shooting: Who Were the Eight Victims?" BBC News, April 18, 2021, https://www.bbc.com/news/world-us-canada-56789254.

14. Not to mention the uptick in racial violence that has targeted non-Asian people of color in the same year.

15. I will not name and shame people, but I will say that I have heard and read comments by prominent national leaders—both Asian American and not— who have, likely unintentionally, perpetuated this ahistorical narrative.

16. Chris Iijima, "Asian Song," *Back to Back*, 1982, available at Sound-Cloud, https://soundcloud.com/buzzlightyearsu/chris-iijima-asian-song.

17. Homewordsound, "We Belong '21 [Music Video]—Magnetic North & Taiyo Na (feat. Ann One/prod. by Chucky Kim)," YouTube, May 19, 2021, https://www.youtube.com/watch?v=2k8euwSwXWU.

18. I use the term "1.5 generation" to describe people who immigrated as young children. Culturally, they are in between the first-generation immigrants—those who migrated as adults—and the second generation—the US-born children of immigrants. Mary Yu Danico, *The 1.5 Generation: Becoming Korean American in Hawaii* (Honolulu: University of Hawaii Press, 2004).

19. Park and Liu, "Interest Convergence or Divergence?"

20. Michele S. Moses, *Living with Moral Disagreement: The Enduring Controversy About Affirmative Action* (Chicago: University of Chicago Press, 2016).

21. Natasha Warikoo, *The Diversity Bargain: And Other Dilemmas of Race, Admissions, and Meritocracy at Elite Universities* (Chicago: University of Chicago Press, 2016), 45.

22. OiYan A. Poon, Megan S. Segoshi, Lilianne Tang, Kristen L. Surla, Caressa Nguyen, and Dian D. Squire, "Asian Americans, Affirmative Action, and the Political Economy of Racism: A Multidimensional Model of Raceclass Frames," *Harvard Educational Review*, 89, no. 2 (2019), doi:10.17763/1943 -5045-89.2.201.

23. Eduardo Bonilla-Silva, *Racism Without Racists: Color-Blind Racism and the Persistence of Racial Inequality in America*, 3rd ed. (New York: Rowman & Littlefield, 2009). I use Bonilla-Silva's race frame of abstract liberalism to categorize one of the two worldviews found among Asian American affirmative action opponents. Abstract liberals tend to use classically liberal ideas (e.g., equal opportunity and individualism) to explain racial disparities.

24. Some of my most progressive friends and I have confessed to each other that when we first registered to vote, we registered as Republicans. For example, Dr. Patrick Camangian, a well-regarded and accomplished education scholar, shared his own story in an official university video celebrating his scholarship,

teaching, and leadership. The video starts with him stating, "I don't think most of my students would know that in one point in my life, I used to be a hard-core Rush Limbaugh follower." This quote is then contrasted with his work and career in advancing racial justice and equity in education. "Meet the Faculty: Patrick Camangian," University of San Francisco, June 14, 2012, https://www .youtube.com/watch?v=qSLj7X1mztY.

25. Liliana M. Garces and Uma M. Jayakumar, "Dynamic Diversity: Toward a Contextual Understanding of Critical Mass," *Educational Researcher* 43, no. 2 (2014), doi:10.3102/0013189X14529814.

26. A basic awareness of the history of struggle for education rights among Black, Indigenous, Latinx, Asian American, and other racially minoritized people would point out how preposterous this racial frame is. Plus, there is an abundance of research that counters this worldview. See, for example, Amanda R. Tachine, *Native Presence and Sovereignty in College: Sustaining Indigenous Weapons to Defeat Systemic Monsters* (New York: Teachers College Press, 2022); Richard R. Valencia, "'Mexican Americans Don't Value Education!': On the Basis of the Myth, Mythmaking, and Debunking," *Journal of Latinos and Education* 1, no. 2 (November 13, 2009): 81–103, doi:10.1207/S1532771XJLE 0102_2; Lauren M. Wells, *There Are No Deficits Here: Disrupting Anti-Blackness in Education* (Thousand Oaks, CA: Corwin Press, 2023).

27. For example, Dean—one of the policy supporters I interviewed—is a Chinese American immigrant who is very active on WeChat. Additionally, during the 2020 California election, notable numbers of Chinese American immigrants actively worked with Chinese for Affirmative Action and a statewide cross-racial coalition to support and advocate for Prop 16 (i.e., a ballot measure aimed at overturning Prop 209, California's affirmative action ban) on WeChat.

28. Terry Stancheva, "21 Mind-Blowing WeChat Statistics in 2021," Review 42, March 31, 2021, https://review42.com/resources/wechat-statistics/#:~:text =WeChat%20has%201%20billion%20monthly,million%20users%20in%20 Q4%202019.

29. Steven Chen, "An Elephant in a China Shop," *Medium*, March 5, 2018, https://medium.com/@crwstrategy/an-elephant-in-a-china-shop-d69c6fccf944.

30. Janelle Wong, S. Karthick Ramakrishnan, Taeku Lee, and Jane Junn, *Asian American Political Participation: Emerging Constituents and Their Political Identities* (New York: Russell Sage, 2011).

31. Aaron Couch, "White House Addresses Jimmy Kimmel's China Joke," *Hollywood Reporter*, January 10, 2014, https://www.hollywoodreporter.com/tv /tv-news/white-house-addresses-jimmy-kimmels-670005.

32. This statement is untrue. See chapter 2.

33. Shout out to Cathy Dang and the team at CAAAV who fearlessly stood up for Akai Gurley's family. Read more about Dang's leadership in Ariella Rotramel, *Pushing Back: Women of Color-Led Grassroots Activism in New York City* (Athens: University of Georgia Press, 2020).

34. Donatella Porta and Alice Mattoni, "Social Movements," in *The International Encyclopedia of Political Communication*, ed. Gianpietro Mazzoleni (West Sussex: John Wiley & Sons, 2015).

35. Chi Zhang, *WeChatting American Politics: Misinformation, Polarization, and Immigrant Chinese Media* (New York: Tow Center for Digital Journalism, 2018), https://www.cjr.org/tow_center_reports/wechatting-american-politics-misinformation-polarization-and-immigrant-chinese-media.php.

36. Cathy Park Hong, "How Fake News Is Hatching in Immigrant Communities," *New York Times*, December 20, 2020, https://www.nytimes.com/2020/12/20/opinion/fake-news-disinformation-immigrants.html.

37. Jennifer Lee, Janelle Wong, and Karthick Ramakrishnan, "Asian Americans Support for Affirmative Action Increased since 2016," *AAPI Data* (blog), February 4, 2021, http://aapidata.com/blog/affirmative-action-increase; Anemona Hartocollis and Ted Siefer, "On Eve of Harvard Bias Trial, Dueling Rallies Show Rifts among Asian-Americans," *New York Times*, October 14, 2018, https://www.nytimes.com/2018/10/14/us/harvard-protest-affirmative-action.html.

38. OiYan Poon and Janelle Wong, "The Generational Divide on Affirmative Action," *Inside Higher Ed*, February 25, 2019, https://www.insidehighered.com/admissions/views/2019/02/25/views-chinese-americans-affirmative-action-vary-age-opinion.

39. Connie Wun, "Ignoring the History of Anti-Asian Racism Is Another Form of Violence," *Elle*, March 1, 2021, https://www.elle.com/culture/career-politics/a35635188/anti-asian-racism-history-violence/.

40. Vigilant Love, https://www.vigilantlove.org.

41. Asian American Pacific Islander Women Lead (AAPI Women Lead), "#YuriTaughtUS feat. Eddy Zheng," May 19, 2020, https://www.imreadymovement.org/post/yuritaughtus-feat-eddy-zheng. For New Breath Foundation, see https://new-breath.org.

42. Alicia Garza, "Wrap It Up and Back It Up with Dr. Connie Wun," *Lady Don't Take No* (podcast), April 2, 2021, https://lady-dont-take-no.simplecast.com/episodes/wrap-it-up-and-back-it-up-with-dr-connie-wun-BKYcCgtk.

43. Kat Chow, "Grace Lee Boggs, Activist and American Revolutionary, Turns 100," *NPR Code Switch*, June 27, 2015, https://www.npr.org/sections/codeswitch/2015/06/27/417175523/grace-lee-boggs-activist-and-american-revolutionary-turns-100.

44. "Detroit Activist, Philosopher Grace Lee Boggs: 'The Only Way to Survive Is by Taking Care of One Another,'" transcript, *Democracy Now!*, April 2, 2010, https://www.democracynow.org/2010/4/2/grace_lee_boggs. All Boggs quotations are from this source.

45. Jason Wu and James McMaster, "Hate-Crime Laws Are Not the Answer to Anti-Asian Violence, Abolition Is," *Teen Vogue*, April 28, 2021, https://www.teenvogue.com/story/anti-asian-hate-crimes-bill-abolition.

46. Mari Matsuda, "Critical Race Theory Is Not Anti-Asian," *Reappropriate*, March 12, 2021, http://reappropriate.co/2021/03/mari-matsuda-critical-race-theory-is-not-anti-asian; Bryan Mena, "Ted Cruz Changes Course and Votes to Support Bill to Address Hate Crimes Against Asian Americans," *Texas Tribune*, April 22, 2021, https://www.texastribune.org/2021/04/22/ted-cruz-asian-american-hate-crimes-vote.

## CHAPTER 4: "IF NOT ME THEN WHO?"

1. The antithesis of Viet Nguyen's concept of narrative plenitude is narrative scarcity.

2. These are just some examples from *People* magazine.

3. I hadn't yet learned about the racist and settler-colonial histories of US higher education. Craig Steven Wilder, *Ebony and Ivy: Race, Slavery, and the Troubled History of America's Universities* (New York: Bloomsbury, 2013); Leigh Patel, *No Study Without Struggle: Confronting Settler Colonialism in Higher Education* (Boston: Beacon Press, 2021).

4. Keitaro Okura, "Stereotype Promise: Racialized Teacher Appraisals of Asian American Academic Achievement," *Sociology of Education* 95 (2022): 302–19.

5. I am convinced that my teachers and school administrators would have punished me had I been a boy, Black, Latinx, Native American, Pacific Islander, or Southeast Asian, based on research documenting disproportionately high rates of school discipline enacted on these populations. For example, see Dolly M. D. Nguyen, Pedro Noguera, Nathan Adkins, and Robert T. Teranishi, "Ethnic Discipline Gap: Unseen Dimensions of Racial Disproportionality in School Discipline," *American Educational Research Journal* 56 (2019): 1973–2003.

6. My dad has a college degree and was a chemical engineer who was often passed over for promotions, because he spoke English with an accent. His supervisors encouraged him to take accent reduction classes. Faced with these xenophobic linguistic barriers at his place of employment, he would regularly pursue new entrepreneurial projects that were rarely profitable. My mom earned a GED after immigrating to the US, and mostly she worked as a seamstress for local dry-cleaning businesses and garment factories.

7. New Order's *Bizarre Love Triangle* has been hailed as the Asian American anthem by some Gen-X Asian Americans. Esther Wang, "How Can I Explain: An Incomplete Oral History of Asian Americans and Our Ineffable Love of New Wave," *Jezebel*, January 25, 2021, https://jezebel.com/how-can-i-explain-an-incomplete-oral-history-of-asian-1845911631.

8. Nana Osei-Kofi, Lisette E. Torres, and Joyce Lui, "Practices of Whiteness: Racialization in College Admissions Viewbooks," *Race Ethnicity and Education* 16 (2013): 386–405.

9. Even though I didn't get into my top-choice colleges, I was still admitted to several selective colleges and universities. Beyond my feelings getting hurt, my postsecondary educational pathway and career trajectory were not harmed. Not getting into an Ivy League institution was not the same as not going to college. Mike Hoa Nguyen and colleagues make a similar argument with empirical evidence. Mike Hoa Nguyen, Connie Y. Chang, Victoria Kim, Rose Ann E. Gutierrez, Annie Le, Denis Dumas, and Robert T. Teranishi, "Asian Americans, Admissions, and College Choice: An Empirical Test of Claims of Harm Used in Federal Investigations," *Educational Researcher* 49 (2020): 579–94.

10. Dana Y. Takagi, *The Retreat from Race: Asian-American Admissions and Racial Politics* (New Brunswick, NJ: Rutgers University Press, 1992).

11. OiYan Poon, "Edward Blum: 'I Needed Asian Plaintiffs,'" YouTube, July 30, 2018, https://www.youtube.com/watch?v=DiBvo-05JRg.

12. Sumi Cho first coined the term "racial mascot" to describe how White anti-equity forces used stereotypes of high-achieving Asian Americans as a discursive tool against campaigns for racial equity. Sumi Cho, "Redeeming Whiteness in the Shadow of Internment: Earl Warren, Brown, and a Theory of Racial Redemption," *Boston College Third World Law Journal* 19 (1998): 73–170.

13. OiYan A. Poon and Megan S. Segoshi, "The Racial Mascot Speaks: A Critical Race Discourse Analysis of Asian Americans and Fisher vs. University of Texas," *Review of Higher Education* 42 (2018): 235–67.

14. I paid this advice forward to my friend Dr. Anthony Ocampo. Leading up to the 2020 US presidential election, he was shocked to learn about a Filipinos for Trump rally near his home in Southern California. Anthony C. Ocampo, "I Went to a 'Filipinos for Trump' Rally. Here's What I Found," *Colorlines*, October 16, 2020, https://colorlines.com/article/i-went-filipinos-trump-rally -heres-what-i-found.

15. Sally Chen, Douglas Lee, OiYan Poon, and Janelle Wong, "Sounding the Alarm and Reclaiming an Asian American Politics for Racial Equity," in *Asian American Rising: Movement Visions and New Directions in the 21st Century*, ed. Diane Wong and Mark Tseng-Putterman (New York: New York University Press, forthcoming).

16. I use rejective to describe colleges that reject more applicants than they admit. In this case, Eric's college rejects over 90 percent of applicants each year.

17. I have provided a description, instructions, and materials for the activity in appendix A (found online at beacon.org/PoonAppendix).

18. Eduardo Bonilla-Silva, *Racism without Racists: Color-Blind Racism and the Persistence of Racial Inequality in the United States* (New York: Rowman & Littlefield, 2006).

19. This is changing. Starting with the high school graduating class of 2030, California is requiring all students to take at least one semester of an ethnic studies class to earn their diploma. Megan Tagami, "California High Schools Are Adding Hundreds of Ethnic Studies Classes. Are Teachers Prepared?" *CalMatters*, March 29, 2023, https://calmatters.org/education/higher-education /college-beat-higher-education/2023/03/california-high-schools-ethnic-studies.

20. Researchers have long documented school racial segregation through tracking. Dania V. Francis and William A. Darity, "Separate and Unequal Under One Roof: How the Legacy of Racialized Tracking Perpetuates Within-School Segregation," *RSF: The Russell Sage Foundation Journal of the Social Sciences* 7 (2021): 187–202.

21. Edward Iwata, "Is It a Clash over Writing . . . ," *Los Angeles Times*, June 24, 1990, https://www.latimes.com/archives/la-xpm-1990-06-24-vw-1117-story .html, accessed January 30, 2023.

22. Christine E. Sleeter, "Critical Race Theory and the Whiteness of Teacher Education," *Urban Education* 52 (2017): 155–69.

23. Juliana Kim, "Florida Says AP Class Teaches Critical Race Theory. Here's What's Really in the Course," NPR, January 22, 2023, https://www.npr .org/2023/01/22/1150259944/florida-rejects-ap-class-african-american-studies.

24. Interestingly, just four years after this interview, the University of California announced that it had admitted more Latinx students than ever before,

making them the largest ethnic group of admitted freshmen. Still, the numbers of California's Latinx college-eligible students are not what one would expect in the University of California in bias-free conditions. To my knowledge, there are no Latinx community-led calls to action against affirmative action.

25. South Cove Community Health Center was founded by Asian Americans in Boston Chinatown in 1972 to serve the healthcare needs of the community. My paternal grandparents and immigrant elders have benefited from their services and programs.

26. Sharon S. Lee, "Over-Represented and De-Minoritized: The Racialization of Asian Americans in Higher Education," *InterActions: UCLA Journal of Education and Information Studies* (2006), doi:10.5070/D422000574.

27. Clara L. Wilkins, Joseph D. Wellman, Laura G. Babbitt, Negin R. Toosi, and Katherine D. Schad, "You Can Win but I Can't Lose: Bias Against High-Status Groups Increases Their Zero-Sum Beliefs About Discrimination," *Journal of Experimental Social Psychology* 57 (2015): 1–14.

28. Howard Shih and Rimsha Khan, *Hidden in Plain Sight: Asian Poverty in the New York Metro Area* (New York: Asian American Federation, 2021), https://www.aafederation.org/hidden-in-plainsight-asian-poverty-in-the-new-york -metro-area.

29. Marco Castillo, *Poverty in New York City: Social, Demographic and Spatial Characteristics, 1990–2019*, ed. Sebastián Villamizar-Santamaría (New York: Center for Latin American, Caribbean and Latino Studies at the CUNY Graduate Center, 2022), https://clacls.gc.cuny.edu/2022/11/28/latinos-continue -to-have-the-highest-poverty-rates-of-all-race-and-ethnic-groups-in-new -york-city.

30. Coalition for Asian American Children and Families, "New York City's Specialized High School Discovery Program Is a Step in the Right Direction but Is Not Enough," press release, April 11, 2019, https://www.cacf.org/resources /new-york-citys-specialized-high-school-discovery-program-is-a-step-in-the -right-direction-but-is-not-enough.

31. Claire Jean Kim, *Asian Americans in an Anti-Black World* (Cambridge: Cambridge University Press, 2023).

32. In my work interviewing college admissions officers about how race-conscious holistic admissions worked, I learned that they understood the importance of understanding students as individuals with multiple identities, whose contexts of educational opportunity were shaped by intersecting social and political systems.

33. Anthony P. Carnevale and Michael C. Quinn, *Selective Bias: Asian Americans, Test Scores, and Holistic Admissions* (Washington, DC: Georgetown University Center on Education and the Workforce, 2021), cew.georgetown.edu /asianadmissions.

34. Jacqueline Yi and Nathan R. Todd, "Internalized Model Minority Myth among Asian Americans: Links to Anti-Black Attitudes and Opposition to Affirmative Action," *Cultural Diversity and Ethnic Minority Psychology* 27 (2021): 569–78.

35. Some have argued that Asian Americans face a racial penalty in race-conscious admissions practices. However, my colleagues and I have pointed out

the fallacies behind such a belief. Margaret M. Chin, OiYan Poon, Janelle Wong, and Jerry Park, "Here Are TEN Reasons NOT to Fall for the 'Asian American Penalty' Trap in Admissions!" *Medium*, February 23, 2019, https://medium.com /@dddefenddiversitydd/anti-asian-american-bias-exists-but-here-are-ten-reasons -not-to-fall-for-the-asian-american-71ef01195189.

36. Phil Yu (www.AngryAsianMan.com) is a popular Asian American blogger and author.

37. David H. Kim, "Freddie Gray Riots Devastated Small Business Owners," *Baltimore Sun*, May 11, 2015, https://www.baltimoresun.com/opinion/op-ed /bs-ed-freddie-gray-stores-20150511-story.html.

38. Heather McGhee, *The Sum of Us: What Racism Costs Everyone and How We Can Prosper Together* (New York: Penguin Random House, 2022).

39. Claire Wang, "Damaged Asian Businesses Show Solidarity with Black Lives Matter Protesters," NBC News, June 4, 2020, https://www.nbcnews.com /news/asian-america/damaged-asian-businesses-show-solidarity-black-lives -matter-protesters-n1224766.

40. Eve Tuck, "Suspending Damage: A Letter to Communities," *Harvard Educational Review* 79 (2009): 409–27.

41. To read more on employment disparities, see Margaret M. Chin, *Stuck: Why Asian Americans Don't Reach the Top of the Corporate Ladder* (New York: New York University Press, 2020); Van C. Tran, Jennifer Lee, and Tiffany J. Huang, "Revisiting the Asian Second-Generation Advantage," *Ethnic and Racial Studies* 42 (2019): 2248–69; Arthur Sakamoto and Sharron Xuanren Wang, "Deconstructing Hyper-Selectivity: Are the Socioeconomic Attainments of Second-Generation Asian Americans Only Due to Their Class Background?" *Chinese Journal of Sociology* 7 (2021): 3–21. Sakamoto and Wang critique the study by Tran and colleagues, and they suggest that Asian Americans may not be facing as much of a glass ceiling as some claim.

42. See, for example, Christopher M. Span, *From Cotton Field to Schoolhouse: African American Education in Mississippi, 1862–1875* (Chapel Hill: University of North Carolina Press, 2012); Richard R. Valencia, "'Mexican Americans Don't Value Education!': On the Basis of the Myth, Mythmaking, and Debunking," *Journal of Latinos and Education* 1, no. 2 (November 13, 2009): 81–103, doi:10.1207/S1532771XJLE0102_2.

43. Matthew Chingos, "Affirmative Action 'Mismatch' Theory Isn't Supported by Credible Evidence," Urban Institute, December 10, 2015, https://www .urban.org/urban-wire/affirmative-action-mismatch-theory-isnt-supported -credible-evidence.

44. See, for example, Shaun R. Harper, Edward J. Smith, and Charles H. F. Davis, "A Critical Race Case Analysis of Black Undergraduate Student Success at an Urban University," *Urban Education* 53 (2018): 3–25; Tara Yosso, *Critical Race Counterstories Along the Chicana/Chicano Educational Pipeline* (New York: Routledge, 2006).

45. Yukong Zhao, a Florida businessman, has even gone so far as to claim that affirmative action in college admissions represented a modern-day Chinese Exclusion Act. Kate Bachelder, "Harvard's Chinese Exclusion Act," *Wall Street*

*Journal,* June 5, 2015, https://www.wsj.com/articles/harvards-chinese-exclusion-act-1433543969.

46. Janelle Wong, "Review of Anti-Asian Hate Incident Reporting and Data Collection 2019–2021," June 7, 2021, https://docs.google.com/document/d/19llMUCDHX-hLKru-cnDCqoBirlpNgFo7W3f-qoJoko4/edit.

47. Nguyen et al., "Asian Americans, Admissions, and College Choice," 579–94.

48. Abigail Noel Fisher v. University of Texas at Austin, No. 09–50822 (5th Cir. 2014), https://www.ca5.uscourts.gov/opinions%5Cpub%5Co9/09-50822-CV2.pdf.

49. I reflected on this interaction with George in an essay for *Reappropriate.* In that essay I had used the name "Stan." OiYan Poon, "Reconnecting Heart and Head: Racism, Immigration Policy, WeChat, and Chinese Americans," *Reappropriate,* May 24, 2018, http://reappropriate.co/2018/05/reconnecting-heart-and-head-racism-immigration-policy-wechat-and-chinese-americans.

50. Chris Fuchs, "California Governor Signs Bill to Disaggregate Asian-American Health Data," NBC News, September 27, 2016, https://www.nbcnews.com/news/asian-america/california-governor-signs-bill-disaggregate-asian-american-health-data-n655361.

51. Jennifer Lee, Karthick Ramakrishnan, and Janelle Wong, "Accurately Counting Asian Americans Is a Civil Rights Issue," *Annals of the American Academy of Political and Social Science* 677 (2018): 191–202; OiYan A. Poon, Jude Paul Dizon, and Dian Squire, "Count Me In! Ethnic Data Disaggregation Advocacy, Racial Mattering, and Lessons for Racial Justice Coalitions," *Journal Committed to Social Change on Race and Ethnicity* 3 (2017): 92–124, https://journals.shareok.org/jcscore/article/view/34.

52. Chris Fuchs, "California Data Disaggregation Bill Sparks Debate in Asian-American Community," NBC News, August 26, 2016, https://www.nbcnews.com/news/asian-america/california-data-disaggregation-bill-sparks-debate-asian-american-community-n638286.

53. See, for example, Jenny Yang, "Today is a sad day for buffet-obsessed immigrant families," Twitter, May 7, 2020, 5:12 p.m., https://twitter.com/jennyyangtv/status/1258519992548515841.

54. Anti-Defamation League, *Audit of Antisemitic Incidents 2022* (March 2023), https://www.adl.org/resources/report/audit-antisemitic-incidents-2022.

55. Many texts have documented Asian American movements and activism, including Daryl Maeda, *Rethinking the Asian American Movement* (New York: Routledge, 2011); Sharon S. Lee, *An Unseen Unheard Minority: Asian American Students at the University of Illinois* (New Brunswick, NJ: Rutgers University Press, 2021); Lori Kido Lopez, *Asian American Media Activism: Fighting for Cultural Citizenship* (New York: New York University Press, 2016).

56. As professor Maxwell Leung reminded me, contemporary Asian American politics has been one of coalition-building since the Third World Liberation Front, through Jesse Jackson's Rainbow PUSH Coalition, and into current politics, as I discuss in the next chapter.

57. Claire Jean Kim, "The Usual Suspects: Asian Americans as Conditional Citizens," in *The State of Asian America: Trajectory of Civic and Political Engagement: A Public Policy Report*, ed. Paul M. Ong (Los Angeles: LEAP, 2008).

58. See, for example, OiYan Poon, "'The Land of Opportunity Doesn't Apply to Everyone': The Immigrant Experience, Race, and Asian American Career Choices," *Journal of College Student Development* 55 (2014): 499–514; Stanley Sue and Sumie Okazaki, "Asian-American Educational Achievements: A Phenomenon in Search of an Explanation," *American Psychologist* 45 (1990): 913–20; Vivian S. Louie, *Compelled to Excel: Immigration, Education, and Opportunity among Chinese Americans* (Redwood City, CA: Stanford University Press, 2004); Jamie Lew, *Asian Americans in Class: Charting the Achievement Gap among Korean American Youth* (New York: Teachers College Press, 2006).

59. Kelly Weill, "Washington Group Fighting Affirmative Action Used Proud Boys as Guards," *Daily Beast*, October 17, 2019, https://www.thedaily beast.com/washington-group-fighting-affirmative-action-referendum-88-used -proud-boys-as-guards; Naomi Ishisaka, "Affirmative Action Debate in Washington Takes an Orwellian Turn," *Seattle Times*, October 21, 2019, https://www .seattletimes.com/seattle-news/opposition-to-affirmative-action-in-washington -evokes-model-minority-myth; Katie Lapham, "Um . . . no. Equity is NOT a code word for anti-Asian," Twitter, March 16, 2019, 6:45 p.m., https://twitter .com/lapham_katie/status/1107065401815515141?s=20.

60. Lisa Lowe offered canonical theorizing to more deeply understand these issues and how the diversity of Asian American perspectives and choices is constituted by history, capital, culture, and other social forces. Lisa Lowe, "Heterogeneity, Hybridity, Multiplicity: Marking Asian American Differences," *Diaspora: A Journal of Transnational Studies* 1, no. 1 (1991): 24–44, doi:10.1353 /dsp.1991.0014.

## CHAPTER 5: "K(NO)W HISTORY, K(NO)W SELF"

1. I was much less involved in Asian American organizations as an undergraduate student than I would become later in graduate school.

2. James Loewen, *Sundown Towns: A Hidden Dimension of American Racism* (New York: New Press, 2018); "Is There Any Truth to the Idea of 'Midwestern Nice'?" *Economist*, December 27, 2018, https://www.economist.com /graphic-detail/2018/12/27/is-there-any-truth-to-the-idea-of-midwestern-nice.

3. Allyson Tintiangco-Cubales, Rita Kohli, Jocyl Sacramento, Nick Henning, Ruchi Agarwal-Rangnath, and Christine Sleeter, "Toward an Ethnic Studies Pedagogy: Implications for K–12 Schools from the Research," *Urban Review* 47 (2015): 104–25, https://doi.org/10.1007/s11256-014-0280-y.

4. One was Chinese and Vietnamese; one, Chinese and Filipino; one Chinese and Korean.

5. Brazilian educator Paulo Freire developed a concept of popular education, documented through his books, including the foundational work *Pedagogy of the Oppressed*. Popular education begins with an affirmation of learners' observations and experiential knowledge of the world. Through collective dialogue, learners analyze and look for patterns in how unjust social, political, and

economic conditions are reproduced. They then develop a theory on which to act to transform structural conditions. Paulo Freire, *Pedagogy of the Oppressed* (New York: Bloomsbury Academic, 2000).

6. Arundhati Roy, "Do Turkeys Enjoy Thanksgiving?," opening plenary address, World Social Forum, Mumbai, India, January 16, 2004.

7. "Mission," AYPAL, https://www.aypal.org/mission.

8. Soo Ah Kwon, *Uncivil Youth: Race, Activism, and Affirmative Governmentality* (Durham, NC: Duke University Press, 2013).

9. Nitasha Sharma, "The Racial Studies Project: Asian American Studies and the Black Lives Matter Campus," in *Flashpoints for Asian American Studies*, ed. Cathy Schlund-Vials (New York: Fordham University Press, 2018), 48–65.

10. Daryl Joji Maeda, *Rethinking the Asian American Movement* (New York: Routledge, 2012).

11. Andy Noguchi, "U.C. Davis Professor Isao Fujimoto (Sept. 28, 1933–Feb. 25, 2022)," JACL Florin Chapter, https://www.florinjacl.com/professor -isao-fujimoto.html.

12. An excellent book to read about disability justice is Alice Wong's memoir *Year of the Tiger: An Activist's Life* (New York: Penguin Random House, 2022).

13. Sharon S. Lee has published an excellent book on student activist campaigns for Asian American studies in the Midwest. Anh was not a student at the University of Illinois, Urbana-Champaign, but Lee's book provides a vibrant history of the 1990s, when Anh joined AASA on her campus. Sharon S. Lee, *An Unseen Unheard Minority: Asian American Students at the University of Illinois* (New Brunswick, NJ: Rutgers University Press, 2022).

14. To learn more about the Vincent Chin case, I highly recommend watching Christine Choy and Renee Tajima-Peña's 1987 documentary *Who Killed Vincent Chin?*

15. To learn more about the concept of racial literacy, check out Dr. Sealey-Ruiz's work. For example, she and her daughter Olivia write about the idea in Olivia I. Ruiz and Yolanda Sealey-Ruiz, "Our Journey toward Racial Literacy: A Mother and Daughter's Story," *Journal of Adolescent and Adult Literacy* 66 (2022): 199–202.

16. Steven Chen, "An Elephant in a China Shop," *Medium*, March 5, 2018, https://medium.com/@crwstrategy/an-elephant-in-a-china-shop-d69c6fccf944.

17. Heather McGhee, *The Sum of Us: What Racism Costs Everyone and How We Can Prosper Together* (New York: One World, 2021).

18. Evelyn Hu-DeHart, "The History, Development, and Future of Ethnic Studies," *Phi Delta Kappan* 75, no. 1 (1993): 50–54, http://www.jstor.org /stable/20405023.

19. Wayne Au, *Unequal by Design: High-Stakes Testing and the Standardization of Inequality* (New York: Routledge, 2022).

20. There is not much information about Kitihawa to document her story, but artists have imagined and represented it. Iris Colburn, "Probing the Surface: Artist Chris Pappan's Material and Conceptual Work with Ledger Art," in *Visualizing Genocide: Indigenous Interventions in Art, Archives, and Museum*, ed. Yve Chavez and Nancy Marie Mithlo (Tucson: University of Arizona Press,

2022), 148–80; Darcel Rockett, "Wonder What That Four-Faced Object Is Outside Your Green Line 'L' Window? The Floating Museum's Latest Art Initiative," *Chicago Tribune*, August 16, 2019, https://www.chicagotribune.com /entertainment/museums/ct-ent-floating-museum-cultural-transit-assembly -20190816-20190816-mr7kxkvjirei7k7w4x6nyiisda-story.html.

21. Jeremy C. Young and Jonathan Friedman, *America's Censored Classrooms* (New York: PEN America, 2022), https://pen.org/report/americas -censored-classrooms.

22. Leigh Patel, *No Study Without Struggle: Confronting the Legacy of Settler Colonialism in Higher Education* (Boston: Beacon Press, 2021).

### CONCLUSION: ASIAN AMERICAN IDENTITY IS A SOLIDARITY ETHIC AND PRACTICE

1. Derrick Bell, *Faces at the Bottom of the Well: The Permanence of Racism* (New York: Basic Books, 1992).

2. Ellen Wu, *Overrepresented: The Surprising Story of Asian Americans and Racial Justice* (Princeton University Press, forthcoming).

3. In 2016, at the height of the protests over the indictment and conviction of former NYPD officer Peter Liang for manslaughter in killing Akai Gurley, I raised questions about the inherent anti-Black ideologies exhibited in these Chinese American community protests. In response, I began receiving hateful threats of violence against me and my family in my email and in the mail from Chinese American Liang supporters. Over the years I have also received threats of violence from others, but the first of these communications came from people who also identified as Chinese.

4. Iyko Day, *Alien Capital: Asian Racialization and the Logic of Settler Colonial Capitalism* (Durham, NC: Duke University Press, 2016).

5. I wrote an op-ed about our trip to DC and how you dressed up as Black Widow that Halloween. OiYan Poon, "If the U.S. Ditches Affirmative Action, All Students Will Lose Out," *Globe and Mail*, October 28, 2022, https://www .theglobeandmail.com/opinion/article-if-the-us-ditches-affirmative-action-all -students-will-lose-out.

6. Lisa Philip, "How Asian Americans Got Wrapped Up in the Affirmative Action Debate—and Why Many Want Out," WBEZ Chicago, June 7, 2023, https://www.wbez.org/stories/supreme-court-affirmative-action-case-centers -asian-americans/0d60209a-7fc2-4194-8b06-133bfe17221c.

7. Thank you to Lisa for your patience and to the WBEZ production team for cutting out most of my sobbing in the story that aired!

8. Sometimes people ask me why I continue to use the social media handle "SpamFriedRice." It has always been an homage to one of my favorite Hong Konger comfort foods my mother would make for me. Before settling on this handle, I had considered "SpamNoodleSoup," which is also a favorite staple in Hong Kong cha chaan tengs, or tea restaurants. Both food items are cultural productions created from humble, colonized conditions. Spam spread through Asian diasporic communities due to Western imperialism. Spam fried rice is a metaphor for the creative energy and productions that come from Asian diasporic communities despite and in spite of challenging conditions. Ang Li, "Asian American Chefs Are Embracing Spam. But How Did the Canned Meat Make

Its Way into Their Cultures?" *Time*, May 26, 2019, https://time.com/5593886 /asian-american-spam-cuisine.

9. Roya Aziz, "Protesters Rally for Tolerance: Students Ask Administrators to Support Ethnic Communities," *California Aggie* 120 (February 9, 2001).

10. "Letter from the Department Chair," UC Davis Asian American Studies Department, https://asa.ucdavis.edu/about.

11. OiYan A. Poon, Jude Paul Matias Dizon, and Dian Squire, "Count Me In! Ethnic Data Disaggregation Advocacy, Racial Mattering, and Lessons for Racial Justice Coalitions," *Journal Committed to Social Change on Race and Ethnicity* 3, no. 1 (2017): 92–124, https://www.jstor.org/stable/48644493.

12. Ian Haney López, *Merge Left: Fusing Race and Class, Winning Elections, and Saving America* (New York: New Press, 2019).

13. "Auntie Sewing Squad," Kristina Wong, https://www.kristinawong.com /projects-blog/auntie-sewing-squad, accessed June 17, 2023.

14. "Mission and Values," VAYLA New Orleans, https://vayla-no.org/about, accessed June 17, 2023.

15. OiYan A. Poon and Jacob Cohen, "Charter School 'Miracle' in Post-Katrina New Orleans? Youth Participatory Action Research and the Future of Education Reform," *Journal of Critical Thought and Praxis* 1 (2012): 144–71.

16. Karen Hua, "'No Arena Save Chinatown' Could Be Read as Protesters Packed the Streets," NBC 10 Philadelphia, June 10, 2023, https://www.nbc philadelphia.com/news/local/no-arena-save-chinatown-could-be-read-as -protesters-packed-the-streets/3583226.

17. Gandhi Mahal Restaurant—Minneapolis, "Hello everyone!" Facebook, May 29, 2020, https://www.facebook.com/GandhiMahalRestaurant/posts /3030378453725259.

18. Catherine Ceniza Choy, *Asian American Histories of the United States* (Boston: Beacon Press, 2022).

# INDEX